IMAGES
of America

SAN FRANCISCO'S VISITACION VALLEY

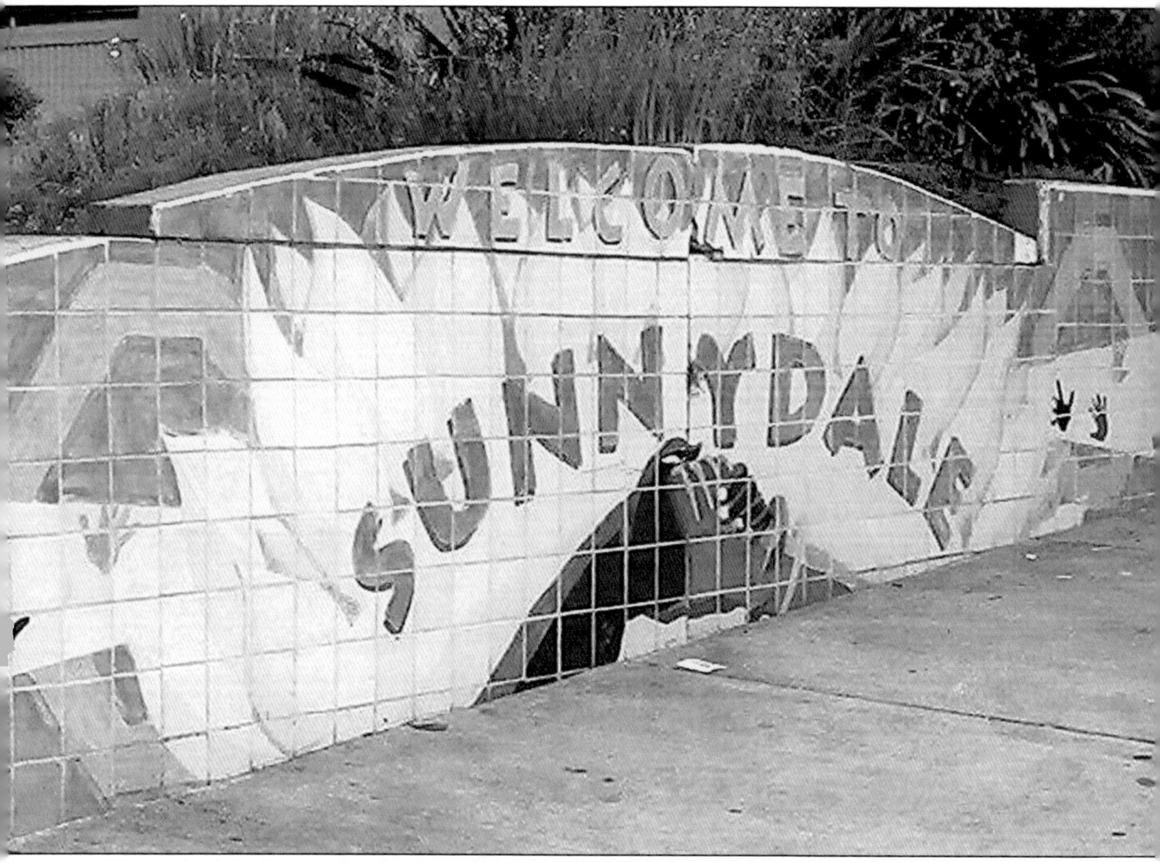

This colorful tile mural welcomes all people to Sunnydale and, by extension, Visitacion Valley. (Courtesy Edie Epps.)

ON THE COVER: In 1927, San Francisco celebrated the opening of its second-largest park with a parade of floats and other festivities. The park, located on the northern edge of Visitacion Valley, is named after John McLaren, the renowned longtime superintendent of Golden Gate Park. (Courtesy Visitacion Valley Community Center.)

IMAGES
of America

SAN FRANCISCO'S VISITACION VALLEY

Visitacion Valley History Project

Cynthia Cox
Edie Epps
Jackie Fishtrom
Russel Morine
Betty Parshall

ARCADIA
PUBLISHING

ISBN 978-0-7385-3041-3

Published by Arcadia Publishing
Charleston SC, Chicago IL, Portsmouth NH, San Francisco CA

Printed in the United States of America

Library of Congress Catalog Card Number: 2005929120

For all general information contact Arcadia Publishing at:
Telephone 843-853-2070
Fax 843-853-0044
E-mail sales@arcadiapublishing.com
For customer service and orders:
Toll-Free 1-888-313-2665

Visit us on the Internet at www.arcadiapublishing.com

This book is dedicated in loving memory of Alma Stevenson Taylor (1911–2004), whose gentle yet fierce spirit and devotion to the Valley live on and continue to inspire.

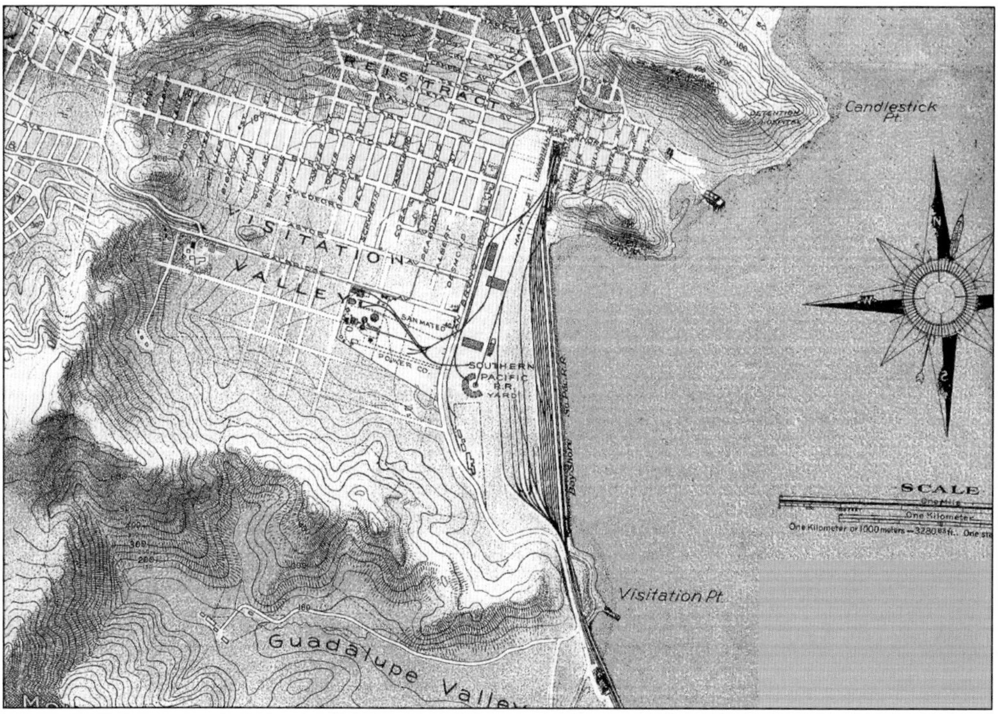

This 1915 map shows San Francisco's street grid, the tracks of Southern Pacific, and the southeastern neighborhood of Visitacion Valley with its vast watershed. (Courtesy Russel Morine.)

CONTENTS

Acknowledgments		6
Introduction		7
1.	The Early Days: Discovery and Settlement	9
2.	Shaping the Valley: Commerce and Transportation	23
3.	Community Life	55
4.	The Valley at Play	87
5.	Homes and Buildings	103
6.	A Few More Faces and Places	123

Acknowledgments

The five authors, who operate collectively as the Visitacion Valley History Project, offer our heartfelt thanks to the many people, organizations, and businesses who so generously contributed to this compilation of images and information about our neighborhood. The list of those who shared is far longer than those formally credited, and we gathered far more material than could possibly fit into 128 pages. We thank you all!

With this book, we continue the important work of the Circle of Elders oral history project, which gathered a wealth of remembrances from seniors who have lived and worked in the Valley and captured them in text and on a video that premiered in summer 2004. It has been a delight for the five of us to meet even more of our neighbors, both former and present. We look forward with anticipation to continuing to conduct interviews and gather memorabilia for a permanent collection to be housed in the Valley and shared among us all. Proceeds from the sale of this book will be earmarked for this ongoing effort.

We simply couldn't fit in everything, everybody, and every organization that make Visitacion Valley what it is today, but we celebrate you all for your outstanding commitment to our favorite community.

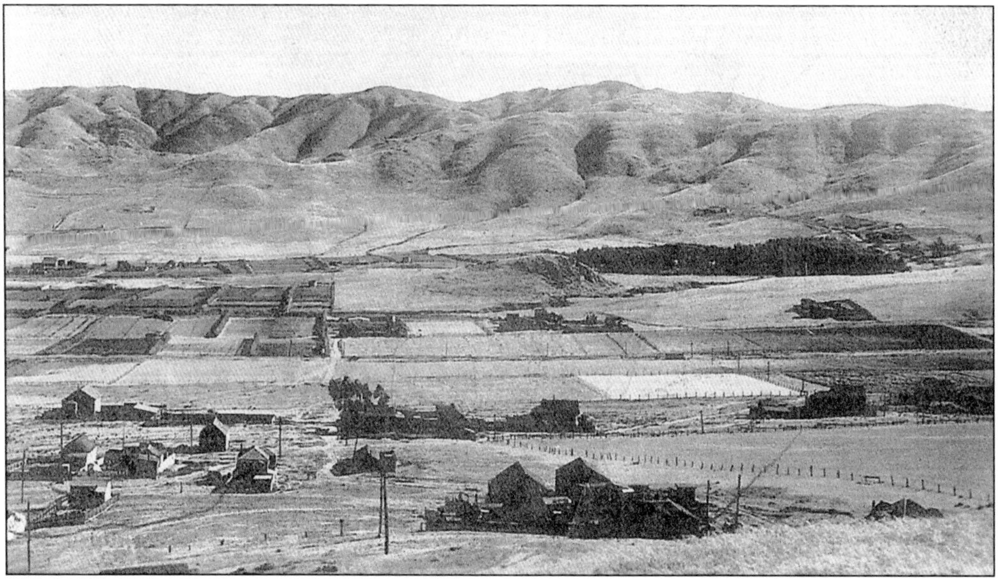

This panorama of early Visitacion Valley looks south to San Bruno Mountain, known locally as the "Blackies," perhaps because of the dark color the hills often assume in varying lights. Written on the back of the photograph is the exclamation "Beautiful!" (Courtesy Jane Bauman Pace.)

INTRODUCTION

For hundreds of years, our southeastern sector—one of San Francisco's three valleys, tucked beneath the San Bruno Mountain range—was inhabited solely by Native Americans who hunted in the hills and fished in the nearby bay. But with the July 2, 1777, "discovery" and naming of Visitacion Valley by Spanish friars and soldiers en route to the Presidio, the land was claimed by the Catholic Church and used to graze herds of livestock. In 1834, the now-Mexican government took back the land that Spain had granted to the church and awarded it instead to prominent Californios. One such grant, the Rancho Canada de Guadalupe, La Visitacion y Rodeo Viejo, was awarded to Jacob Primer Leese, a trader from Ohio married to a sister of the powerful Gen. Mariano Vallejo.

After 1848 and the American annexation of former Mexican territory throughout the West, acreage began to be sold off. Among the earliest landowners in Visitacion Valley were Francois Pioche, a *bon vivant* whose "French Gardens" specialized in roses, and Henry Schwerin, a German whose extensive acreage supported a dairy farm, a nursery specializing in ferns and tulips, and honey bees. Other Europeans, including numerous Italians and Maltese, established truck farms, whose irrigation systems led to the neighborhood's being nicknamed the "Valley of the Windmills."

By the 1870s, industry had come to the Valley: William Ralston's silk ribbon factory, followed by several breweries (including Mission Brewery, noted for its steam beer); two quarries; a gas plant and a fertilizer company; and the Southern Pacific Railroad, which filled in the bay for its tracks and tunnels and from which American soldiers embarked for overseas duty during World War I. Schlage Lock was a major employer between 1925 and 1999, and Silvestri's statuary has been a business neighbor since the 1960s. The Five, Six, and Seven Mile Houses, named for their supposed distance from the original city hall at Portsmouth Square, offered lodging and recreation to both travelers and San Franciscans over a period of many years. With business came transportation, evolving from the original one-track streetcars that cost 5¢ each way, to the MUNI buses that replaced them, to the light rail system now under construction.

In 1905, the Reis-Paul Tract sold lots for \$125 throughout the Valley—\$1 down and \$1 a week. The Sunnydale and Candlestick Cove housing projects were erected for World War II defense workers. Noted developer Joseph Eichler's 1960s plan for luxury housing in two 20-story high-rises evolved instead into Section Eight housing at Geneva Towers, imploded in 1998 and replaced by the attractive townhouses known as Heritage Homes. Both the Visitacion Valley Community Center, spearheaded in 1918 by beloved neighborhood leader Florence Friedman, and the more recent John King Senior Center, now offering a childcare center and 91 assisted living units, continue to meet a variety of neighborhood needs. The classrooms of the Valley's two elementary schools, as well as those at the middle and high schools, are also filled to capacity, as approximately a third of our residents are age 18 and under.

Local churches include the Church of the Visitacion, founded by the Valley's Catholics in 1907. In 1952, its fourth and current building was erected on what was once the six-acre estate of Peter Burnett, California's first governor, and subsequently the San Francisco Auto Camp, the city's first motel. St. James Presbyterian was founded in 1906; Julia Morgan, the famed Hearst Castle architect, designed the present building in 1923. In 1954, Valley Baptist on Raymond purchased its building, erected in 1919, from the Catholics; today Sunday morning services are in English and the afternoon ones in Vietnamese. More than 50 percent of the Valley's current population is comprised of those of Asian and Pacific Islander heritage, and the Valley's rich diversity is further reflected in the ethnic congregations who worship here, including those at Korean First Presbyterian, Indian Baptist, Iglesia El Espiritu Santo, Visitacion Chinese Baptist, and others.

Nearly 230 years after the Spanish travelers celebrated their discovery of this beautiful valley by saying mass, using a huge rock as an altar, our community retains its original name and spelling. Although the area has changed in countless ways, the "Valley of the Good Neighbor" still harkens back to the past. Where herds of livestock once grazed on our windswept hills, we have the Cow Palace. Landscaped greenways and community parks have taken the place of dairy farms and nurseries. Although the Valley no longer "runs around to the sound of Southern Pacific's whistle," residents eagerly await the opening of the new light rail system along Bayshore Boulevard. Industry no longer defines the neighborhood, but the willingness of neighbors to help neighbors remains as strong as ever. And yes, "The Rock" that served as an altar in 1777 still stands, strikingly linking the past with the present!

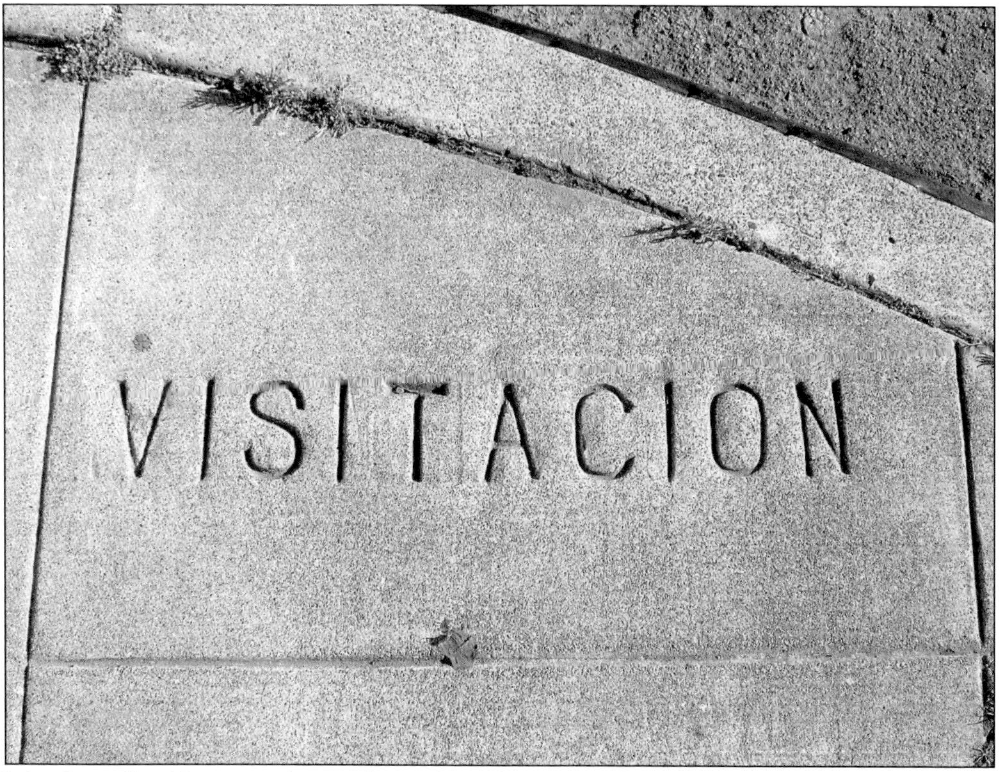

Like the valley, Visitacion Avenue loops down from Mansell Boulevard to Bayshore Boulevard, and retains the Spanish spelling.

One

The Early Days
Discovery and Settlement

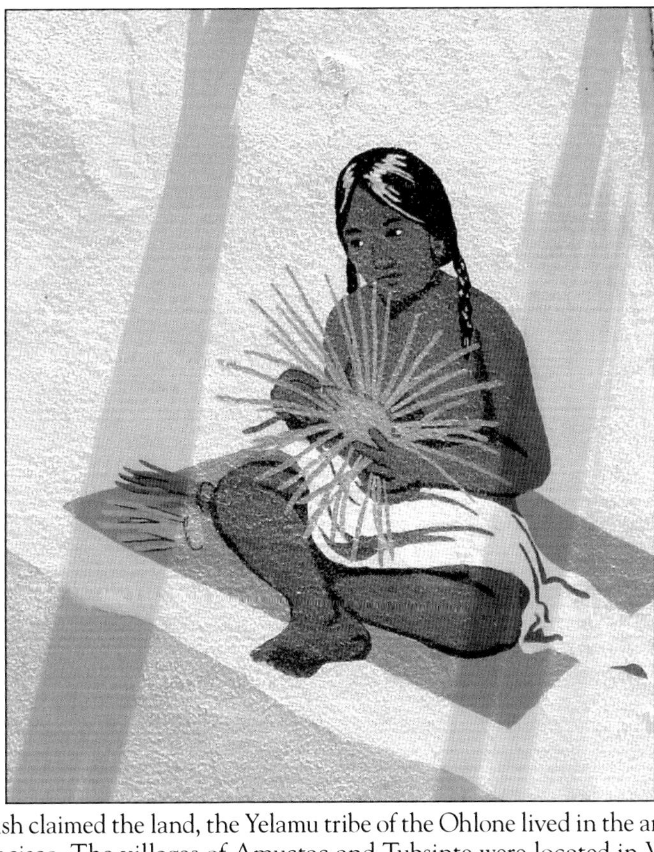

Before the Spanish claimed the land, the Yelamu tribe of the Ohlone lived in the area encompassing today's San Francisco. The villages of Amuctac and Tubsinte were located in Visitacion Valley. The 1987 mural on the side of the neighborhood's current library branch acknowledges this important part of our history. (Courtesy Russel Morine.)

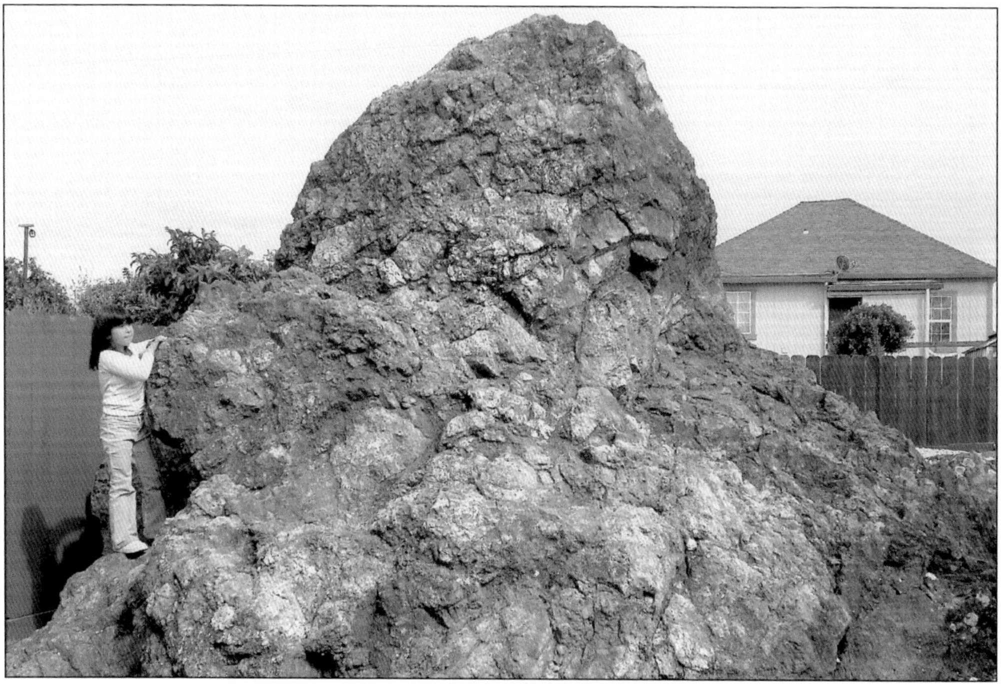

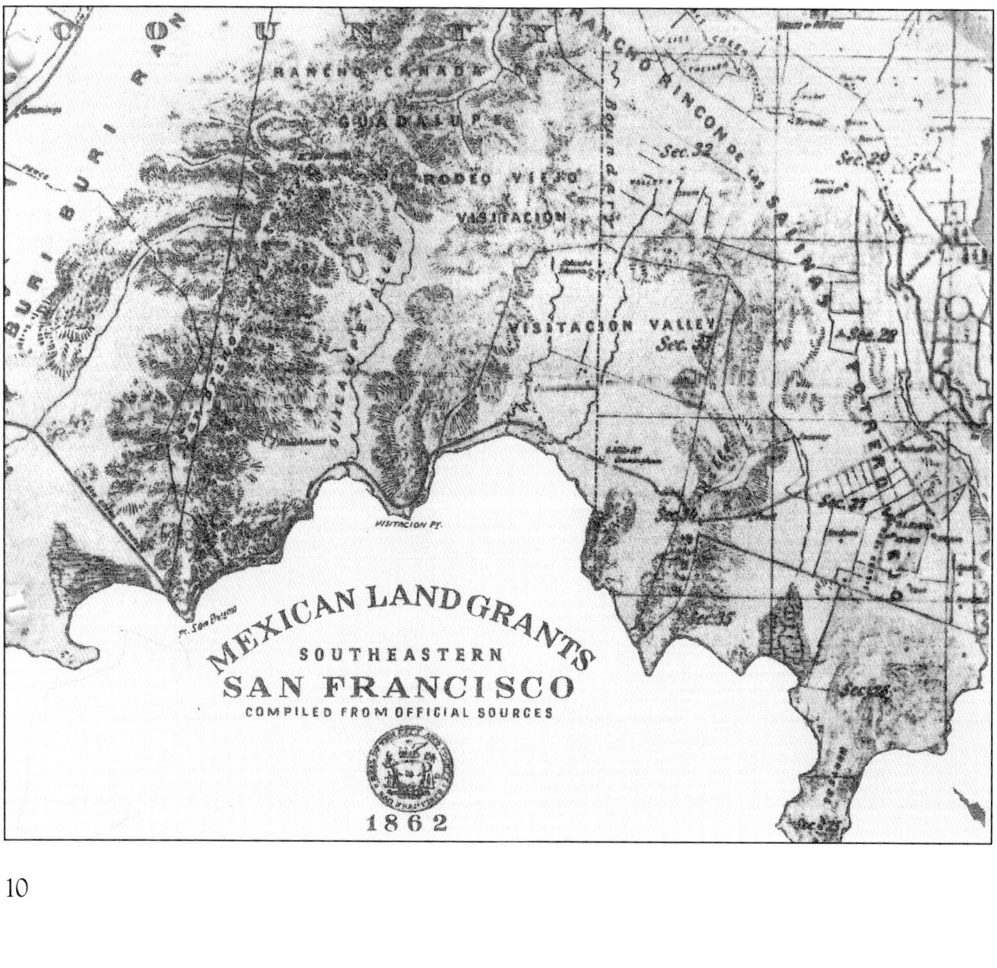
RANCHO CANADA DE GUADALUPE
RODEO VIEJO
VISITACION
RANCHO RINCON DE LAS SALINAS
Sec. 32
Sec. 29
VISITACION VALLEY
Sec. 37
Sec. 28
POTRERO
Sec. 27
Sec. 35
VISITACION PT.
MEXICAN LAND GRANTS
SOUTHEASTERN
SAN FRANCISCO
COMPILED FROM OFFICIAL SOURCES
1862

OPPOSITE ABOVE: In 1777, a party of Spanish soldiers and Franciscan friars traveling north to the Presidio in San Francisco became lost in heavy fog and determined to camp overnight. They awoke the next morning to find a beautiful valley beneath their gaze. They named their discovery Visitacion Valley, as the date was July 2, when Catholics celebrate the Feast of the Visitacion of the Most Blessed Virgin to her cousin St. Elizabeth. According to local lore, before continuing their journey the priests in the party offered a mass, using this large rock as their altar. Just as Visitacion Valley retains the Spanish spelling of its name, this massive rock still stands in a private backyard in the heart of the Valley, pictured here in 2005. (Courtesy Russel Morine.)

OPPOSITE BELOW: In 1834, the Mexican government, which controlled California, secularized all the property given by Spain to the Catholic Church and began making grants of this land to prominent Mexican citizens. Among them was the 1841 grant of the Rancho Canada de Guadalupe, La Visitacion y Rodeo Viejo, encompassing vast acreage in the southeastern sector of today's San Francisco and Brisbane. (Courtesy *Lock and Key*, Schlage Lock, January–February–March 1967.)

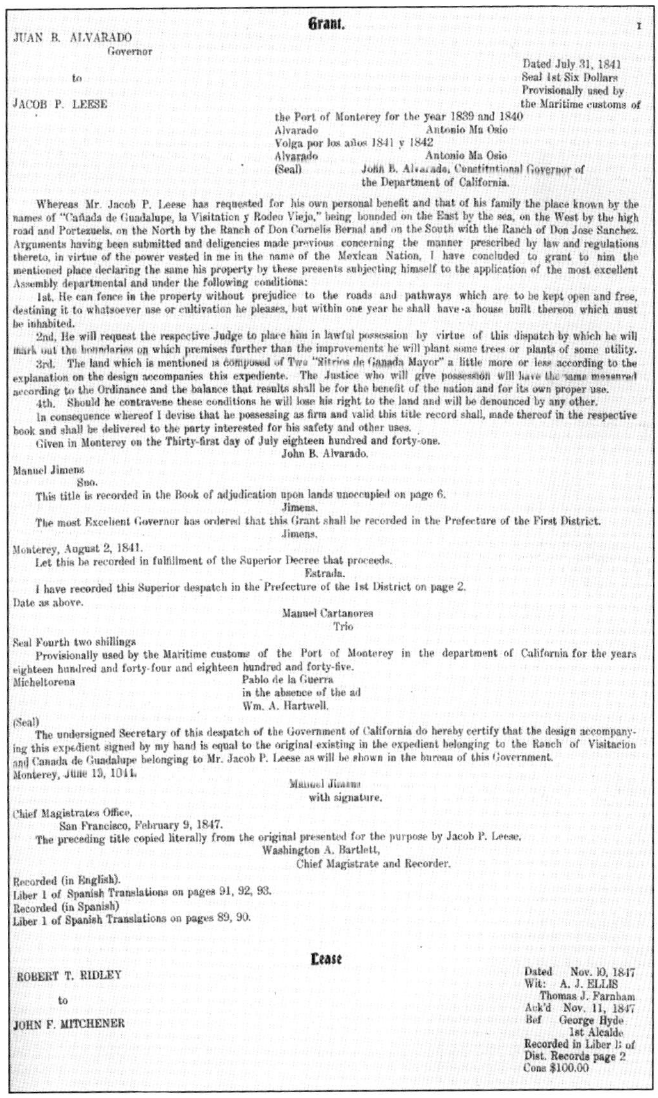

Grant. 1

JUAN B. ALVARADO
Governor
to
JACOB P. LEESE

Dated July 31, 1841
Seal 1st Six Dollars
Provisionally used by
the Maritime customs of
the Port of Monterey for the year 1839 and 1840
Alvarado Antonio Ma Osio
Volga por los años 1841 y 1842
Alvarado Antonio Ma Osio
(Seal) John B. Alvarado, Constitutional Governor of
the Department of California.

Whereas Mr. Jacob P. Leese has requested for his own personal benefit and that of his family the place known by the names of "Cañada de Guadalupe, la Visitation y Rodeo Viejo," being bounded on the East by the sea, on the West by the high road and Portezuels, on the North by the Ranch of Don Cornelis Bernal and on the South with the Ranch of Don Jose Sanchez. Arguments having been submitted and deligencies made previous concerning the manner prescribed by law and regulations thereto, in virtue of the power vested in me in the name of the Mexican Nation, I have concluded to grant to him the mentioned place declaring the same his property by these presents subjecting himself to the application of the most excellent Assembly departmental and under the following conditions:

1st. He can fence in the property without prejudice to the roads and pathways which are to be kept open and free, destining it to whatsoever use or cultivation he pleases, but within one year he shall have a house built thereon which must be inhabited.

2nd. He will request the respective Judge to place him in lawful possession by virtue of this dispatch by which he will mark out the boundaries on which premises further than the improvements he will plant some trees or plants of some utility.

3rd. The land which is mentioned is composed of Two "Sitrios de Ganada Mayor" a little more or less according to the explanation on the design accompanies this expediente. The Justice who will give possession will have the same measured according to the Ordinance and the balance that results shall be for the benefit of the nation and for its own proper use.

4th. Should he contravene these conditions he will lose his right to the land and will be denounced by any other.

In consequence whereof I devise that he possessing as firm and valid this title record shall, made thereof in the respective book and shall be delivered to the party interested for his safety and other uses.

Given in Monterey on the Thirty-first day of July eighteen hundred and forty-one.

John B. Alvarado.

Manuel Jimens
Sno.

This title is recorded in the Book of adjudication upon lands unoccupied on page 6.

Jimens.

The most Excelient Governor has ordered that this Grant shall be recorded in the Prefecture of the First District.

Jimens.

Monterey, August 2, 1841.

Let this be recorded in fulfillment of the Superior Decree that proceeds.

Estrada.

I have recorded this Superior despatch in the Prefecture of the 1st District on page 2.

Date as above.

Manuel Cartanores
Trio

Seal Fourth two shillings

Provisionally used by the Maritime customs of the Port of Monterey in the department of California for the years eighteen hundred and forty-four and eighteen hundred and forty-five.

Micheltorena Pablo de la Guerra
in the absence of the ad
Wm. A. Hartwell.

(Seal)

The undersigned Secretary of this despatch of the Government of California do hereby certify that the design accompanying this expedient signed by my hand is equal to the original existing in the expedient belonging to the Ranch of Visitacion and Canada de Guadalupe belonging to Mr. Jacob P. Leese as will be shown in the bureau of this Government.

Monterey, June 13, 1844.

Manuel Jimene
with signature.

Chief Magistrates Office,
San Francisco, February 9, 1847.

The preceding title copied literally from the original presented for the purpose by Jacob P. Leese.

Washington A. Bartlett,
Chief Magistrate and Recorder.

Recorded (in English).
Liber 1 of Spanish Translations on pages 91, 92, 93.
Recorded (in Spanish)
Liber 1 of Spanish Translations on pages 89, 90.

Lease

ROBERT T. RIDLEY
to
JOHN F. MITCHENER

Dated Nov. 10, 1847
Wit: A. J. ELLIS
Thomas J. Farnham
Ack'd Nov. 11, 1847
Bef George Hyde
1st Alcalde
Recorded in Liber B of
Dist. Records page 2
Cons $100.00

Although Jacob Primer Leese, the recipient of this major land grant from Governor Alvarado, was an Anglo trader from Ohio, he met the qualifications—being a Spanish-speaking and Catholic Mexican citizen—because he had married the sister of Gen. Mariano Vallejo. (Authors' collection.)

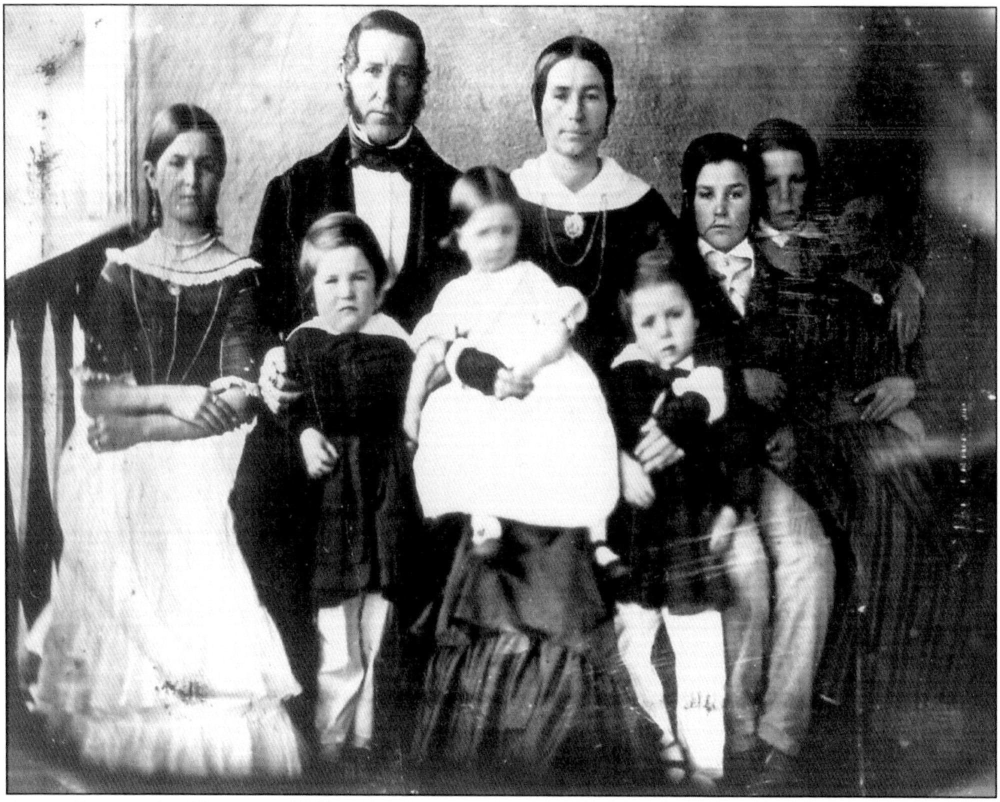

According to the *Visitacion Valley Grapevine*, in 1836, Jacob P. Leese "sailed into the Bay aboard the barque *Don Quixote* with a six-piece orchestra and the lumber to build a mansion on the southwest corner of Clay Street and Grant Avenue." The first Fourth of July celebration in San Francisco was held in his home. He subsequently married Rosalia Vallejo, and together they raised a large family. In 1845, Leese exchanged his rancho for one in Sonoma belonging to Robert Ridley. After 1848, however, the United States controlled California and most former grantees lost their land. (Courtesy San Francisco History Center, San Francisco Public Library.)

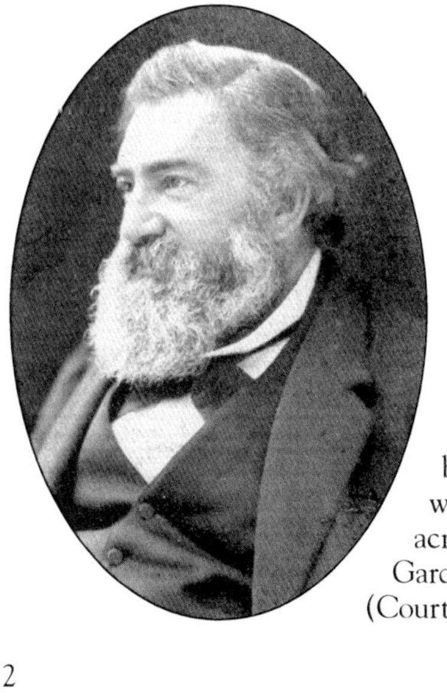

Frenchman Francois Louis Alfred Pioche arrived in San Francisco in 1849, investing in multiple business ventures and patronizing the arts. He gained distinction by importing 40 Parisian chefs and a boatload of French wines. He bought up an impressive amount of land, including acreage in Visitacion Valley, where he established the French Gardens, specializing in roses that were sold at the flower markets. (Courtesy Chamber of Commerce, Pioche, NV.)

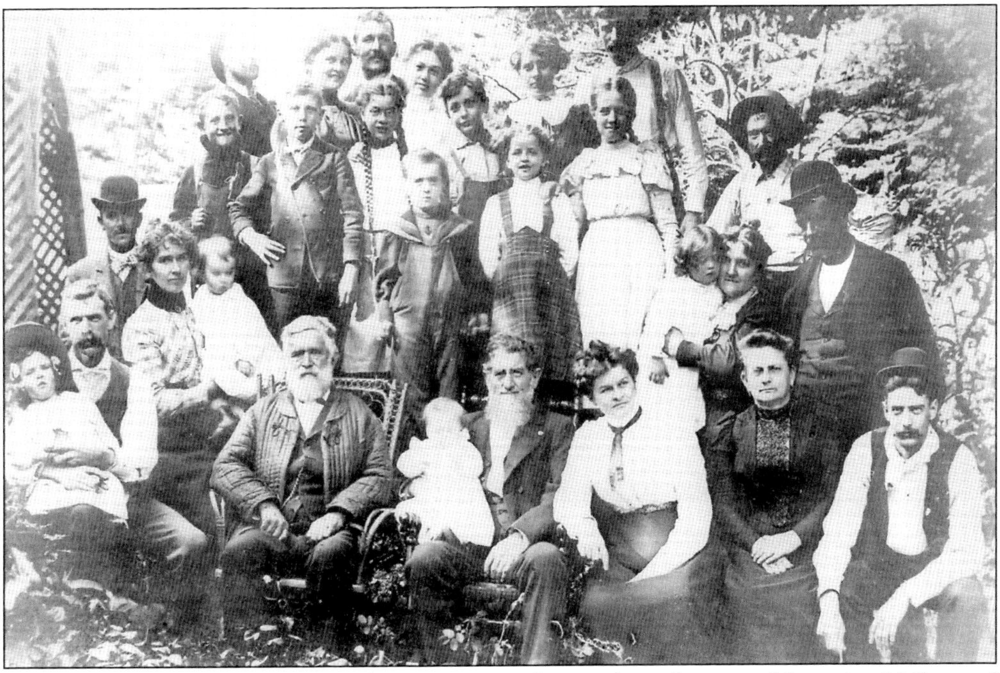

In 1854, German emigre Henry Schwerin acquired a number of acres in Visitacion Valley and what is now Daly City. Ironically his large herd of dairy cows grazed on the site of today's Cow Palace parking lots. Schwerin and his sons also established a horticultural nursery, specializing in ferns and tulips that were sold at the Flower Mart along with Pioche's roses. (Courtesy San Francisco History Center, San Francisco Public Library.)

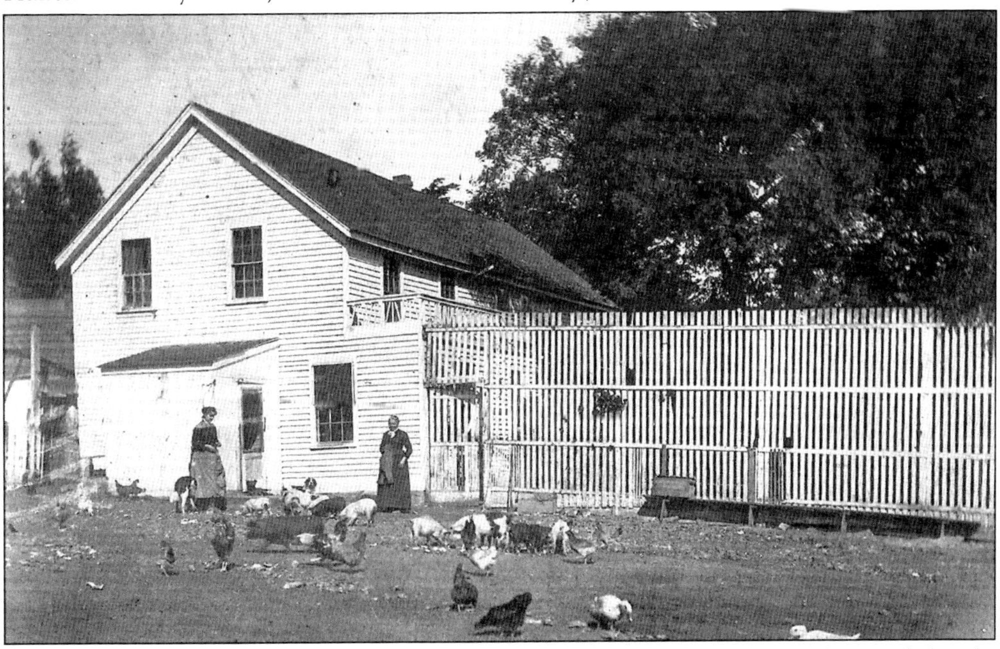

The lumber for the Schwerin family home was brought from France on three ships and then by wagon to the Valley. Henry and Ottilia Schwerin raised their eight children in this home, which was torn down in 1922. (Courtesy Taylor family.)

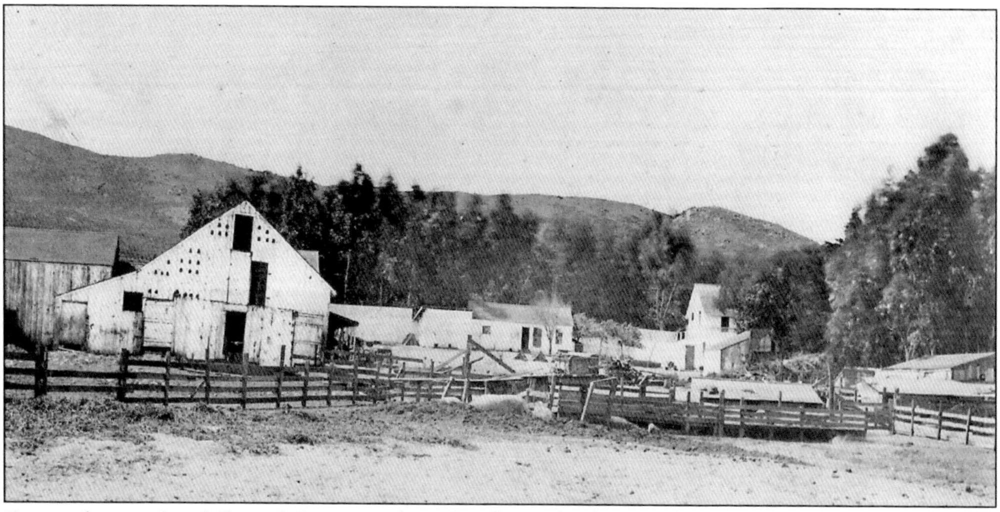

Soon other settlers followed the example of Pioche and Schwerin, farming the large truck gardens and nurseries that flourished until World War II and becoming known for the picturesque—and practical—windmills that pumped the water used for irrigating crops. By the late 1890s, the cattlemen were ordered to remove the fences that blocked roads, and soon streets opened the Valley to roadhouses, restaurants, and saloons. (Courtesy a private collector.)

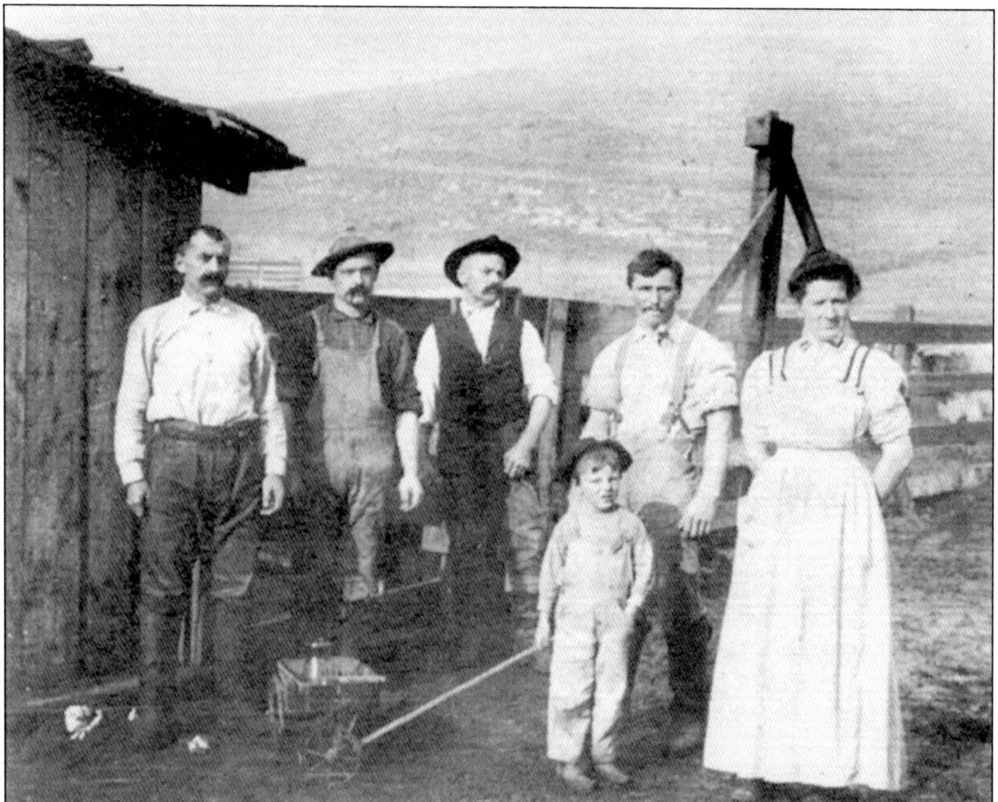

The Johnson and Brown Dairy employed 35 milkers, such as those pictured here, and the woman who cooked for them. (Courtesy *Lock and Key*, Schlage Lock, January–February–March 1967.)

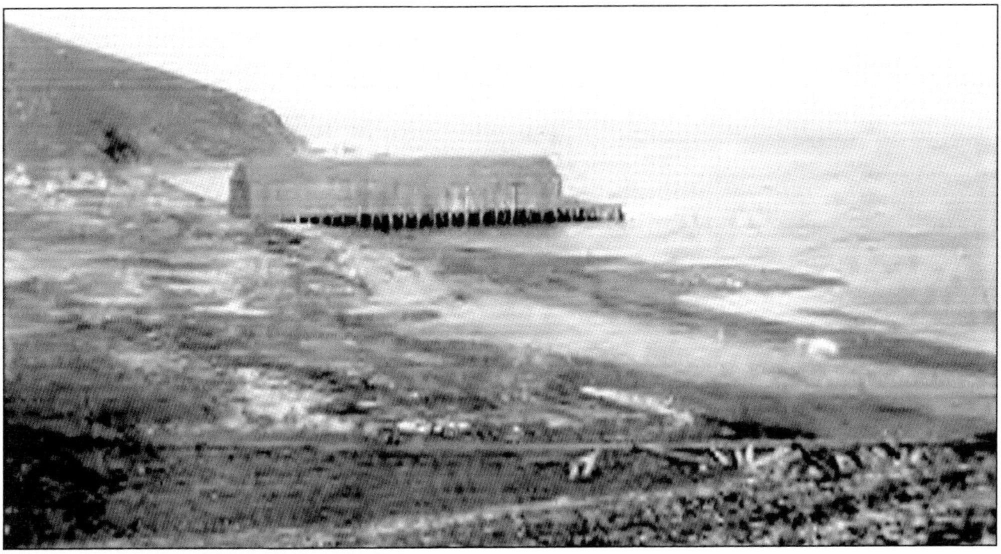

Near today's Candlestick Park, the Johnson and Brown Dairy also built a wharf barn in order to store bales of hay brought by barge from Marin and Sonoma Counties. Justine Baron Marcelli remembers another attraction at the cove: "My father used to take us to Candlestick— we would never go alone—as he loved the water. We used to go a lot . . . At one time there were clams and oysters . . . It was fun to grow up here." (Courtesy Taylor family.)

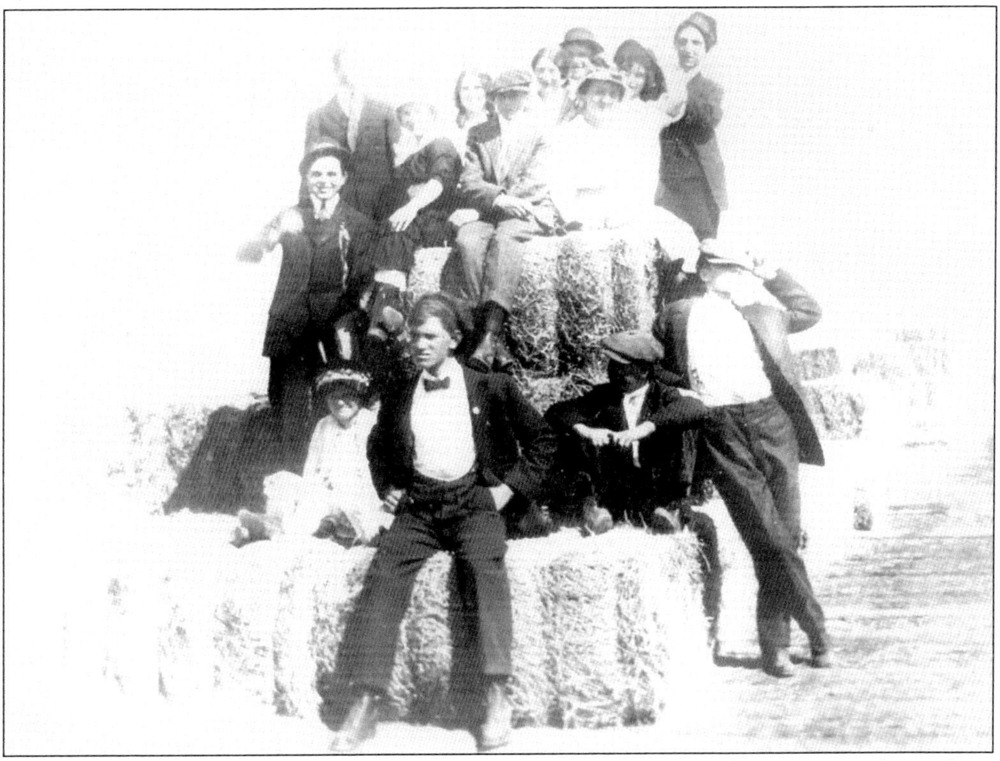

The Johnson and Brown wharf also proved to be a popular spot for these 1918 graduates from Visitacion Valley School. The only identified celebrant is Johnny Tanner of the Tanner Welding Company, sitting on bales of hay in the forefront of the group. (Courtesy Taylor family.)

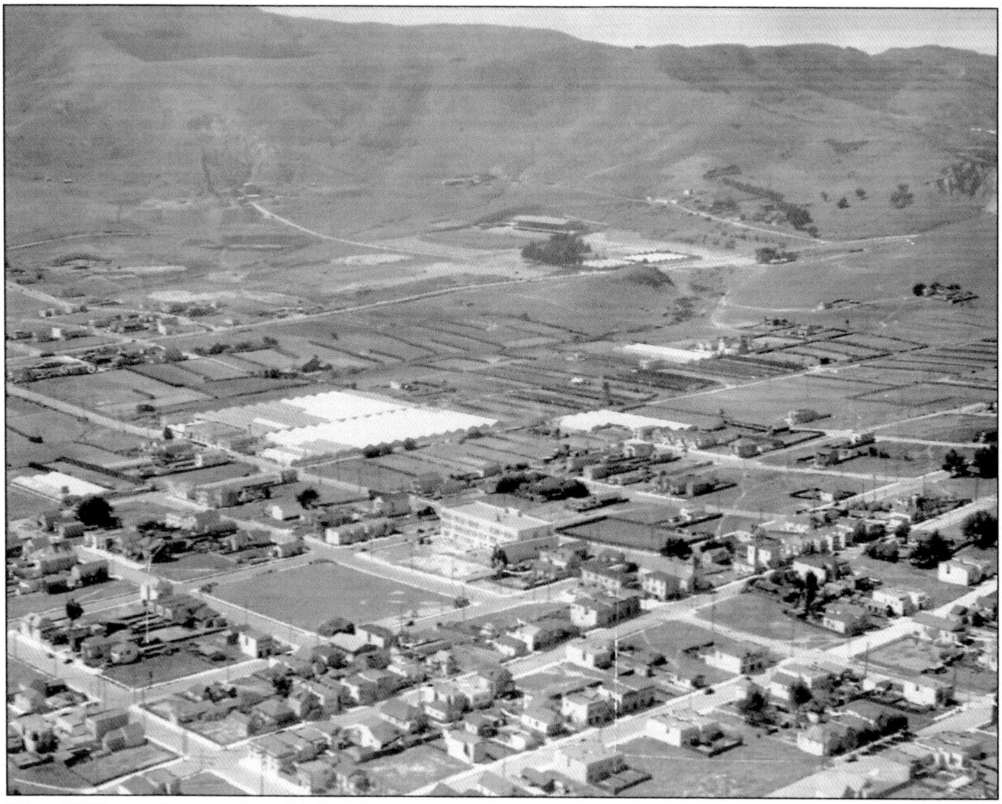

This 1936 aerial view of the Valley shows San Bruno Mountain in the background. The dog racing track on Geneva Avenue is in the upper center, and the blocks of white buildings are nursery greenhouses. Housing had begun to fill in the open space. (Courtesy Richard Gatti.)

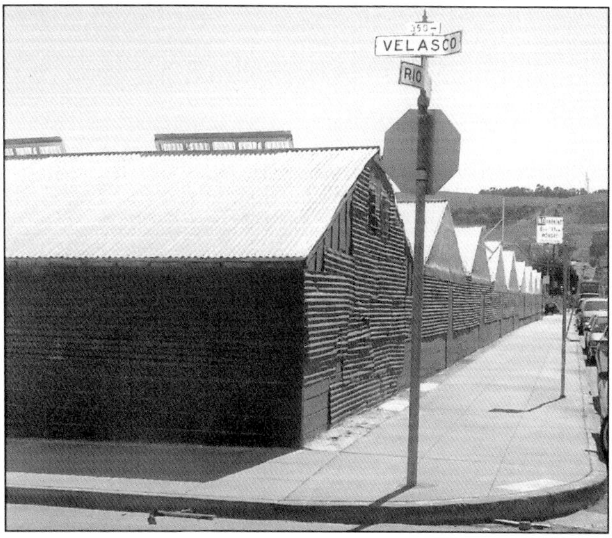

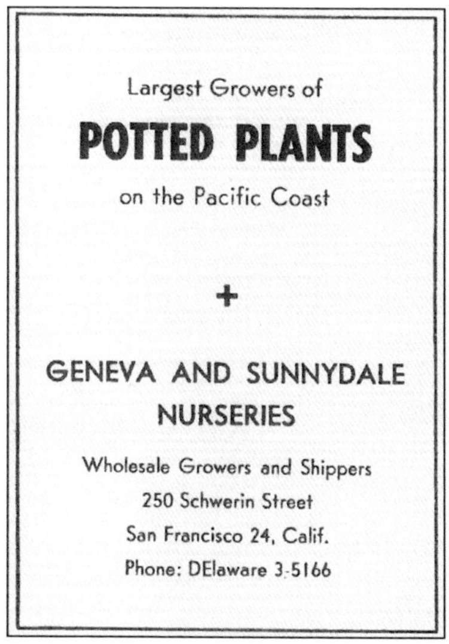

Well-known landowner Cesare Restani operated the Geneva and Sunnydale Nurseries, which broke ground in 1927 on the site where Heritage Homes are today. Golden Gate Flowers at Velasco and Rio Vista Streets is one of the few reminders of Visitacion Valley's rich horticultural past. (Courtesy Restani family.)

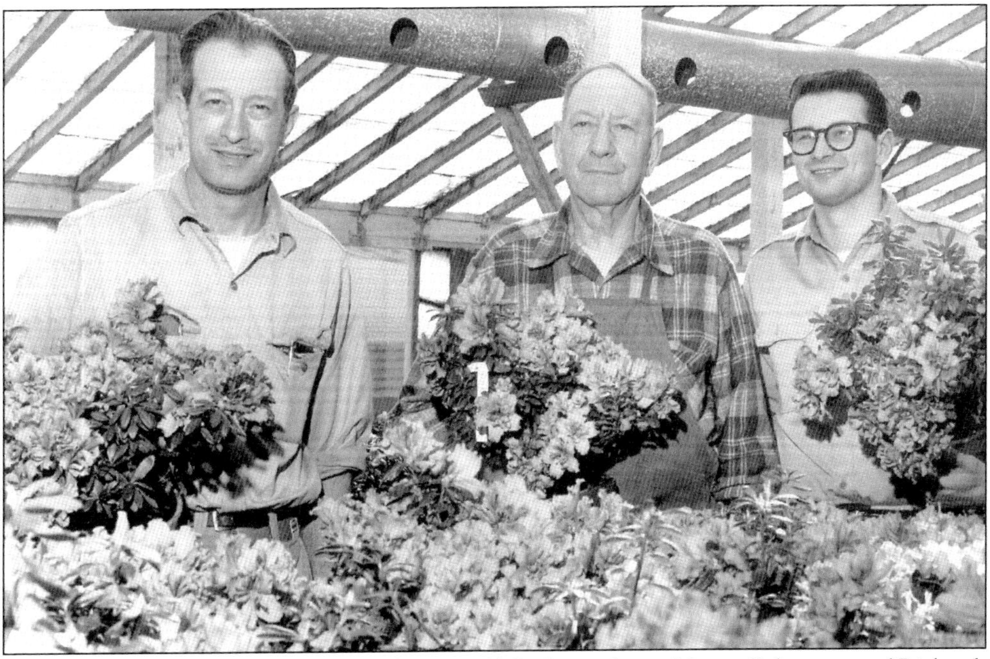

Three generations of Gattis stand together in 1963. Left to right are Victor, Salvatore, and Richard. Salvatore established the nurseries known for azaleas and ferns in 1929. Today Richard and his sons continue the business elsewhere but still sell at the San Francisco Flower Mart. (Courtesy Gatti family.)

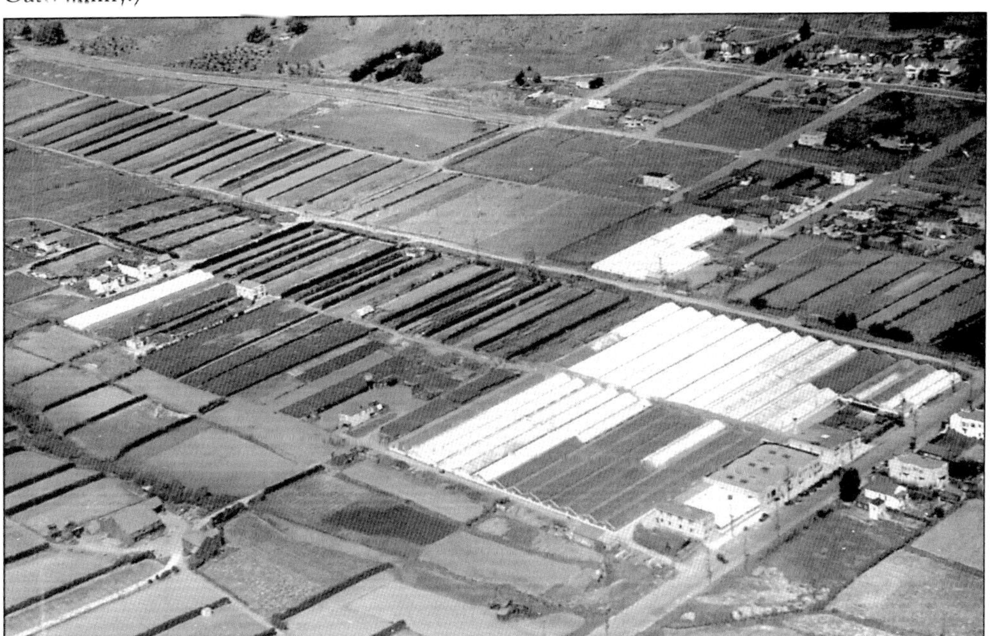

Shown here in the late 1920s are the Gatti nursery buildings, located along Sunnydale Avenue near Britton. Oral historian Clarence Wikse recalls as a boy hearing the young Italian workers strolling back to their quarters on Sunday evenings after an afternoon of bocce ball and wine, singing arias as they walked. (Courtesy Gatti family.)

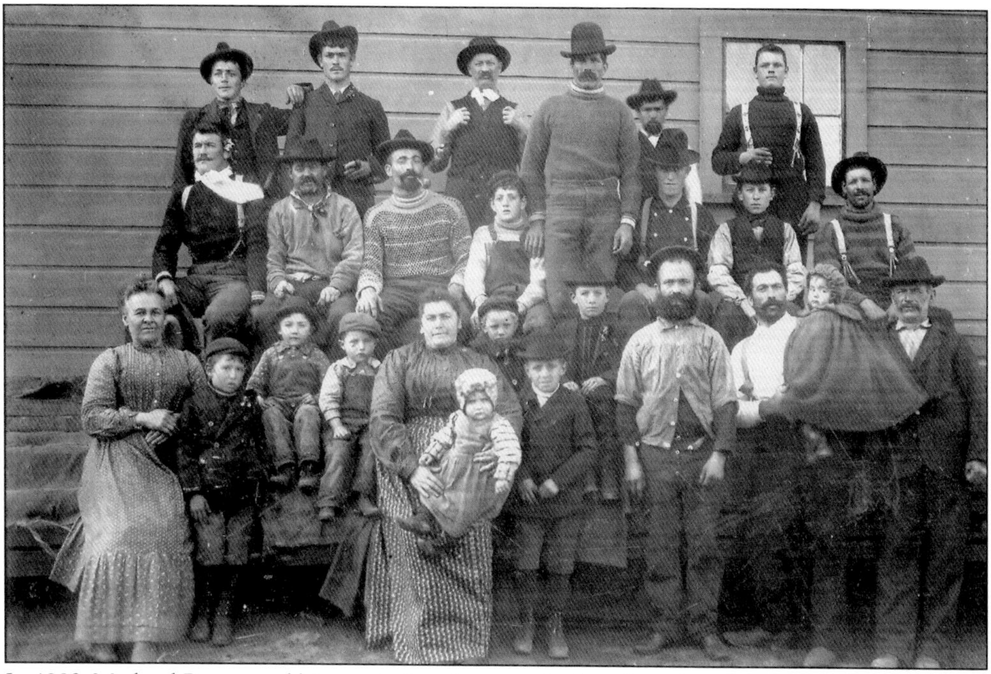

In 1883, Michael Perata and his son-in-law Antonio Sechini bought a ranch in Visitacion Valley for $5,541 in gold coin. Every Sunday, the family matriarch, Rose Sechini (front row left), prepared dinner for the extended family and the ranch hands. Pictured here around 1901 are members of the Sechini, Piasoni, and Armanino families, as well as the workers who helped on the ranch, located in the southern sector of the valley. (Courtesy Richard Brandi.)

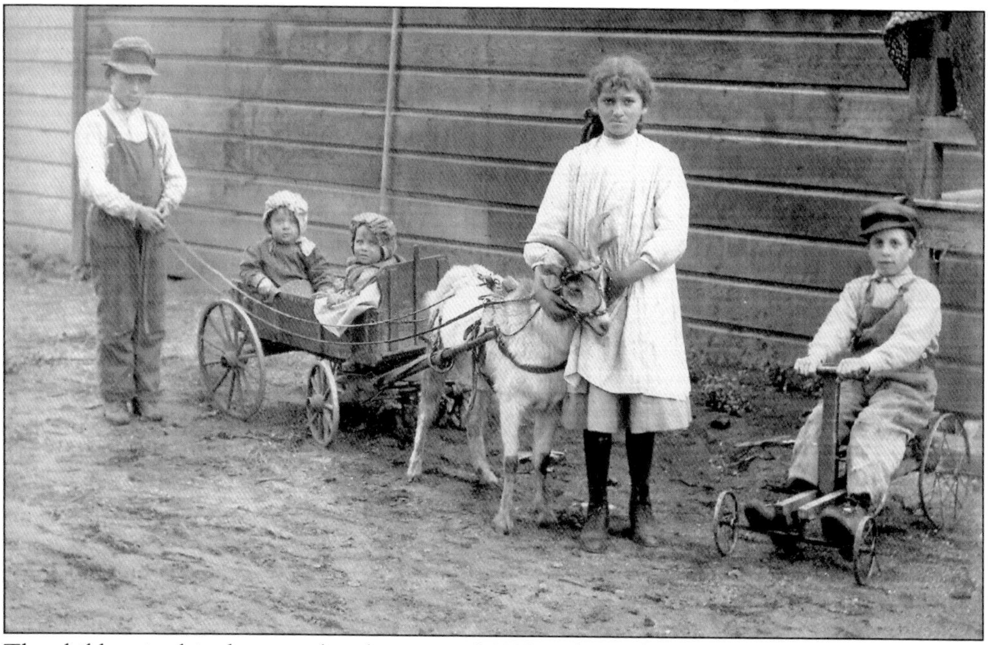

The children in this photograph, taken around 1910 at the Sechini Ranch, from left to right, are Albert Armanino, twins Edna and Ed (Bill) Armanino, an unidentified girl, and cousin Steve Garassino. (Courtesy Richard Brandi.)

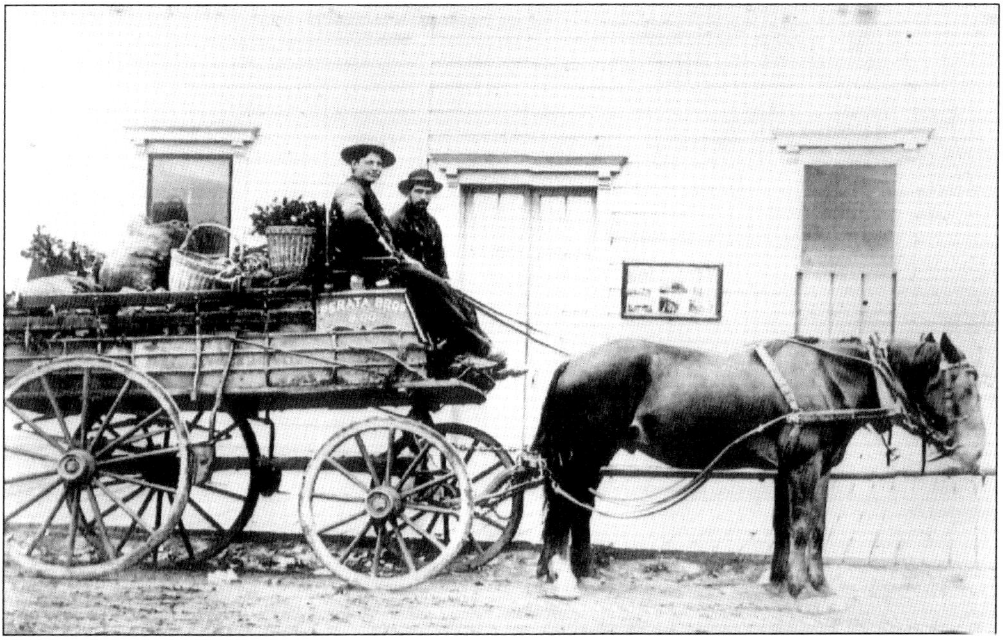

The Sechini Ranch's herbs and vegetables were transported by wagon to the Colombo Market in downtown San Francisco. After the long ride and day at the market, the horse knew which local saloon to stop at on the way home. (Courtesy Richard Brandi.)

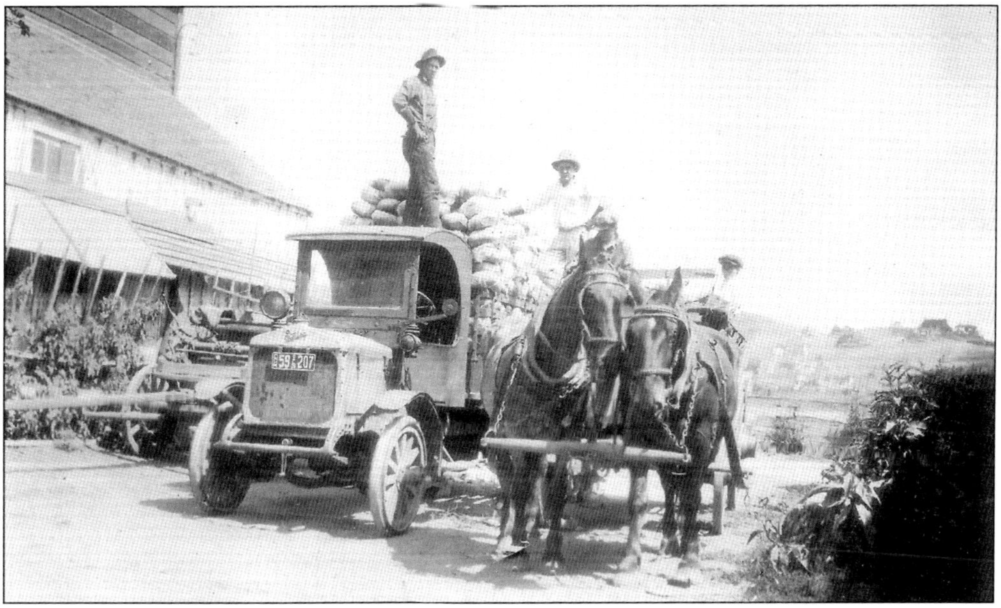

Eventually the Sechini Ranch acquired a truck, shown here being loaded with cabbages in the mid-1920s. As Clarence Wikse recalls, the Sechini, Armanino, and Ferrari ranches in the Valley grew good sauerkraut cabbages that were processed and stored in a barn in Colma. "When the heads had been harvested, kids would gather leaves left on stalks and take them home to be cooked for the family pigs." (Courtesy Richard Brandi.)

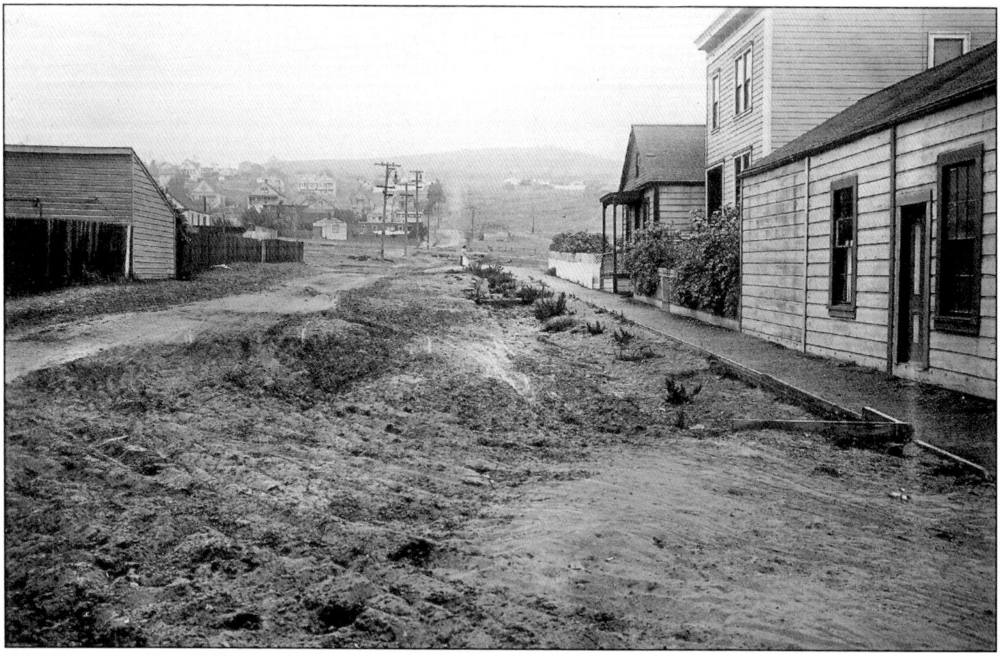

Al Cinti recalls, "When I first came here Leland wasn't all the way paved, just up to Rutland, and they had wooden sidewalks. Mr. Rossi [the pharmacist] was here on Leland, and then the water pump company was down the street, and the hotel and bar on the corner. Across the street where the bank is now they had a hotel. That's where we spent our first night when we arrived." This 1915 photograph shows the intersection of Rutland and Leland, looking north. (Courtesy a private collector.)

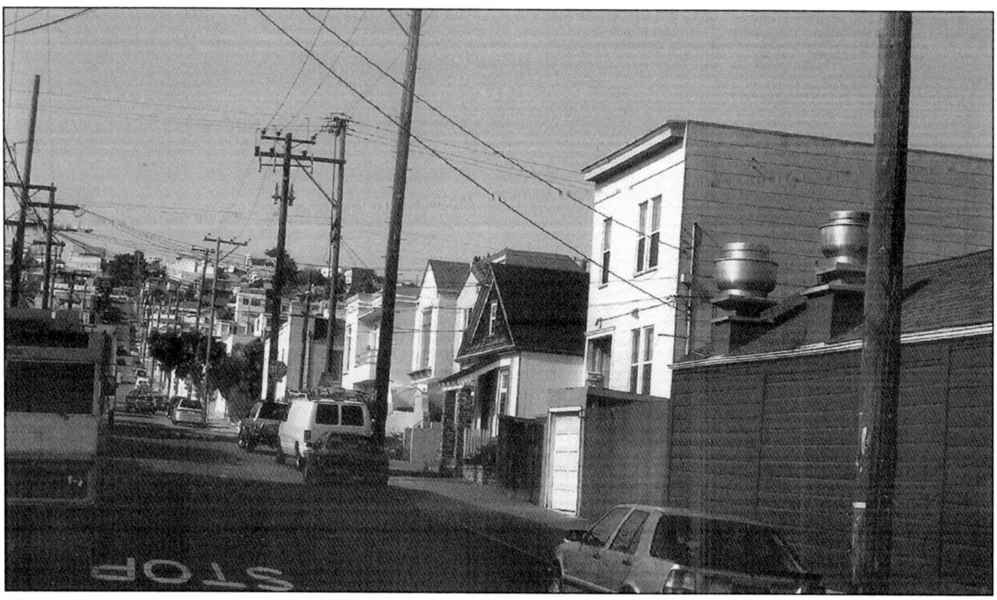

The same three structures on the right in the above picture have survived, while the neighborhood is now filled with homes. (Courtesy Edie Epps.)

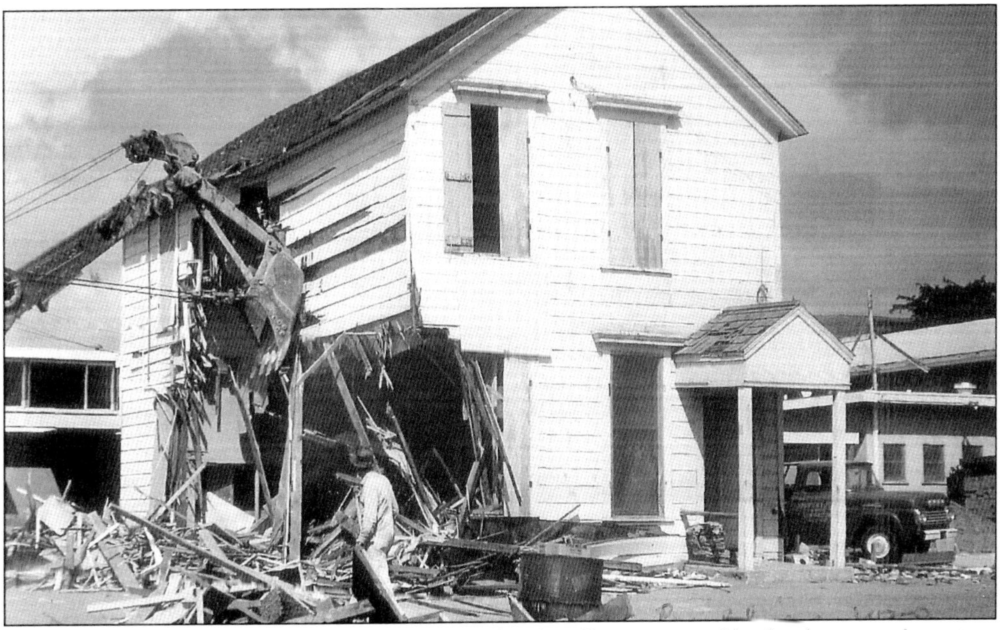

Peter Burnett, California's first governor, moved to San Francisco and built a home and carriage house with its own windmill and water pump on six acres in Visitacion Valley. Burnett developed a grove of over 200 trees. Viola Rusca notes, "At the time President McKinley and Admiral Byrd visited and they planted trees on the property." (Courtesy Church of the Visitacion.)

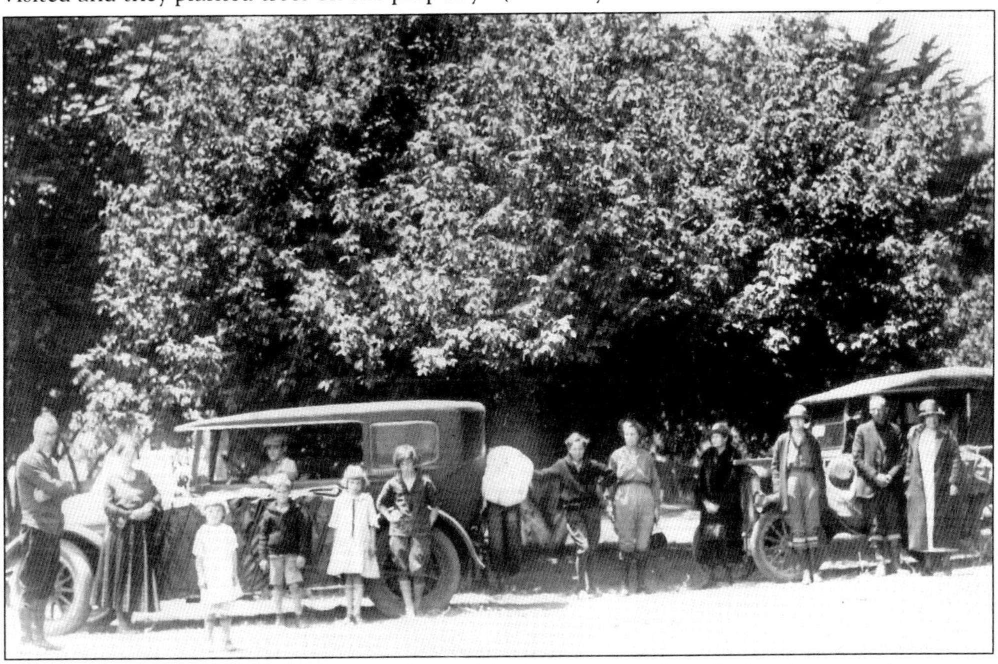

In the 1920s, the governor's house on Sunnydale Avenue served as the headquarters for an auto camp with 40 cabins, tent spaces, its own recreation hall, an outdoor dance platform, and store. The auto camp closed in the mid-1950s and later was razed to make way for a parish school. Church of the Visitacion catechism classes were held in the governor's home until it was demolished. (Courtesy San Francisco History Center, San Francisco Library.)

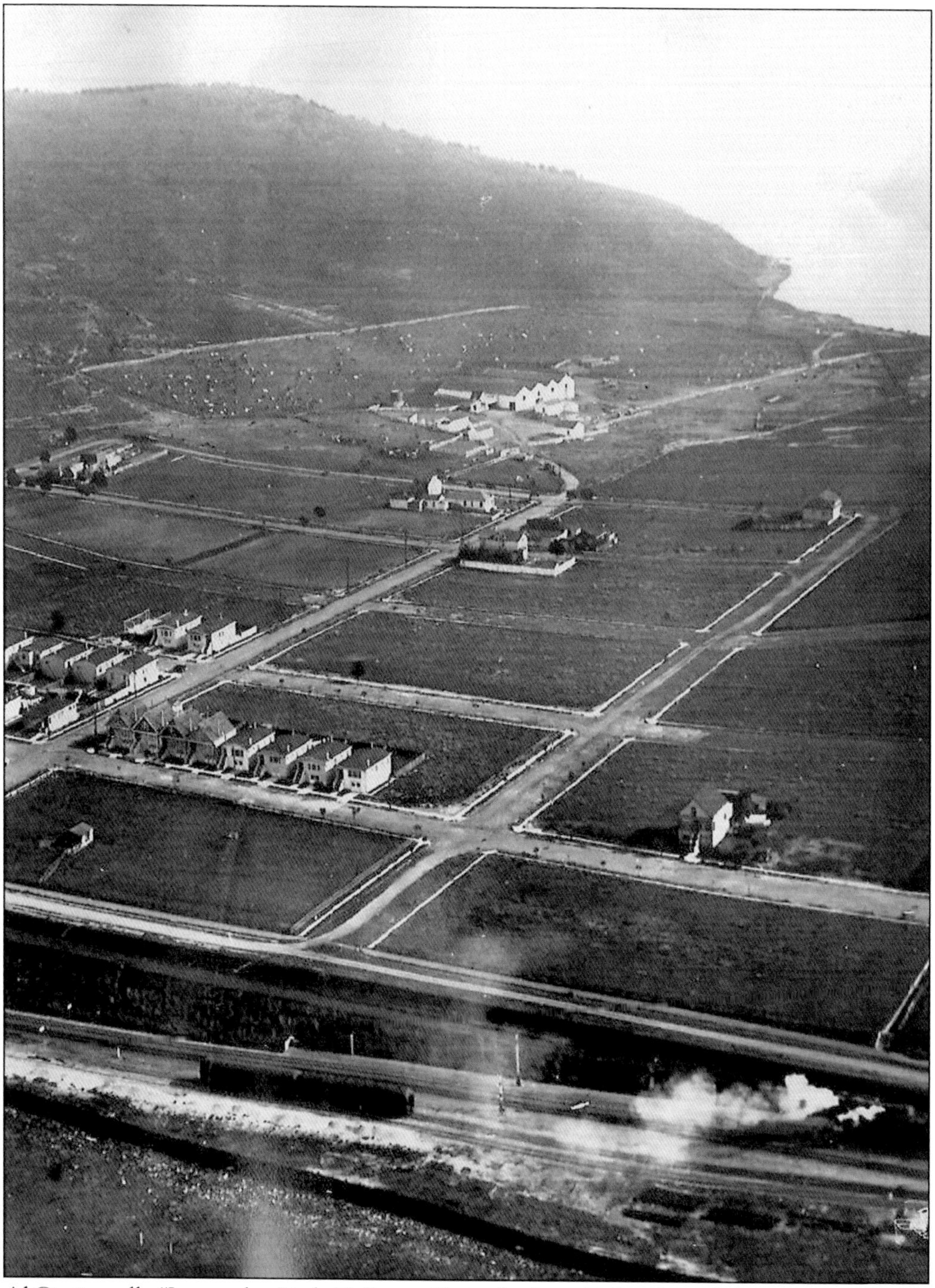

Al Cinti recalls, "I remember Little Hollywood being built up. Before then all that area was gardens and they had to fence it to keep people from helping themselves." And Alma Taylor remembered her mother sending one of her brothers for a bucket of milk from the Johnson and Brown Dairy, located on the south slope of what today is called Bayview Hill. This 1926 photograph looks north at the slope and shows Candlestick Point, the dairy and the first group of Little Hollywood houses. (Courtesy a private collector.)

Two

Shaping the Valley

Commerce and Transportation

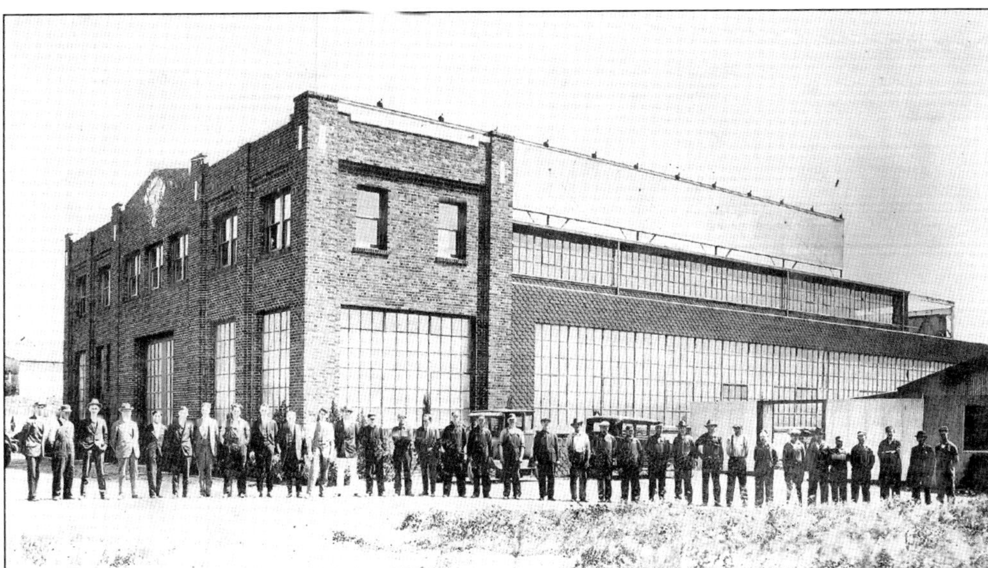

In the early part of the 20th century, the Bodinson Manufacturing Company, which produced custom mining machinery and material handling equipment, bought property in Visitacion Valley. The plant employed about 50 men, with a weekly payroll of approximately $2,000. Schlage Lock purchased its first piece of Valley property from Bodinson and went on to become a major presence in the neighborhood for the next seven decades, while Bodinson moved out of our area. (Courtesy San Francisco History Center, San Francisco Public Library.)

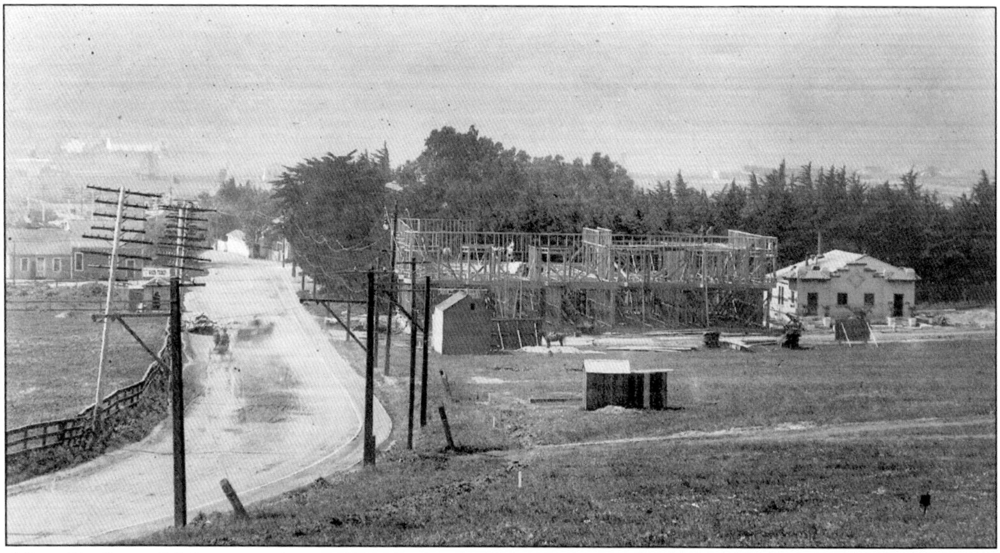

Alma Taylor, a lifelong resident of Visitacion Valley, wrote on the back of this c. 1905 image, "First building on Leland Avenue and Bayshore." Under construction on the left is the Bayshore Hotel. To the right is the Bay Shore Water Company pump house. The main road was San Bruno Road, now Bayshore Boulevard. (Courtesy San Francisco History Center, San Francisco Public Library.)

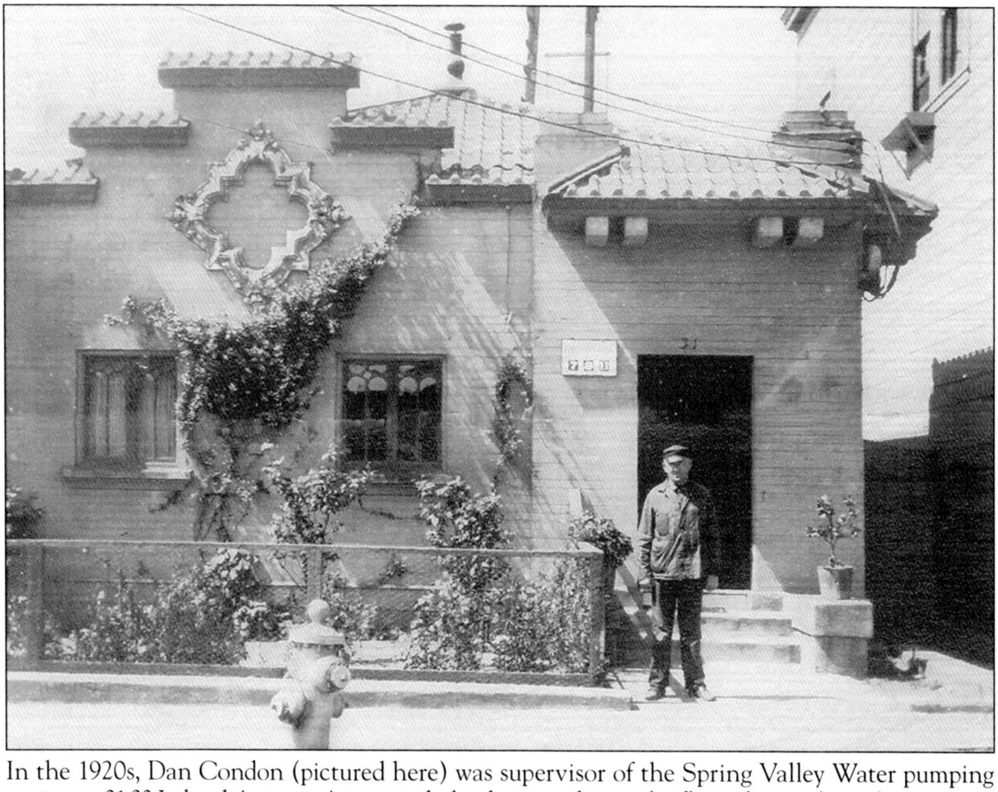

In the 1920s, Dan Condon (pictured here) was supervisor of the Spring Valley Water pumping station at 31-33 Leland Avenue. A woman helped to coordinate the flow of water from the reservoir atop the hill where Mansell Street is today. When signaled, the water would flow into the pumping station. Another signal indicated when the station was full. (Courtesy Danny O'Sullivan.)

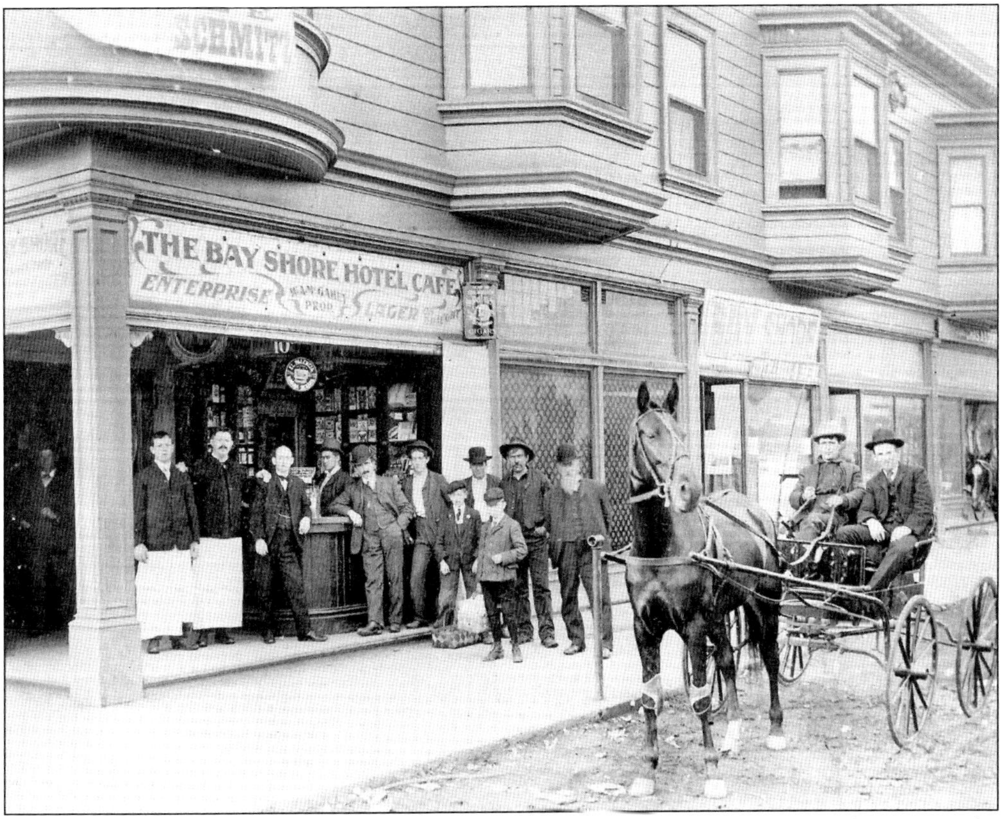

Alma Taylor, Clarence Wikse and Harry Pierce all remembered the excitement when scenes for a silent movie—either *Ten Nights in a Bar Room* or *A Half-Dollar Bill*, starring the Swedish-born actress Anna Q. Nilsson—was filmed at the Bayshore Hotel in the early 1920s. An unscripted comic bit occurred when a local resident known as Gerky appeared for his evening refreshment, saw a fight scene being shot, tried to break it up, and had to be forcibly removed from the set. (Courtesy San Francisco History Center, San Francisco Public Library.)

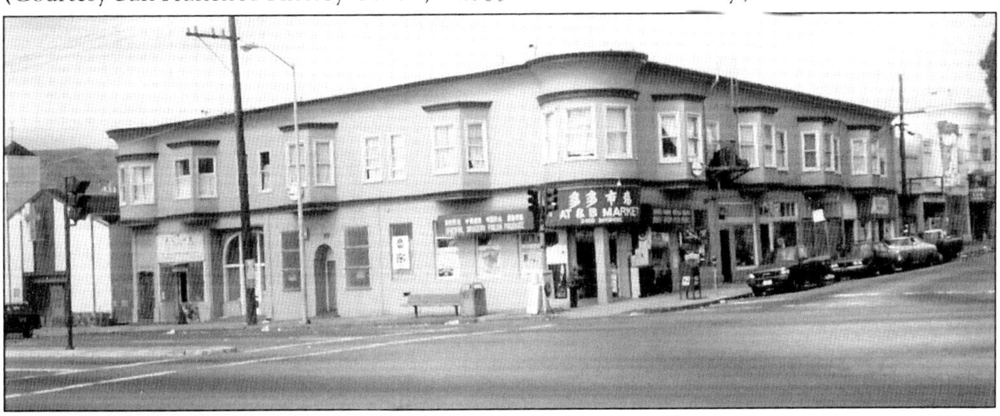

The former hotel at the corner of Bayshore and Leland, now with a market on the ground floor and apartments above, anchors Visitacion Valley's small business district. Leland Avenue was most likely named for prominent San Francisco investor Leland Stanford. Although many establishments along Leland have come and gone, this street remains the backbone of the community. (Courtesy Taylor family.)

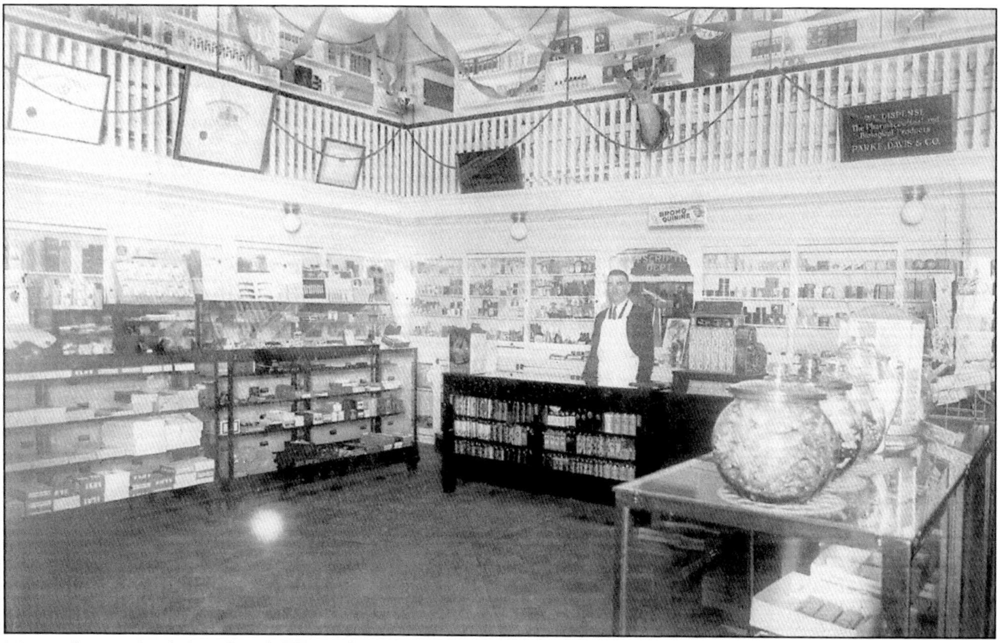

Near the end of the Civil War, the Rossi family established large vegetable gardens worked by hand. Later they joined other landowners in Visitacion Valley in an association and hired farm hands to do the heavy work. Virginio Rossi, pictured above, owned the Visitacion Valley Pharmacy on Leland until 1970, when his daughter took over. (Courtesy Rossi family.)

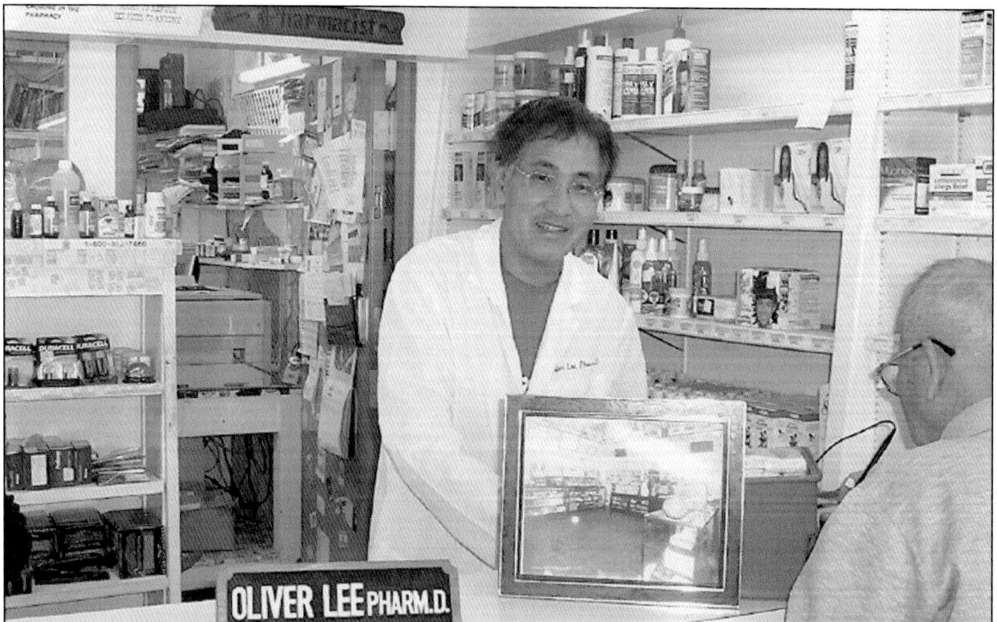

Oral historians Mary Leotta Schwartz, Anna Stuart Johnson, and Viola Cuccaro Rusca all remembered when the only library in the Valley was a bookshelf in the pharmacy. People simply borrowed books and returned them to the shelf when read, with no library card or fines. Today the drugstore has new owners, but the name remains the same. Pharmacist Oliver Lee holds the photograph of the store's original interior. (Courtesy Edie Epps.)

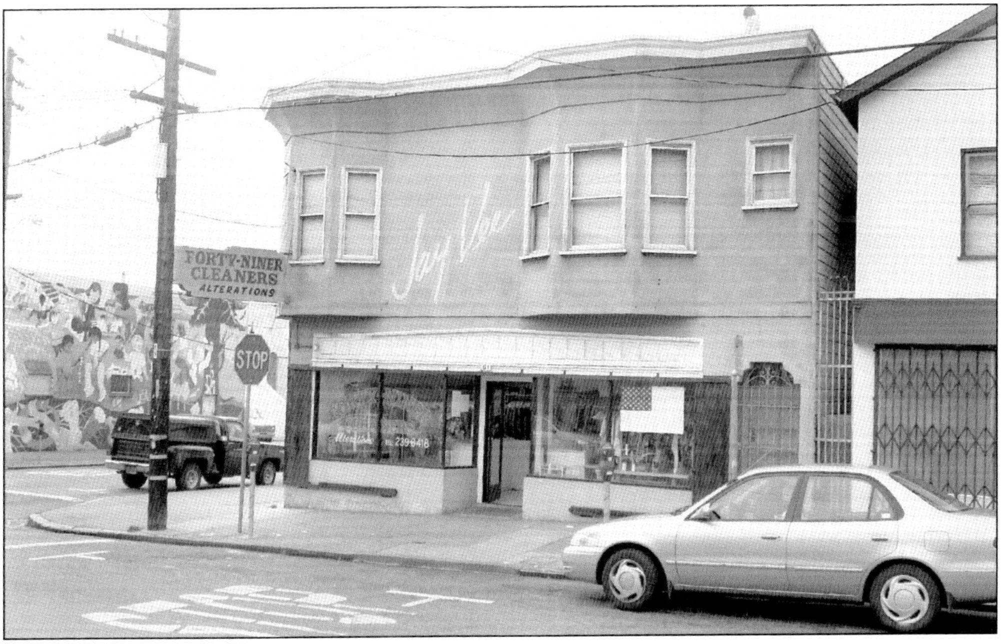

Over the years, a variety of shops have opened and closed along Leland Avenue. The Forty-Niner Cleaners at 51 Leland was once the site of the Jay Vee clothing store, whose sign is still visible across the building's front. Note the mural "Valley Vision" that decorates the library's west side, pictured on the left. (Courtesy Russel Morine.)

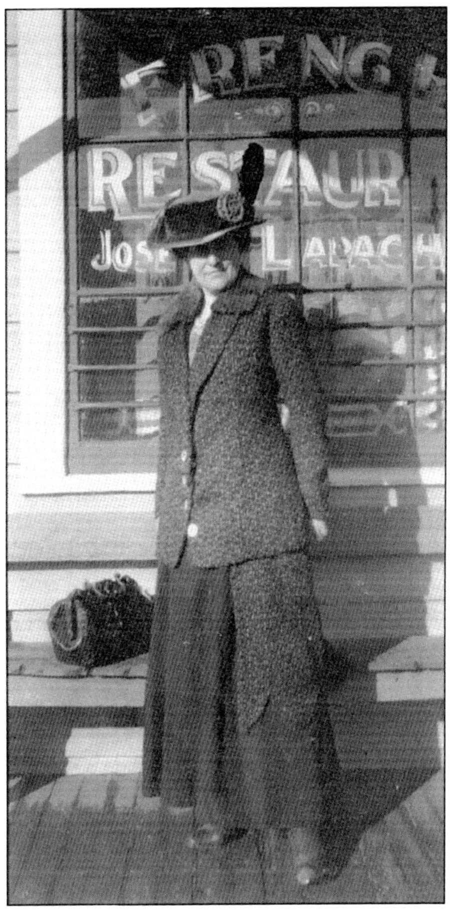

The Lapachet family lived in the Valley for almost 100 years and still owns property here. In the early 20th century, Rose Lafon Lapachet (pictured here) and her husband Joseph ran a combination boardinghouse/restaurant on Bayshore Boulevard as the Southern Pacific rail yards were being constructed. Joseph was also a co-owner of the Franco-American Dairy in the Excelsior neighborhood, and his half-brother ran horses and cattle on the hills where the Cow Palace now stands. (Courtesy San Francisco History Center, San Francisco Public Library.)

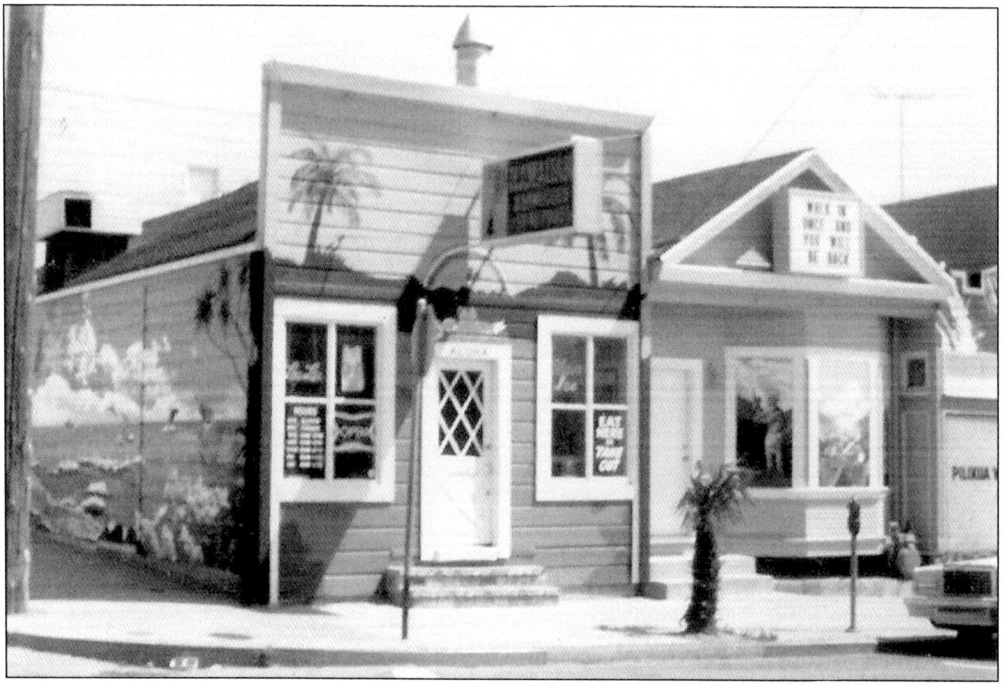

In the early 1900s, Dougherty's Grocery was at 198 Leland. George Gibson helped with deliveries and kept a wagon, horses, and a 1914 Overland truck across the street. The truck was fitted with shelves that could be removed and replaced with seats for a Sunday drive. Residents remember George, who lived to be 98, traveling through sand, rocks, mud, and slush to make deliveries. In the 1970s, the building housed a Samoan barbecue, pictured here. Today it is the G&L Bakery and Restaurant. (Courtesy Betty Parshall.)

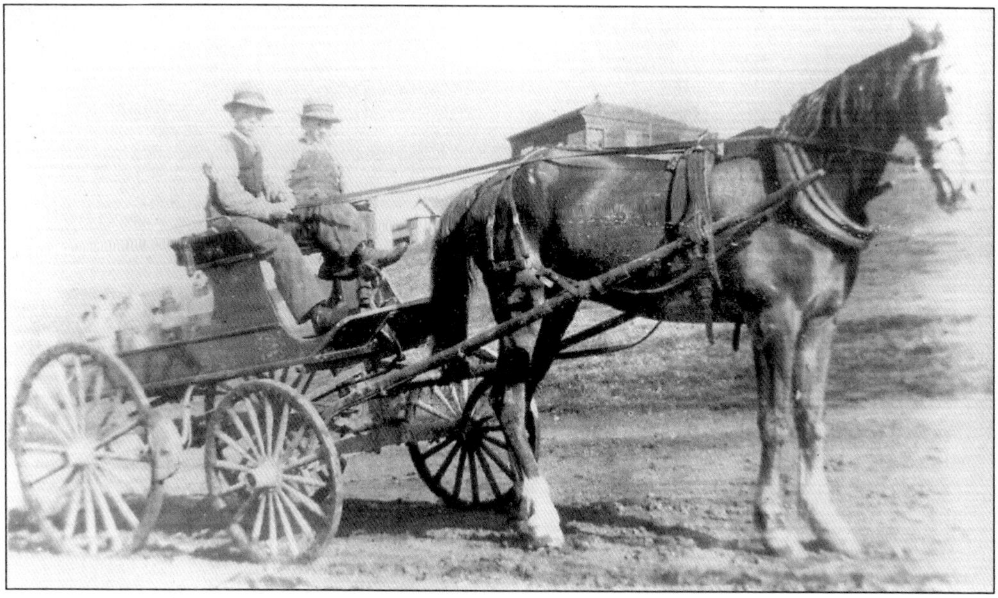

Customers would place their orders with Valley stores in the morning, to be delivered in the afternoon rounds. It took a strong horse to pull a loaded wagon over the dirt roads and up the steep hills. (Courtesy Taylor family.)

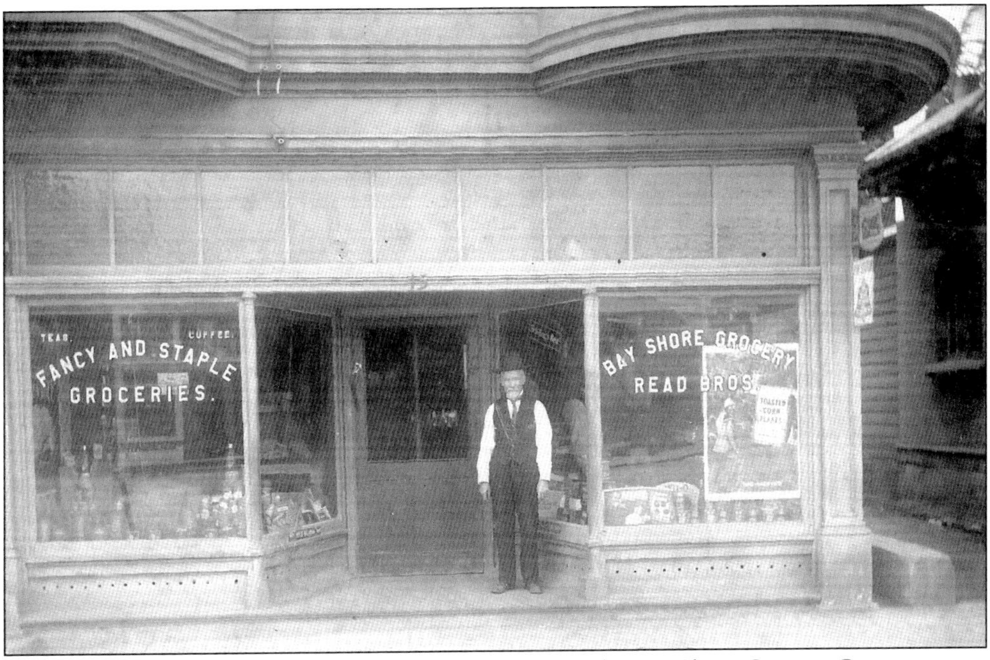

Read Brothers Grocery at 15 Leland, alternatively called the Bay Shore Grocery Company, was operated by Walter and Robert Read and Robert's wife, Mary, throughout the early years of the 20th century. In this photograph, an unidentified man stands in the doorway of the store where both "fancy and staple groceries" were sold. (Courtesy Visitacion Valley Community Center.)

Leland Children's Shop *Infant's, boy's, and girl's wear, nursery furnitures* 15 Leland Ave. Henry Metz JU. 7-8149	**Arthur Resnick** REALTOR Arthur Realty Co. 2320 BAYSHORE BLVD. Off. JU. 5-7345 Res. JU. 7-0394	**FOX'S RESTAURANT & FOUNTAIN** * * * 73 Leland Ave. JU 6-5753	**TEDDY GROCERY** *John and Violet Rado* 296 Teddy Avenue JU. 5-1604
Guttner's Grocery *Groceries & School Supplies* Edna & Clarence Guttner 351 Wilde Avenue JU. 5-6645	**B. S. C.** CLEANERS & LAUNDRY * * * 29 Leland Ave. JU. 7-6464	**Torino Ravioli** *Groceries* 2458 Bayshore Blvd. DE. 3-3578	**norma's beauty shop** 186 Leland Ave. JU 6-6630
Johnson & Son Hardware Co. *Hardware & Builders' Supplies, Paints and Glass* 34 Leland Ave. JU. 5-4958	**Jerry's Texaco Service** *Lubrication, Tune-Up* *Tires — New & Recaps* *Batteries & Accessories* Bayshore & Raymond JU. 4-7511	**Brown Jewelers** *L. Danielson* *Watch repair, diamonds, watches & gifts* 10 Leland Ave. JU. 4-4079	**Forty Niner Cleaners** *Cleaning — Pressing* *Alterations* * * * 93 Leland Ave. JU. 4-3322
VERDA'S BEAUTY SALON *Open Thurs. eve. by appointment* 9:00 to 5:30 170-B Leland Ave. Closed Mon. DE. 3-4045	**Campbell Grocery** BILL & EVELYN DALY 523 Campbell Avenue DE. 3-9866	**Annette's Beauty Service** *Everything for Beauty* 21 Leland Ave. JU. 4-5148	**Bay Shore Grocery** *Groceries, fresh fruits & vegetables* * * * 45 Leland Ave. JU. 5-4897 *Free Delivery*

This display of advertisements from St. James' 50th-anniversary booklet indicates the wide variety of businesses patronized by Valley residents in 1956. (Courtesy St. James Presbyterian.)

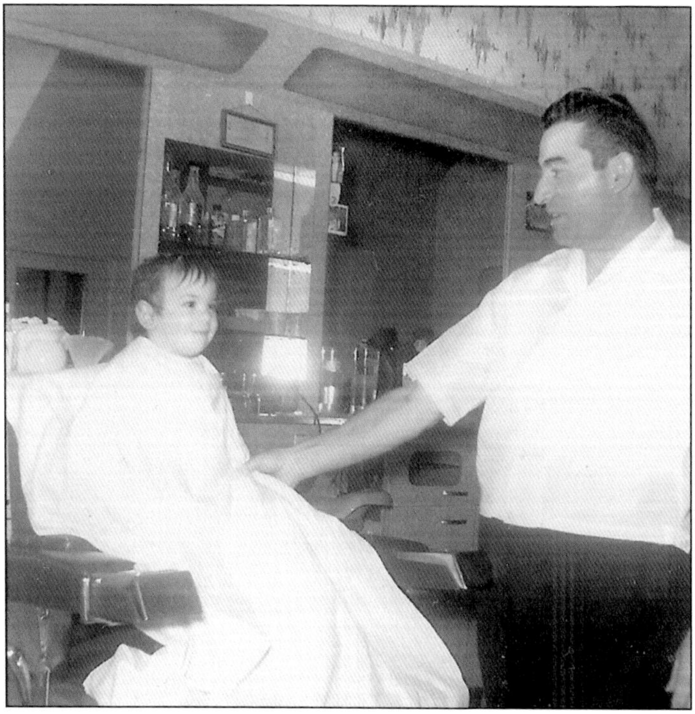

Al Cinti owned the barbershop at 130 Leland. In this 1965 photograph, he is pictured with his son Raymond, who has just had one of his father's good haircuts. (Courtesy Al Cinti.)

Another thriving business on Leland was Brown Jewelers, owned by Louis and Olga Brown. In 1958, Governor Edmund Brown (no relation) stopped by to admire the merchandise. Today the Bank of America parking lot occupies the site. (Courtesy Charles Arosio.)

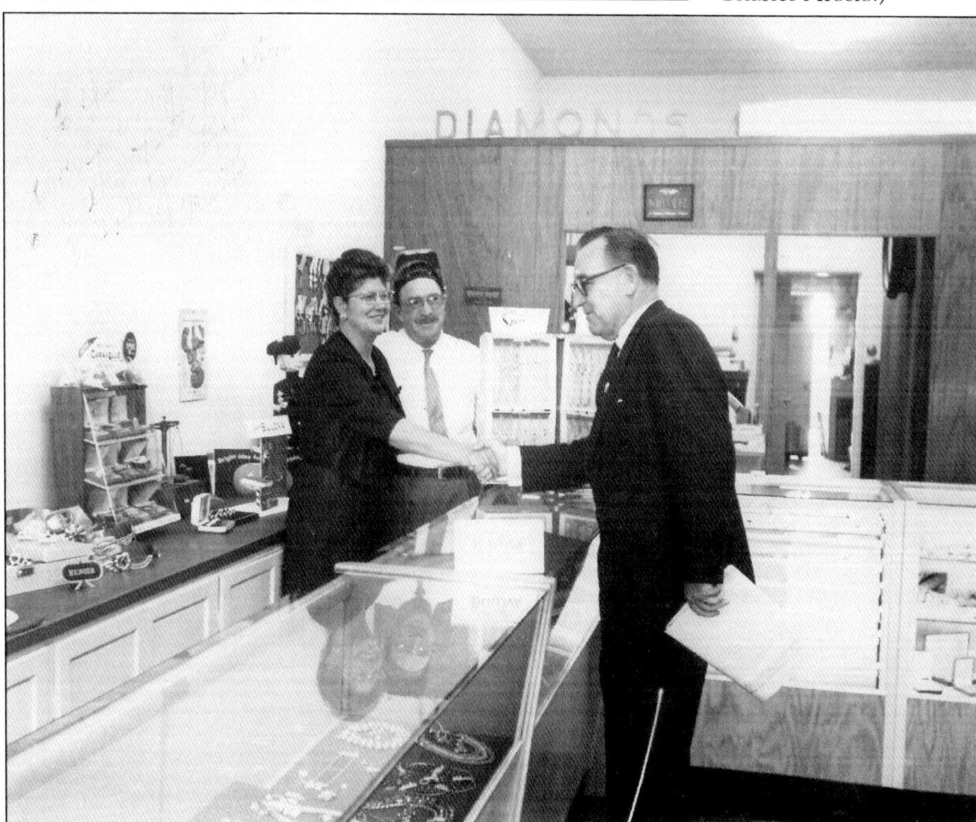

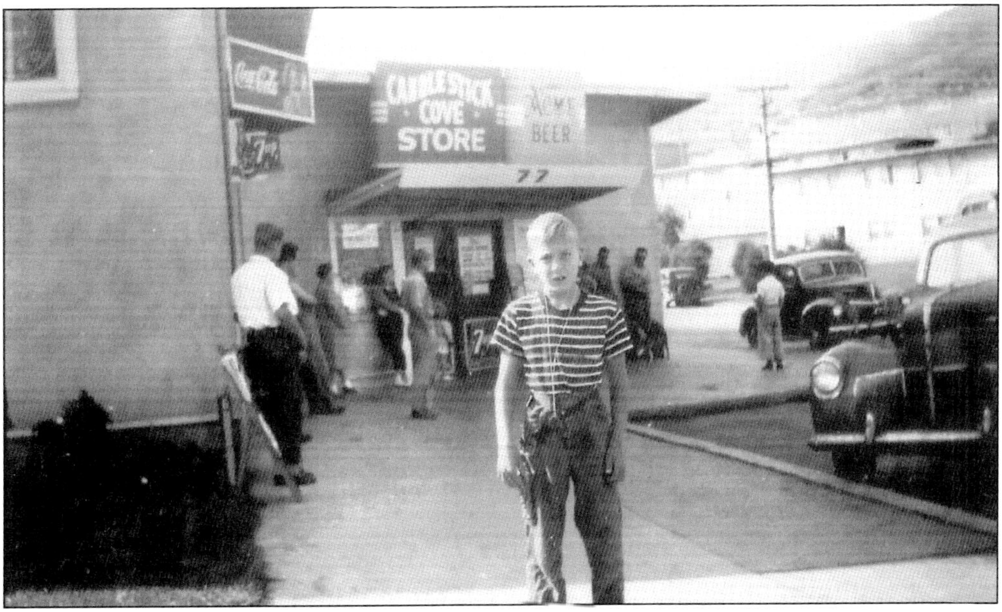

Longtime Valley residents might recall the Candlestick Cove Store and Fox's Creamery as part of the Candlestick Cove housing project. The project was erected for core craftsmen working at Hunter's Point Naval Shipyard. Hank Guernsey stands in front of the store, located where Little Hollywood's Executive Park stands today. In later years, Fox's Creamery moved to Leland Avenue. (Courtesy Hank Guernsey.)

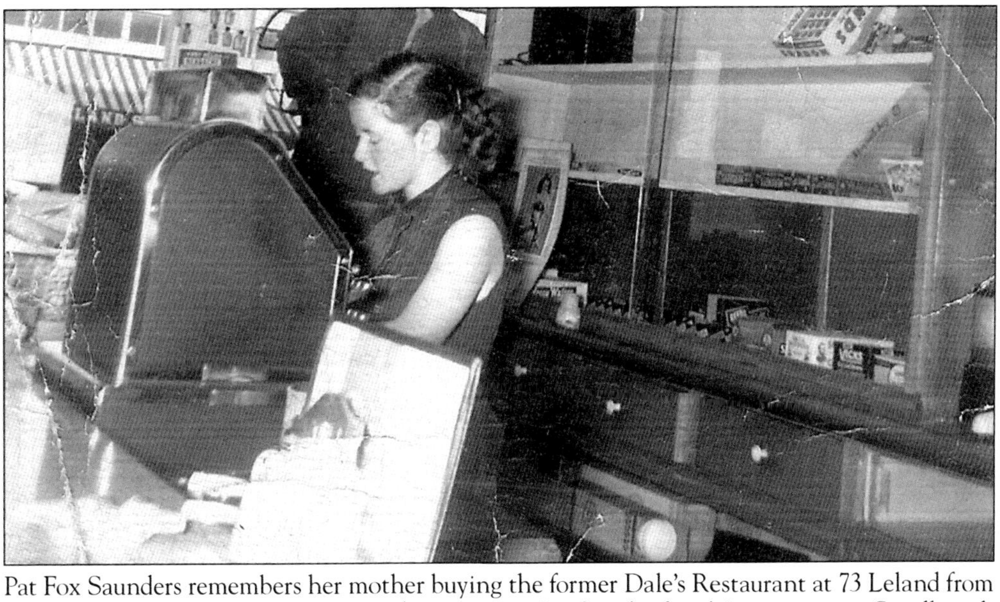

Pat Fox Saunders remembers her mother buying the former Dale's Restaurant at 73 Leland from the Leonetti family for approximately $2,000 in 1953, after the family's creamery at Candlestick Cove was closed to make way for the new freeway. The new space continued to fill at lunchtime with factory and office workers, and Pat helped out after school and on Saturdays. Today a Vietnamese restaurant is located here. (Courtesy Pat Fox Saunders.)

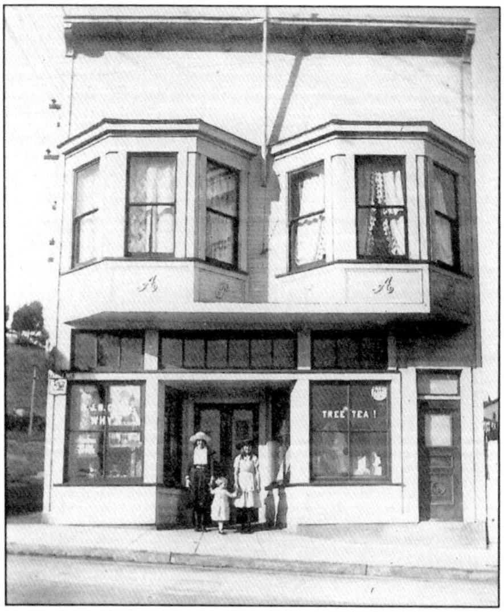

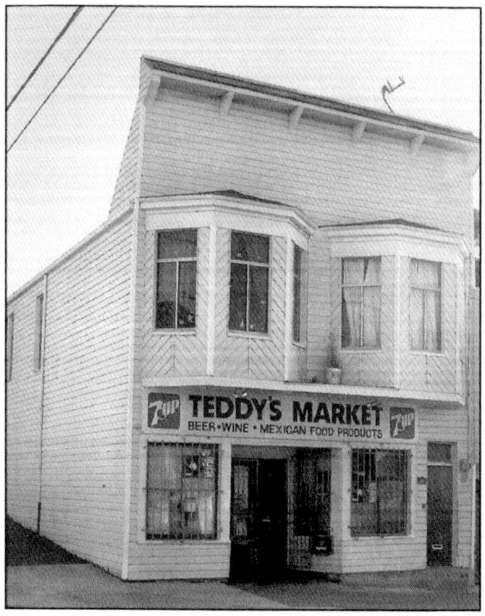

Pictured above left in this c. 1910 shot, Peterson's grocery store was one of dozens of corner markets in Visitacion Valley. Pictured above right, Teddy's Market at the corner of Teddy and Delta Streets is still in business, now owned by the Torres family. (Left photograph courtesy Harry Pierce; right photograph courtesy Edie Epps.)

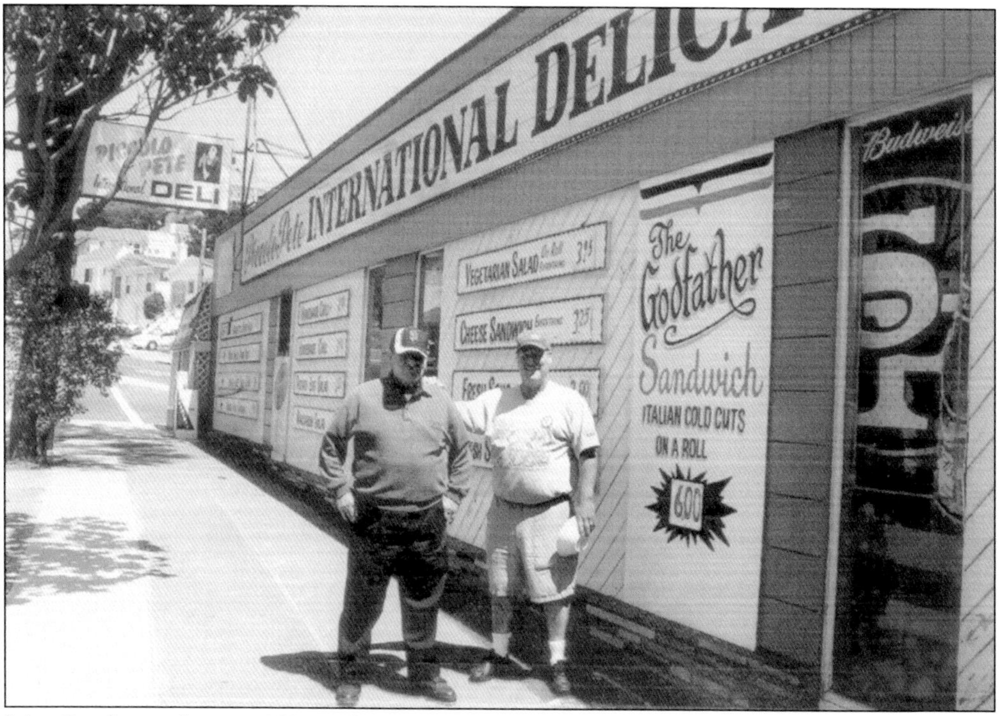

John Siri Sr. was born in 1921 on his parents' vegetable farm, where the Cow Palace is today. At a young age, he purchased his own produce market on Geneva and Mission, and later opened Siri's Markets throughout the San Francisco area. Pictured here with his son John Jr., they opened Picolo Pete International Delicatessen in 1987 and have sold over 200,000 sandwiches to sports fans and locals. "As long as the teams are doing well, then sandwiches sell!" proclaims Senior. (Courtesy Edie Epps.)

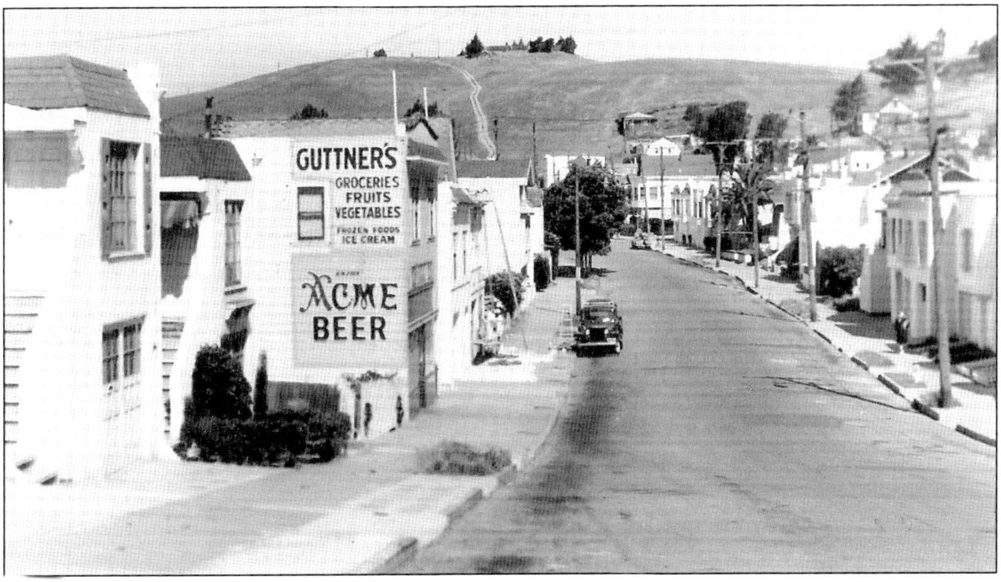

One of two small stores on the 300 and 400 blocks of Wilde (pronounced "Wild-ie" by the locals) Avenue was Guttner's Grocery. The ladder of painter Tom Taylor is propped against the house next door to Guttner's. Further along the street was a store at 400 Wilde, still in business as the KC Market. At the top of the hill is the old reservoir in McLaren Park. Current residents wish the street were still as empty of parked cars! (Courtesy Taylor family.)

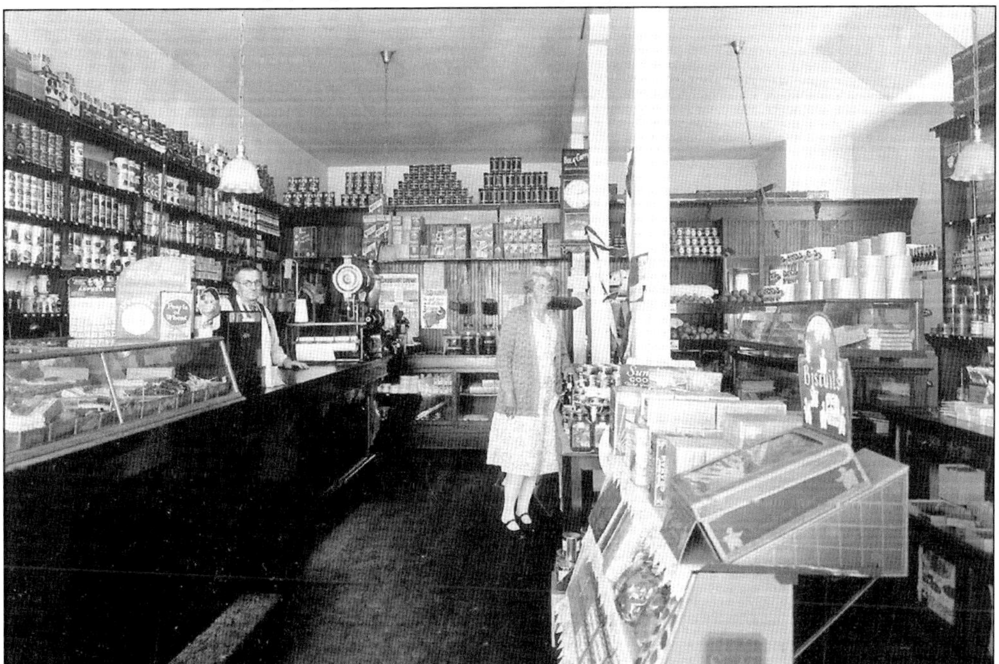

Proprietor Clarence Guttner, active in Valley civic affairs throughout his lifetime, stands behind the counter of his store, as his mother-in-law, Mrs. Hayes, decides on her purchase. On the left is the penny candy case where the neighborhood children pondered how to spend their precious coins. (Courtesy Taylor family.)

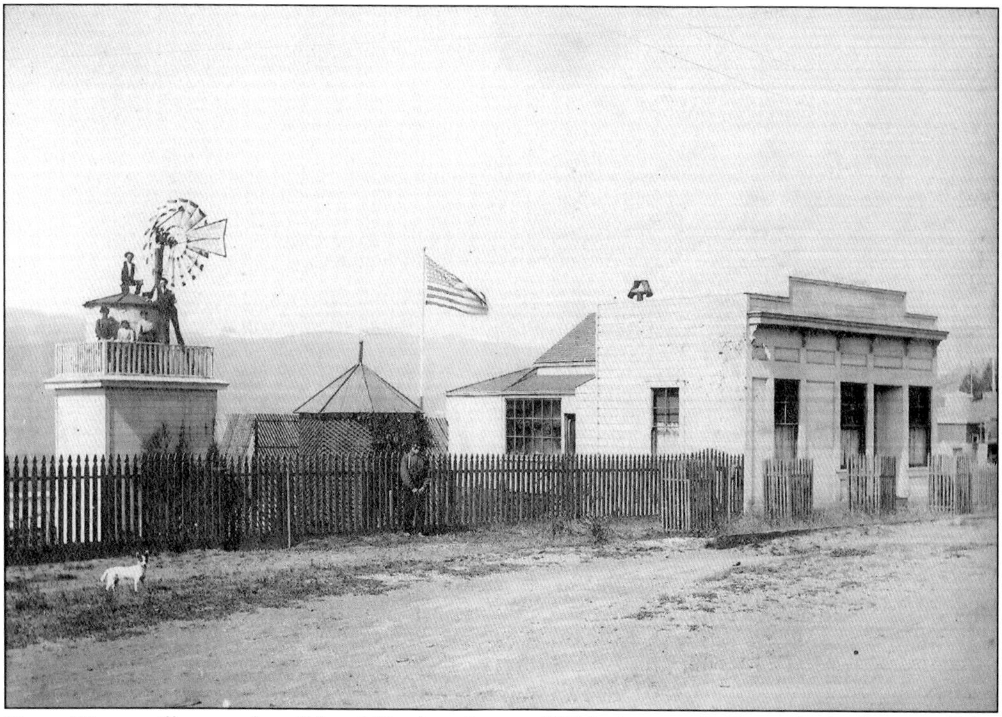

Harry Pierce still remembers "the old barber shop on Wilde Avenue. Bill was the barber—well, he didn't make all his money from barbering—he was a bootlegger. But at Bill's place you never saw any trouble, only his regular customers. I don't know what he charged for his shots [of liquor] but my father always came home happy when he had a haircut." Windmills such as the one pictured here were once common in the Valley. (Courtesy Taylor family.)

REAL ESTATE
INSURANCE

OFFICE
JUNIPER 4-9155

LEONETTI REALTY CO.

BUY OR SELLS - LOANS OR EXCHANGES

NOTARY PUBLIC

REPRESENTED BY
VINCENT LEONETTI

57 LELAND AVENUE
SAN FRANCISCO, CALIF. 94134

The Leonettis still own property in the Valley. The site of their former real estate company at 57 Leland now serves as the youth center for the Chinese Baptist church. (Courtesy Mary Schwartz.)

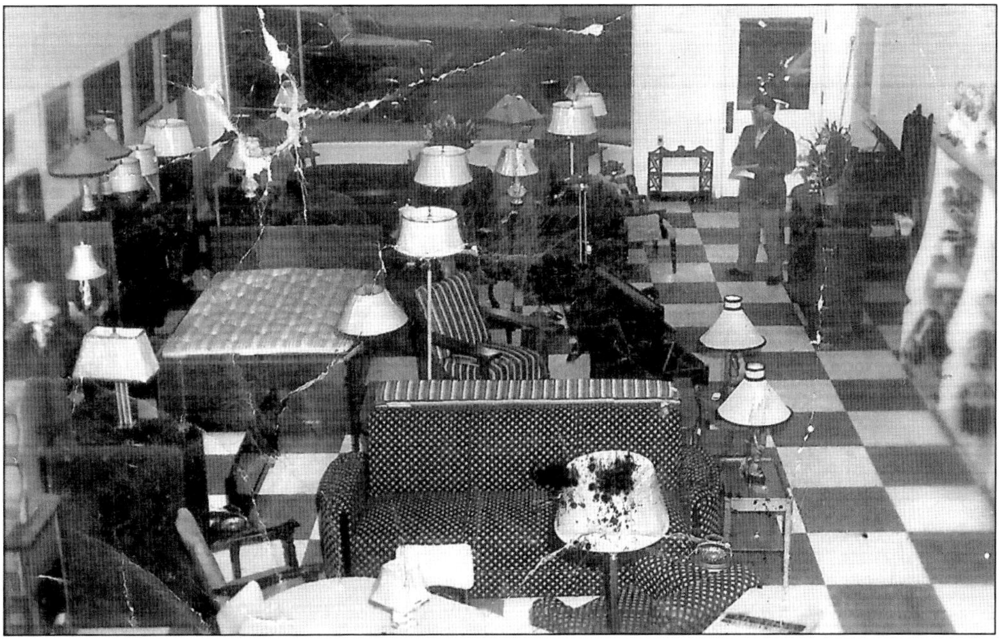

Henry Schindel and his wife, Molly Leonetti, lived on Schwerin Street, where they raised two daughters. In 1950, he opened the first of what would eventually total six successful businesses on Leland Avenue, including this furniture store. He served as president of the merchants association and as president of the Visitacion Valley Improvement Association, and also worked closely with the community center. Anna Stuart Johnson still uses the washing machine she purchased from Schindel's many years ago. (Courtesy Harriet Schindel Newhart.)

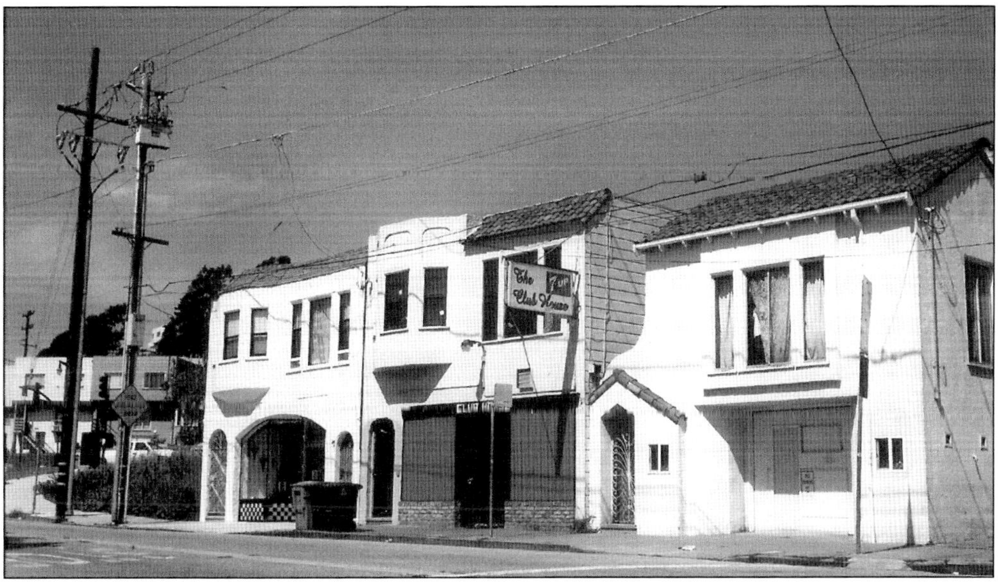

Today the Club House stands in the first block of Blanken off Bayshore. Built in the 1940s as the Hillside Market by Salvador Jimenez's father, which subsequently moved across the street just east of Tunnel, for many years the Club House was the lunch stop for the workers at Schlage Lock and Sunset Scavenger. The beauty salon that currently occupies the ground floor space to the right has also served as a meat market and a pharmacy. (Courtesy Edie Epps.)

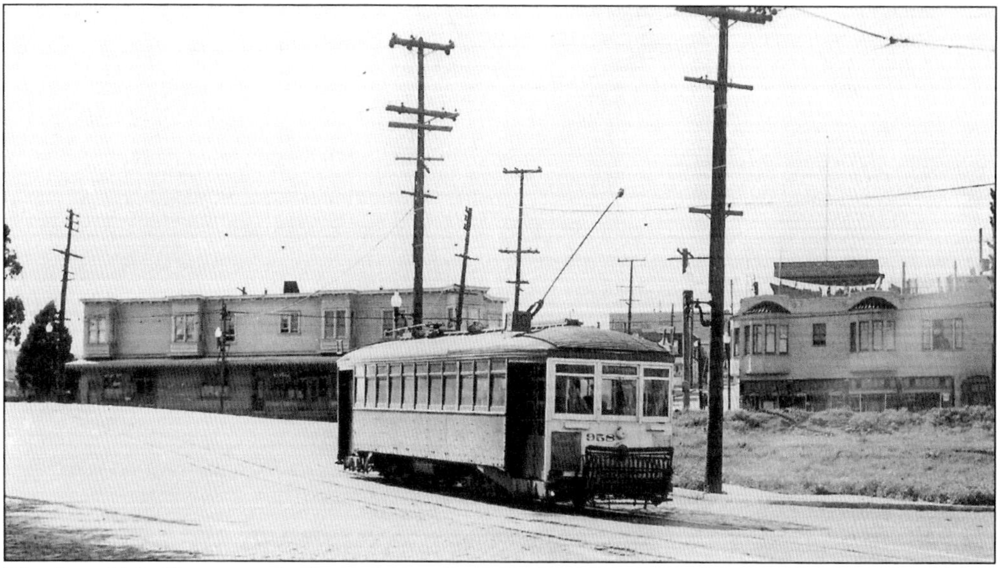

The Five Mile House marked a major stop at the intersection of San Bruno Road and Third Street, pictured here. This line came from downtown to Visitacion Valley, and oral historian Mary Schwartz recalls, "Sometimes the motorman declared the Five Mile House the end of the line, and those who lived in the Valley had to walk over the hills to home. But this was so common no one thought anything of it." (Courtesy a private collector.)

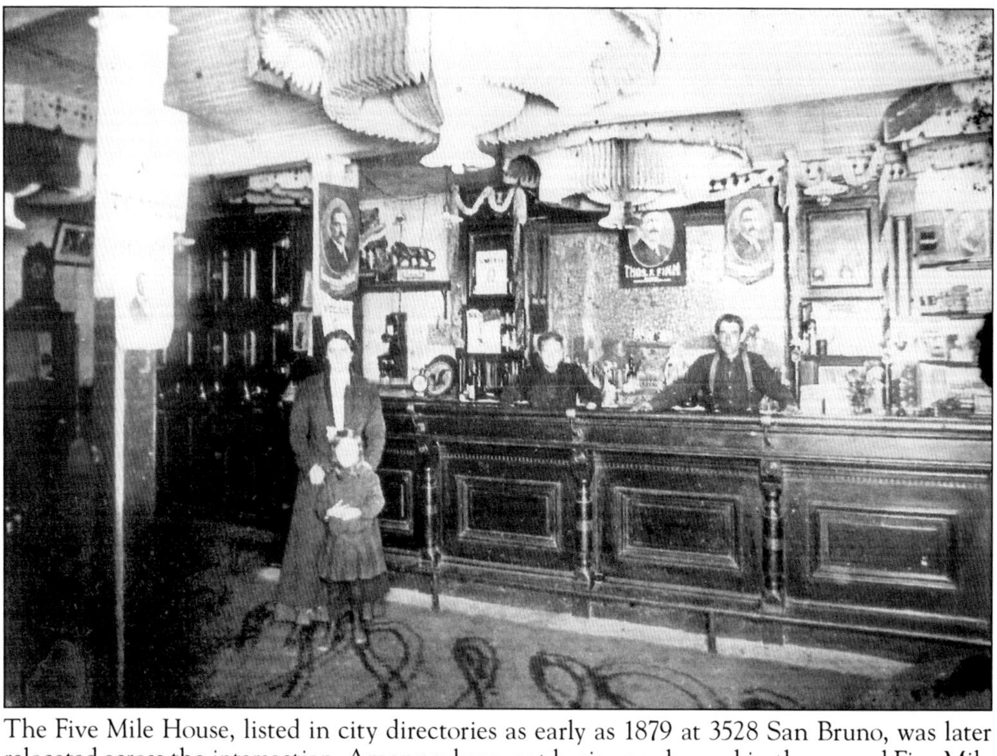

The Five Mile House, listed in city directories as early as 1879 at 3528 San Bruno, was later relocated across the intersection. Among subsequent businesses housed in the second Five Mile House were Riley's Saloon (pictured here), a grocery store owned by Mr. and Mrs. Fanning, and a Mexican restaurant. Today the building serves as private apartments. (Courtesy Taylor family.)

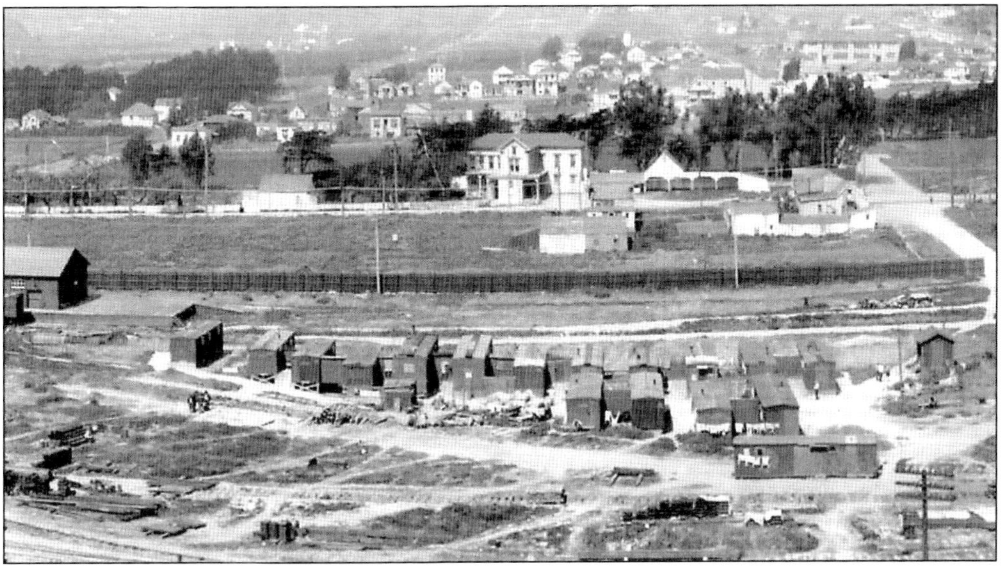

"Pop" Blanken's Six Mile House, located on Bayshore Boulevard near today's county line, was for many years a place popular with businessmen and politicians. As shown in center of this panorama, it was a "rural resort" that provided the usual food, drink, and lodging. In addition, the Six Mile House offered recreational opportunities like trap and rifle shooting, shuffleboard, and bowling, and served as the training headquarters for prize boxers, including "Gentleman Jim" Corbett. (Courtesy a private collector.)

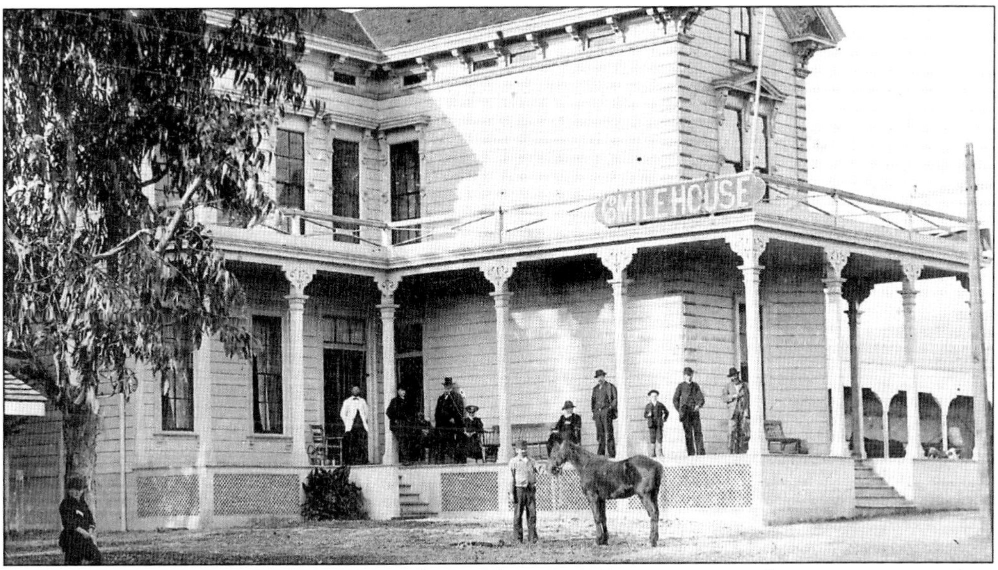

In 1938, the Six Mile House was razed to make space for a garage and gas station, another piece of history lost to "progress." (Courtesy San Francisco History Center, San Francisco Public Library.)

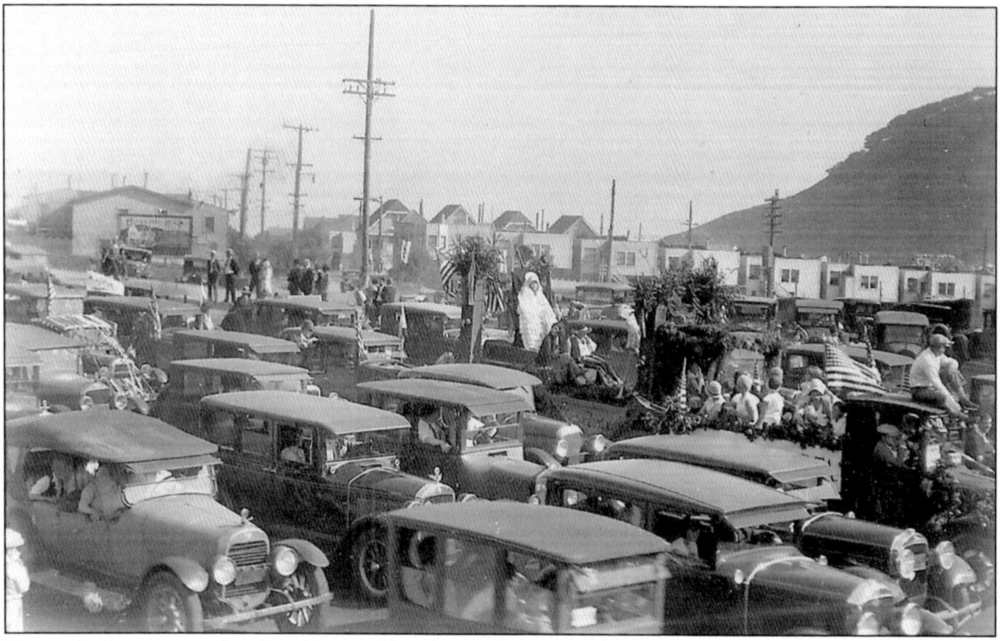

Formerly known as the San Bruno Road, Bayshore Boulevard was widened and reconfigured in an attempt to relieve heavy traffic on El Camino Real, the major thoroughfare connecting San Francisco and San Jose. This photograph of the grand opening ceremonies in 1929, when Elizabeth Ghirado served as queen of the parade, demonstrates the heavy turnout of both cars and residents on this occasion. (Courtesy George Siebel.)

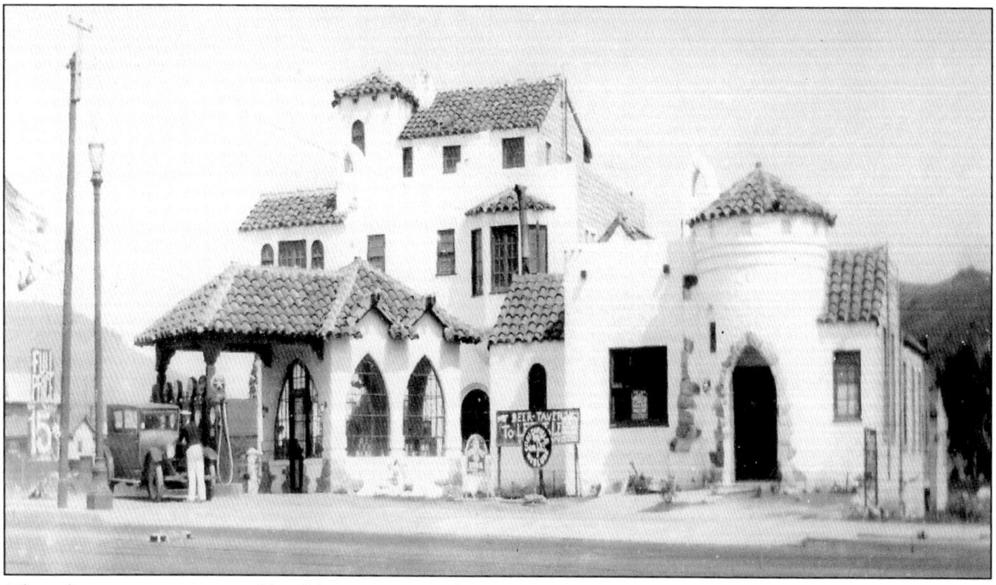

This distinctive group of buildings on Bayshore at Visitacion was built for the Rodiack family between 1933 and 1935. The gas station and rental apartments were designed by Charles Schultz, while Joseph Rodiack himself designed the tavern to the right in the same style. Note that at the time this photograph was taken, gas was selling for 15¢ a gallon, and that the tavern, which eventually became the Tower Inn, where locals could enjoy a meal and a drink, was for lease. (Courtesy Carol Sheehan.)

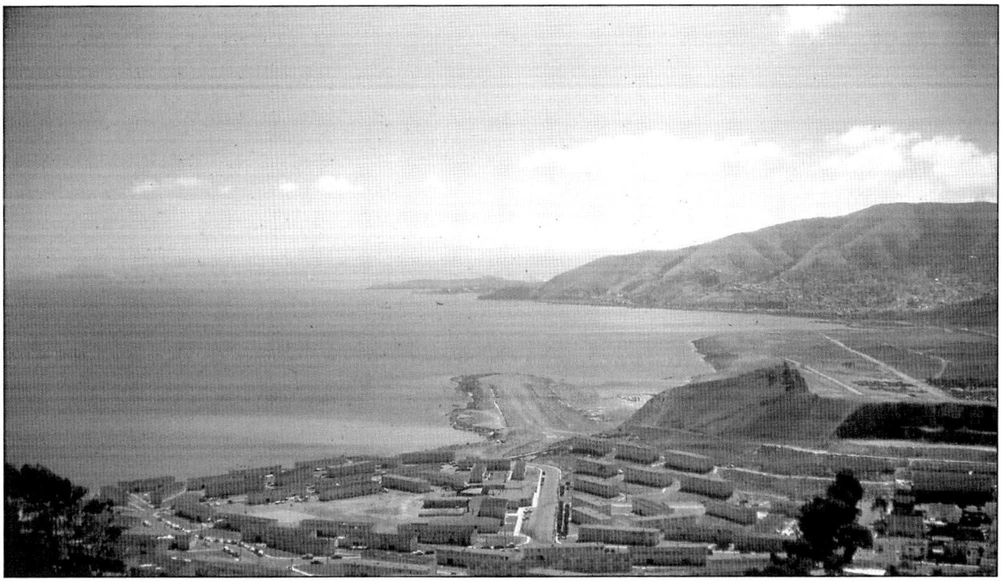

Highway 101 opened in 1954 and continues to serve as one of the Bay Area's major freeways. This photograph shows the beginning of the construction process, which was built on landfill and led to the demolishment of Candlestick Cove housing. (Courtesy Andrew J. Brandi.)

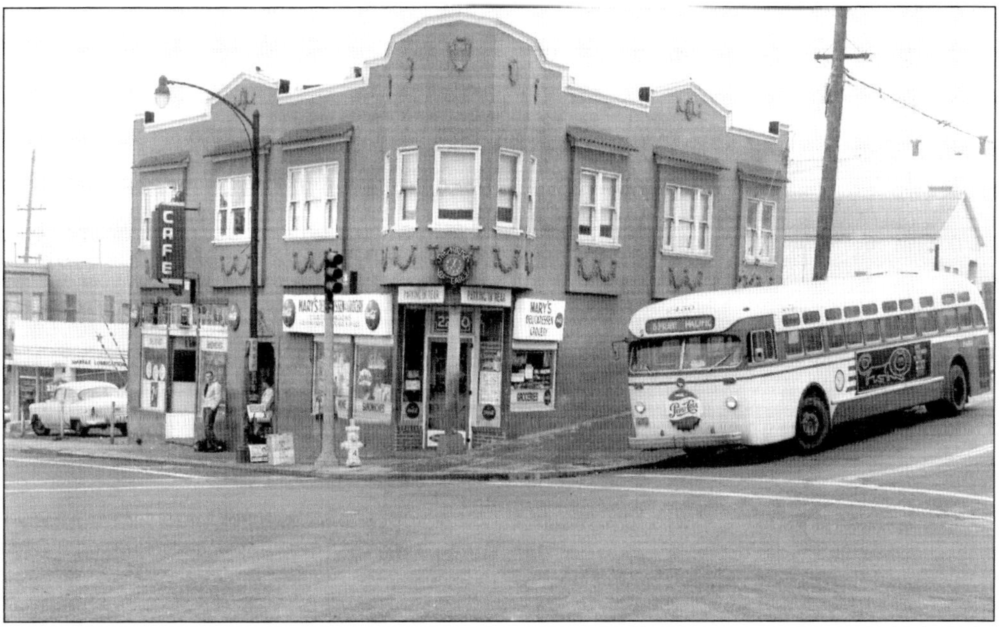

Arleta Avenue, at the San Bruno and Bayshore intersection, has been a MUNI transfer hub for many years. This 1962 photograph shows the corner grocery store, cafe, and apartments that were later replaced by the parking lot for a 7-Eleven convenience store. (Courtesy San Francisco History Center, San Francisco Public Library.)

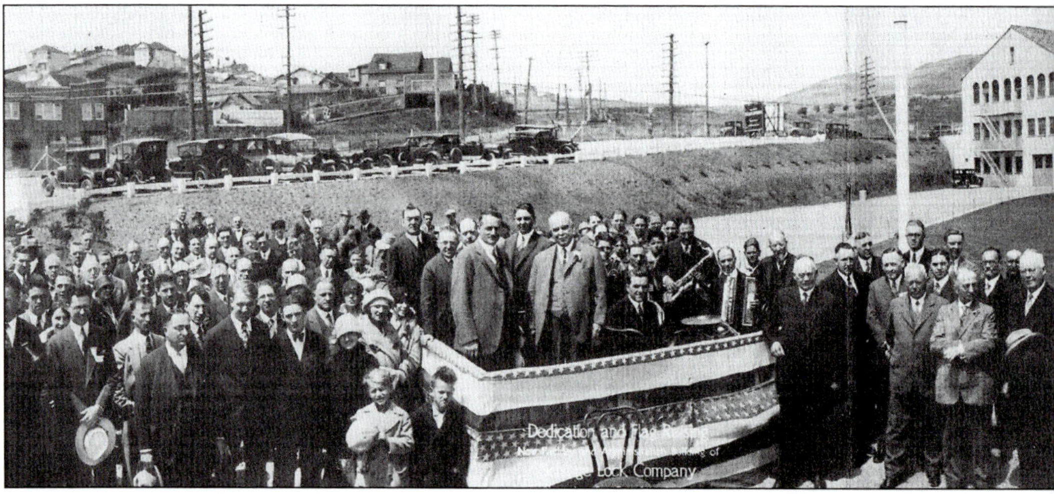

On June 25, 1926, Schlage Lock celebrated its new factory and administrative headquarters with a dedication and flag-raising ceremony. Mayor James Rolph Jr. addressed the crowd, as did the heads of the downtown association and the chamber of commerce. Southern Pacific transported guests

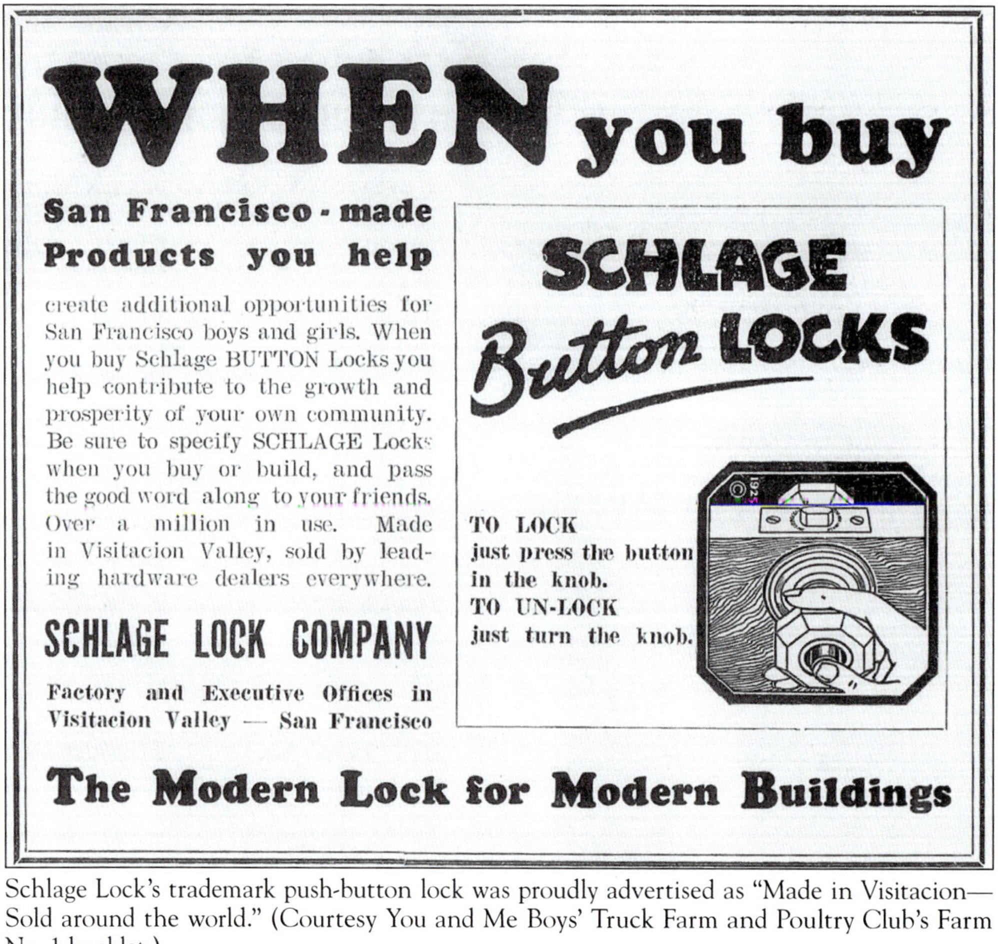

Schlage Lock's trademark push-button lock was proudly advertised as "Made in Visitacion—Sold around the world." (Courtesy You and Me Boys' Truck Farm and Poultry Club's Farm No. 1 booklet.)

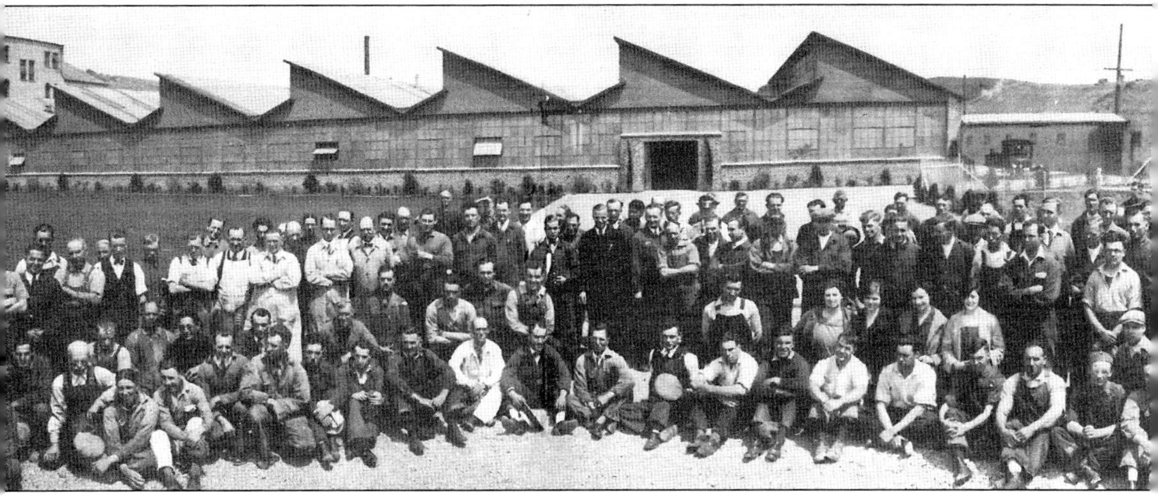

via a special train from Third and Townsend, while many workers and local residents also joined in the festivities. (Courtesy *Lock and Key*, Schlage Lock, January–February–March 1967.)

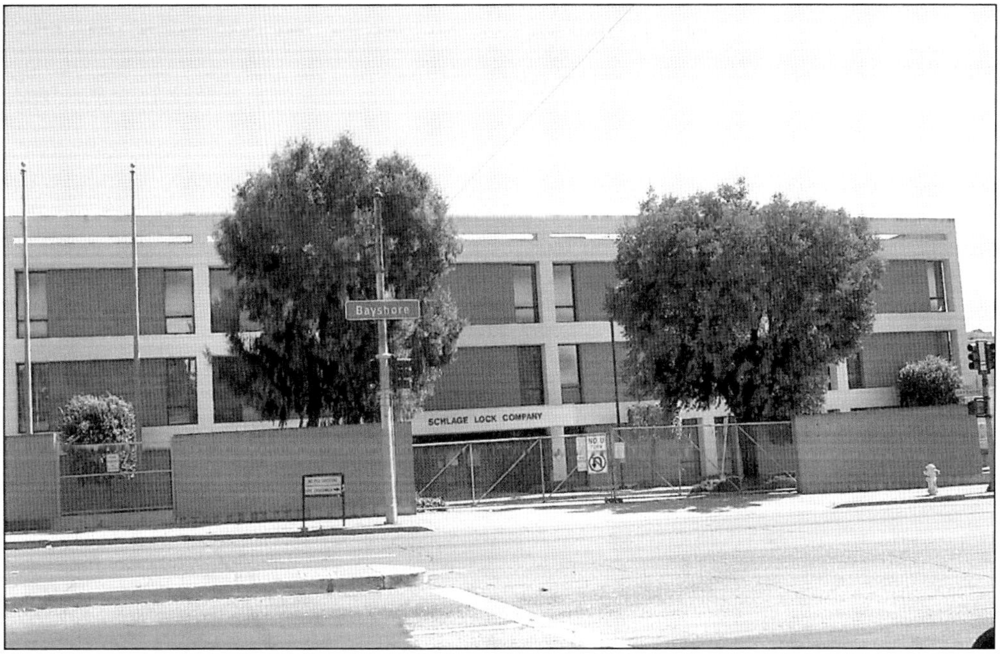

Since the late 1990s, the Schlage buildings have been locked and deserted. In response to Home Depot's proposal to build a megastore at this site, the Visitacion Valley Planning Alliance was formed to work together to bring a variety of smaller retail-serving businesses to the neighborhood instead. (Courtesy Taylor family.)

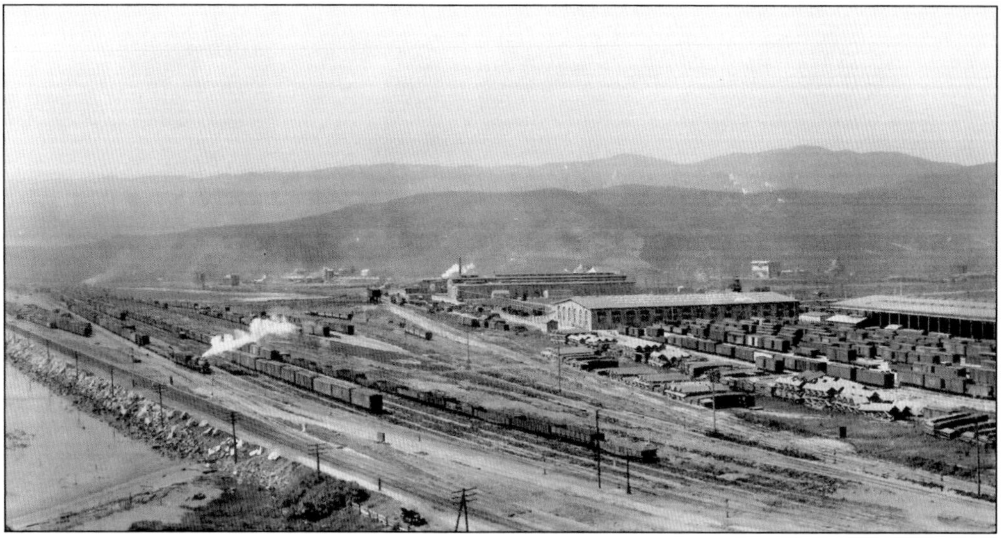

Southern Pacific was a major employer in the Valley in the first half of the 20th century. According to the 1926 Reis Tract's sales brochure, Southern Pacific's "shop and yards cover 226 acres. There are 1,196 employees; the average monthly pay is $164.31." Men worked on the trains and in the yards, the major repair and maintenance center for the Coast Division. (Courtesy a private collector.)

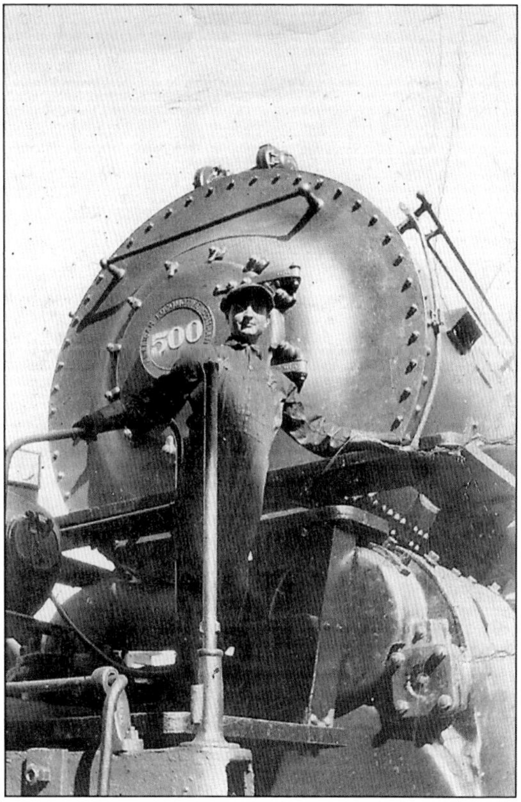

In this 1940s photograph, machinist Peter Sutti services Engine No. 500 at Southern Pacific's Bayshore yard. During World War II, he and others in the Valley worked double shifts for the war effort. For decades, hundreds of people were employed by Southern Pacific and Schlage Lock, and a great many of them lived in Visitacion Valley. (Courtesy Edie Epps.)

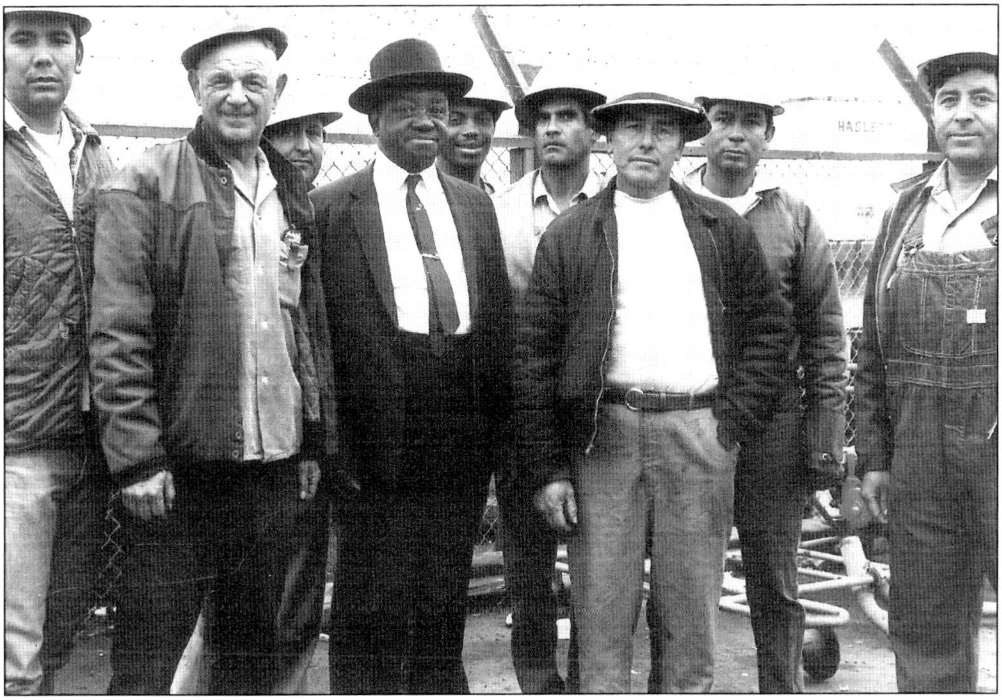

Shown here, second from left, is Charles Arosio with his Southern Pacific "gang" of workers. At least four Valley men, Stanley Livingston, Leslie Keating, Politini, and Seghieri, were engineers, according to Clarence Wikse, who recalled that "the SP yard whistle could be heard throughout the Valley to mark the shifts, morning, noon, and night. The whole Valley ran on that whistle. And the quarry on Geneva blasted with dynamite every day, seven days a week, at 3 p.m. You could hear that too." (Courtesy Arosio family.)

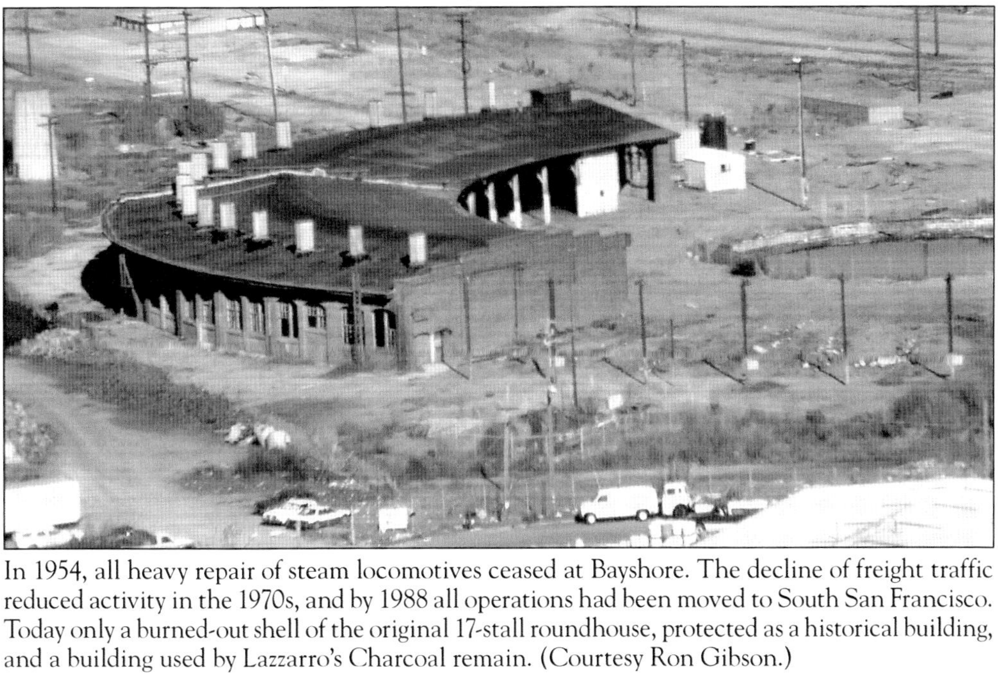

In 1954, all heavy repair of steam locomotives ceased at Bayshore. The decline of freight traffic reduced activity in the 1970s, and by 1988 all operations had been moved to South San Francisco. Today only a burned-out shell of the original 17-stall roundhouse, protected as a historical building, and a building used by Lazzarro's Charcoal remain. (Courtesy Ron Gibson.)

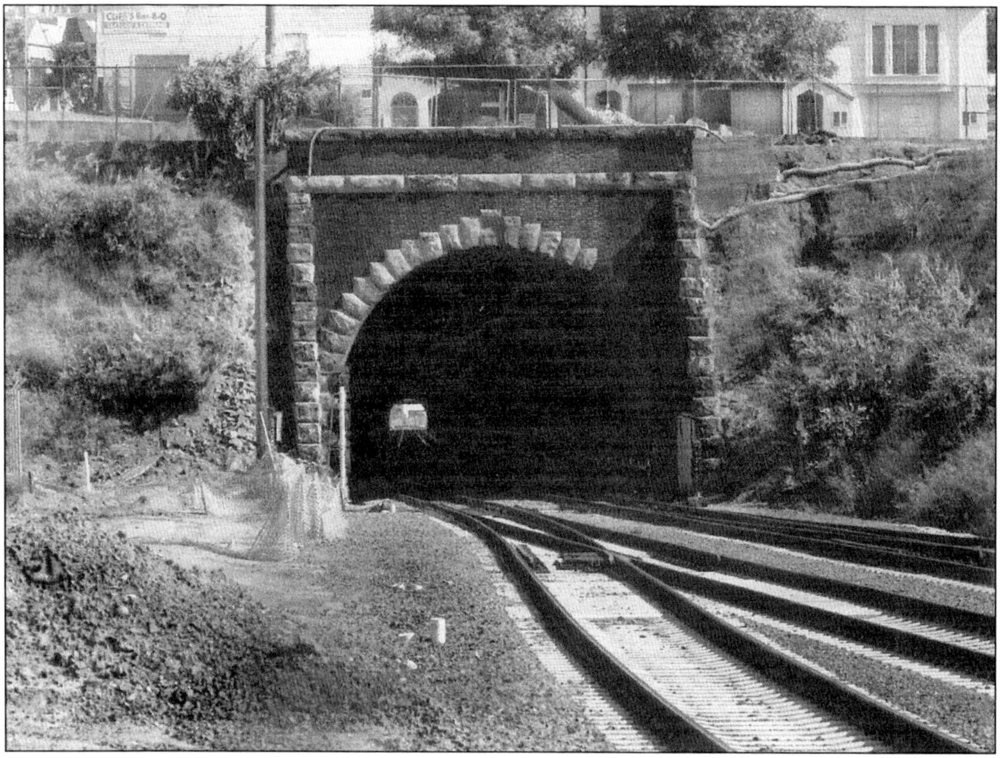

Tunnel No. 4, built around 1905 by Southern Pacific, is still used by CalTrain. Jackie Bauman recalls, "My sister and I could sit and watch the trains come out of the tunnel. Only God kept me from being killed while I was growing up. We climbed over the black thing over the tunnel and were sitting there with our feet hanging over and I said 'Look!' and a train came. We nearly died, the smoke that came out." (Courtesy Anthony Janigian.)

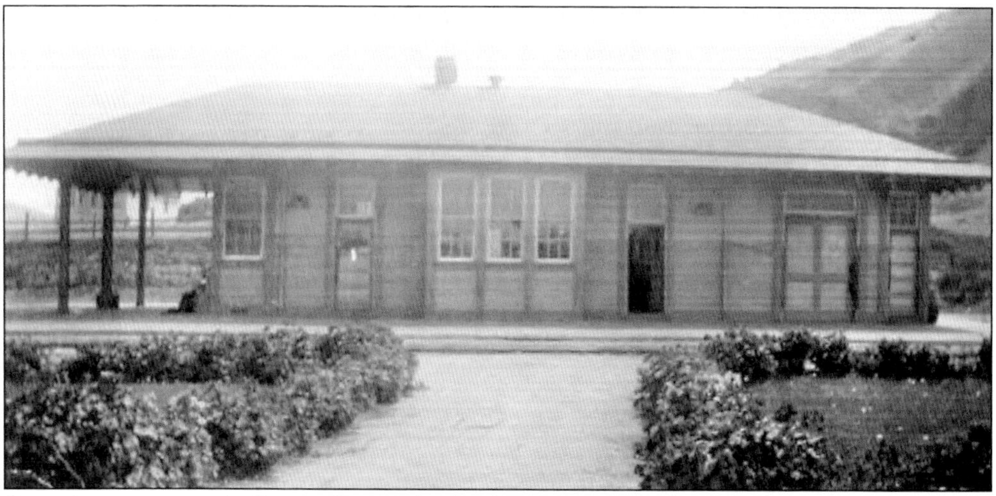

Passenger service on the Peninsula corridor first began in 1863. When Southern Pacific took over, track was laid for the cutoff that served Visitacion Valley, and a commuter depot called Bay Shore Park was constructed. (Courtesy *Lock and Key*, Schlage Lock, January–February–March 1967.)

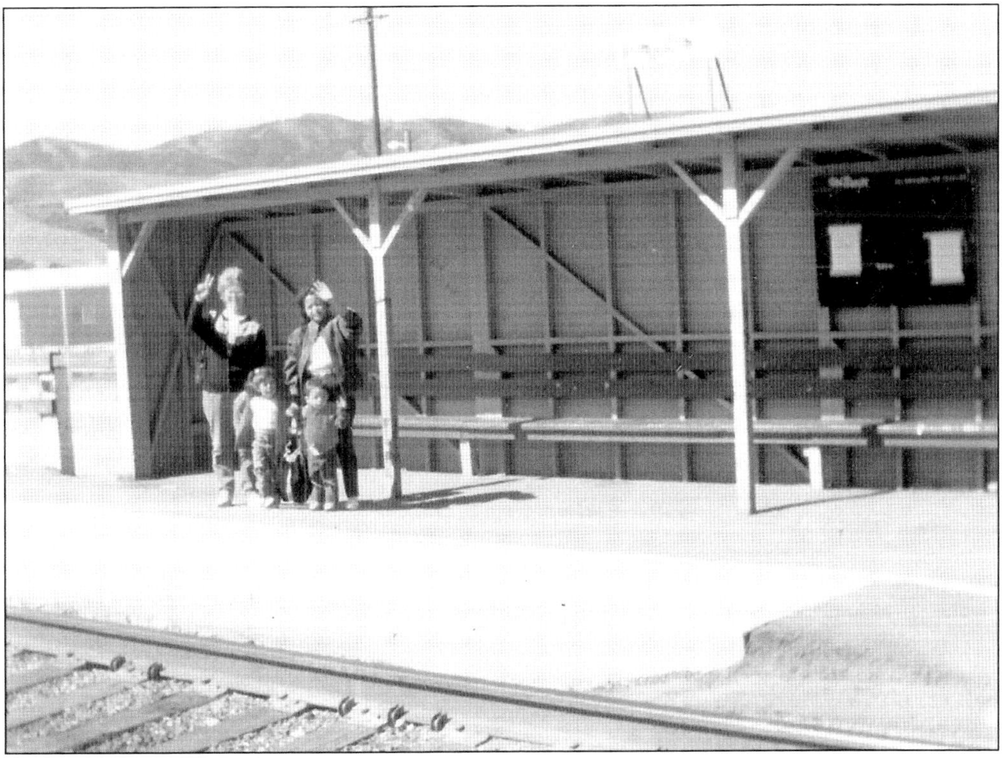

The original Bay Shore Park station was later replaced by open sheds, as pictured in this 1986 photograph in which the Parshall family waits for a southbound train to San Jose's flea market. (Courtesy Betty Parshall.)

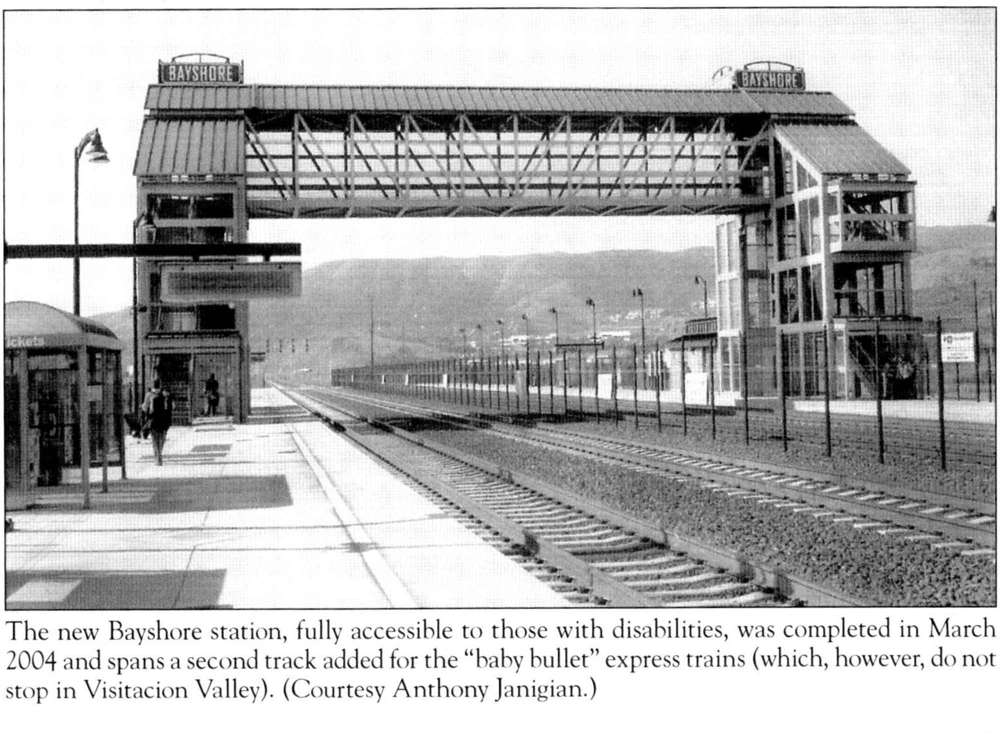

The new Bayshore station, fully accessible to those with disabilities, was completed in March 2004 and spans a second track added for the "baby bullet" express trains (which, however, do not stop in Visitacion Valley). (Courtesy Anthony Janigian.)

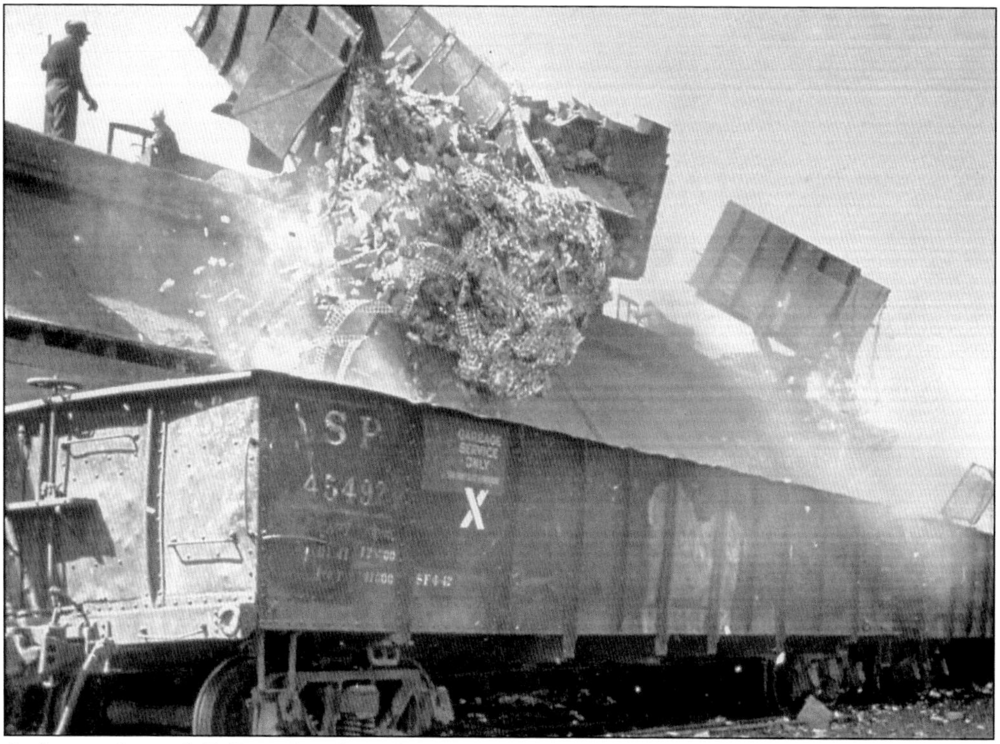

As late as the mid-1960s, refuse from San Francisco was dumped along the shoreline of the bay. Garbage trucks would empty their loads into waiting rail cars, which would then transport the waste to the ever-advancing shoreline. This material would be covered daily with rock and soil quarried from nearby hills. (Courtesy NorCal Waste Systems, Inc.)

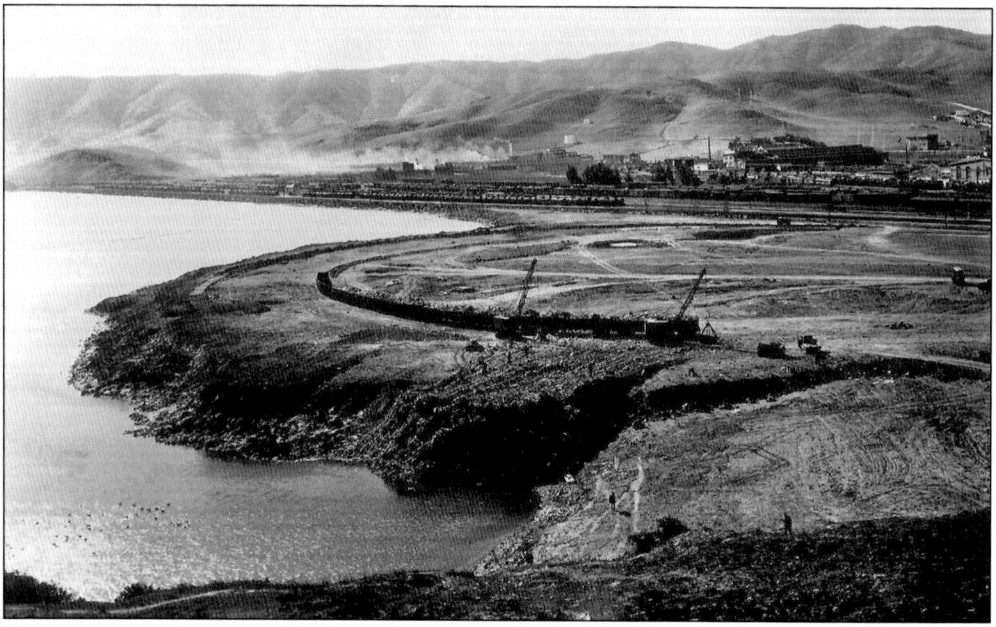

This image from the early 1920s shows the gradual filling of the bay. All the water seen in this image has been replaced by over 500 acres of landfill in Brisbane. (Courtesy a private collector.)

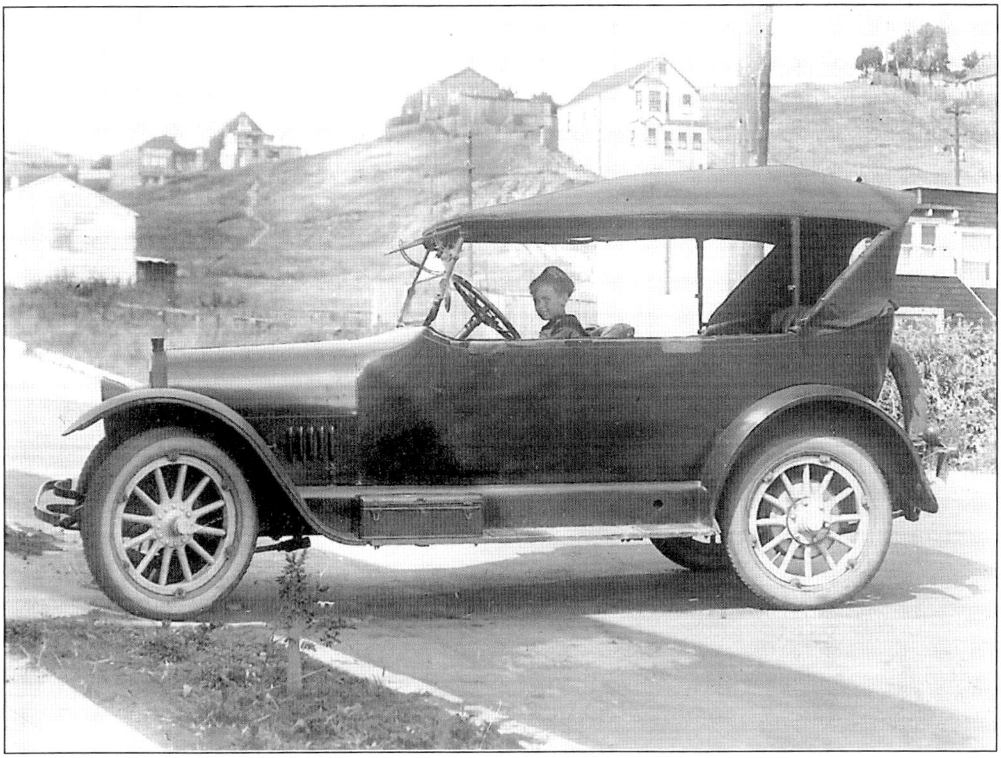

George Siebel sits in the driver's seat on Teddy Avenue, around 1925. On the back of this family photograph is the caption, "The day we sold the Kissel." (Courtesy George Siebel.)

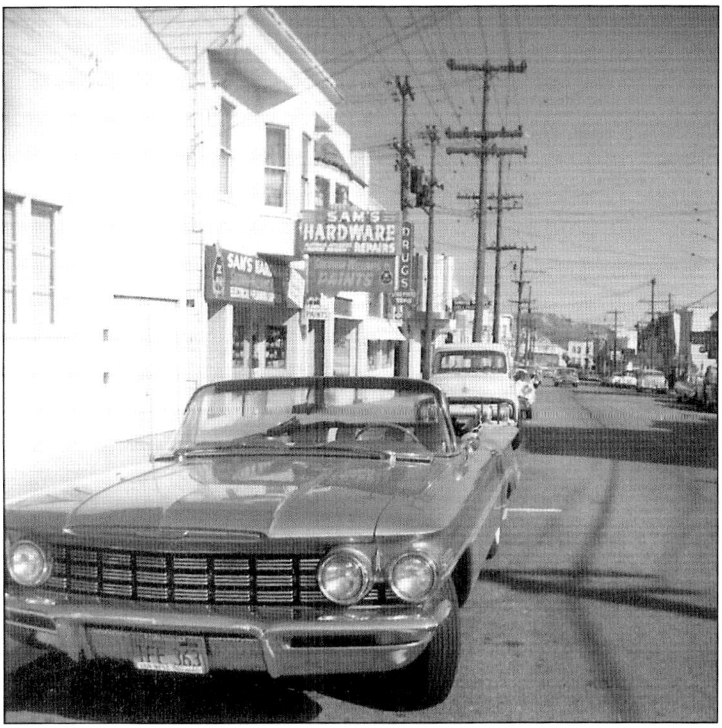

This 1960s photograph shows vehicles parked along Leland Avenue, the neighborhood's primary commercial corridor. To the east are the original Schlage Lock buildings.

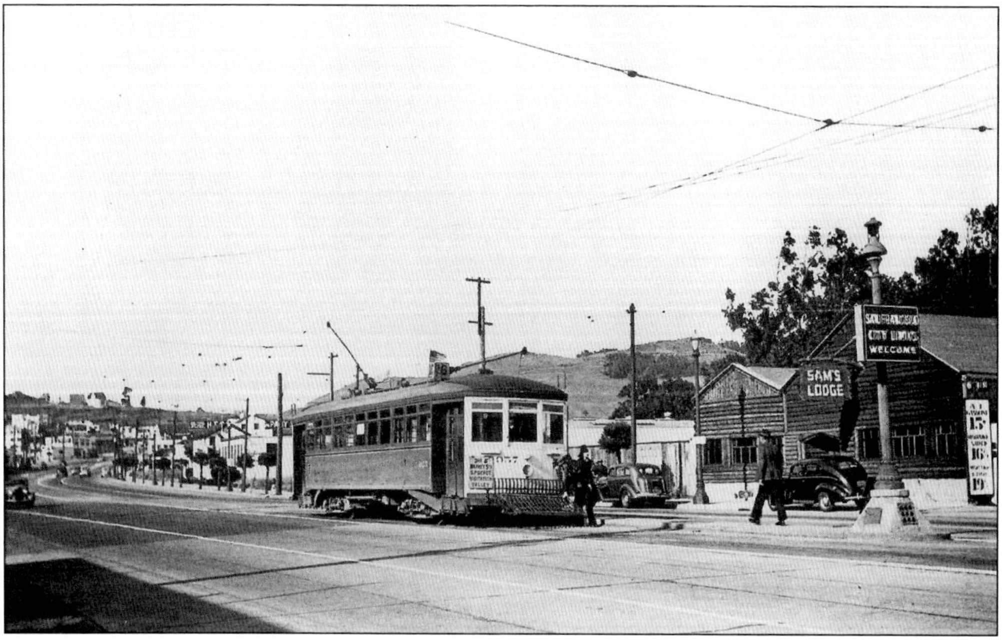

The rustic log cabin that still stands at the county line has been the venue of assorted business ventures. A streetcar makes its final stop outside Sam's Lodge, with the sign indicating the city limits clearly displayed. (Courtesy a private collector.)

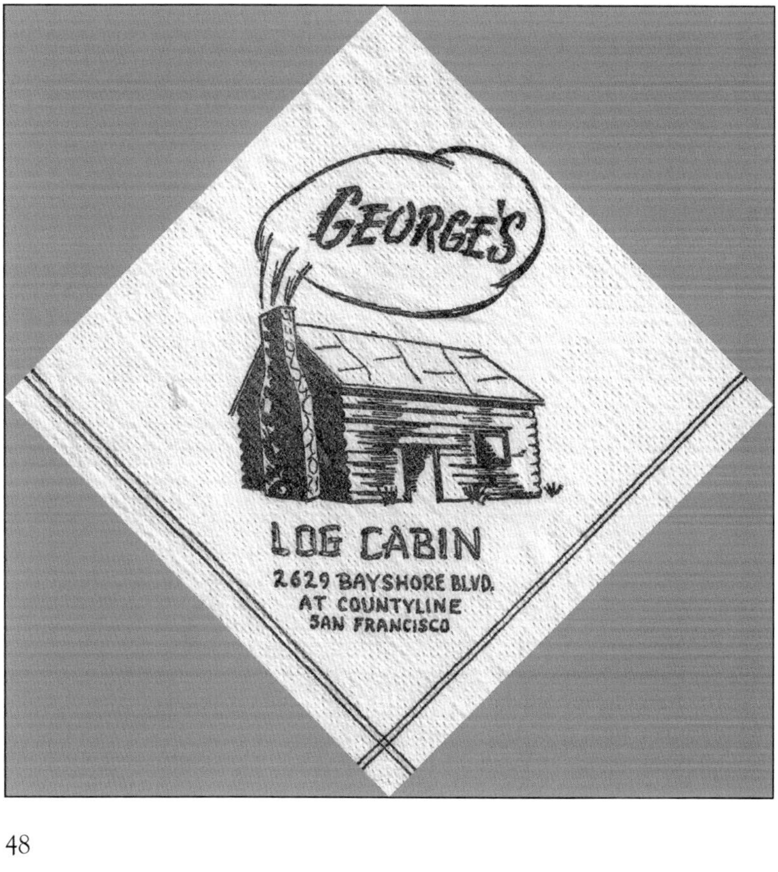

Harry Pierce recalled the line painted across the floor of George's Log Cabin on Bayshore. "If you were on the south side of the line in San Mateo County, you could gamble and drink to all hours, but on the north side you'd be in San Francisco, where gambling was illegal and there was a time limit on drinking." This cocktail napkin is a memento of fun times at George's. (Courtesy Cris Sutti-Janigian.)

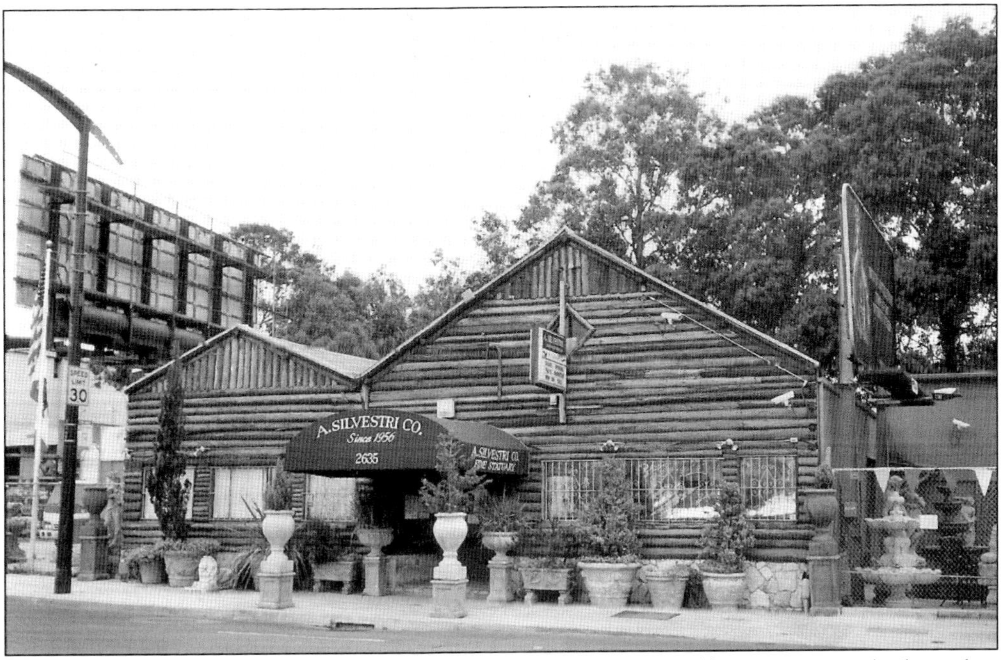

In the mid-1960s, Silvestri's Statuary Company moved into the Valley, occupying the log cabin formerly known as George's. Silvestri's was founded in San Francisco in 1900 by Italian brothers who sold Kewpie dolls and other items door to door. (Courtesy Edie Epps.)

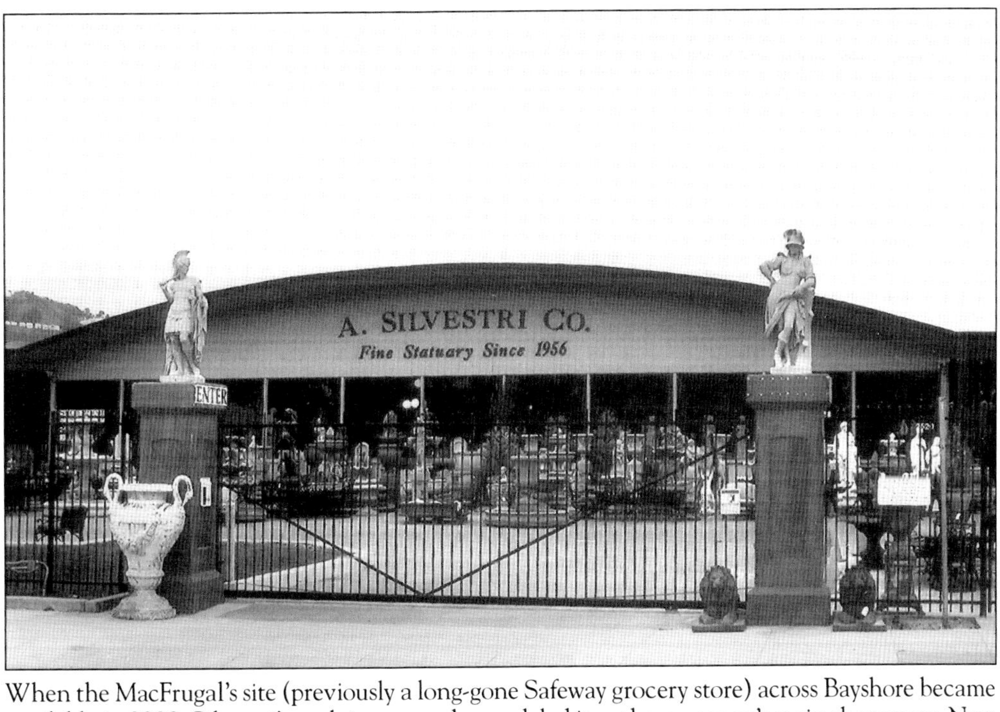

When the MacFrugal's site (previously a long-gone Safeway grocery store) across Bayshore became available in 2000, Silvestri's took it over and remodeled it as the company's main showroom. Now the historic cabin across the street is used to display their line of garden furniture. (Courtesy Edie Epps.)

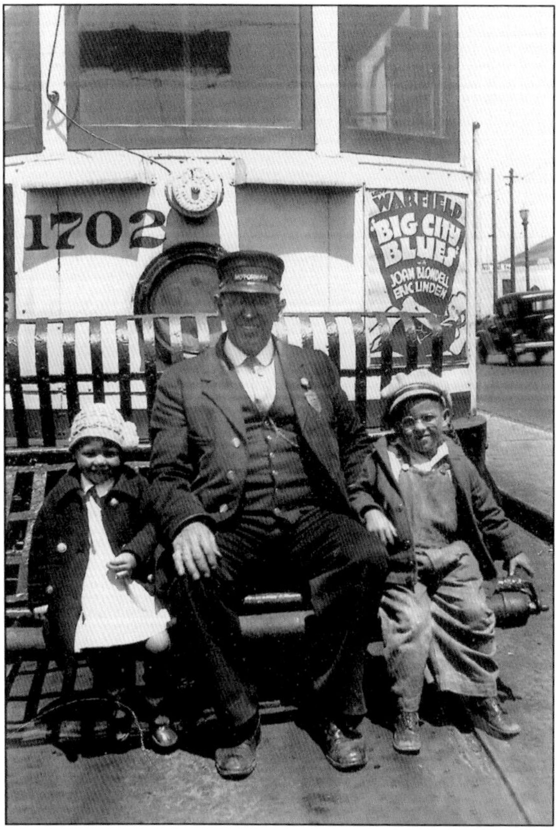

Many local residents worked for the railway today known as MUNI. In the early 1930s, Mr. Voelker, a motorman for the Market Street Railway, took a break at the city limits on Bayshore to pose with his children Mary and Jack. The Voelker family continues as longtime residents of Visitacion Valley. (Courtesy Mark Voelker.)

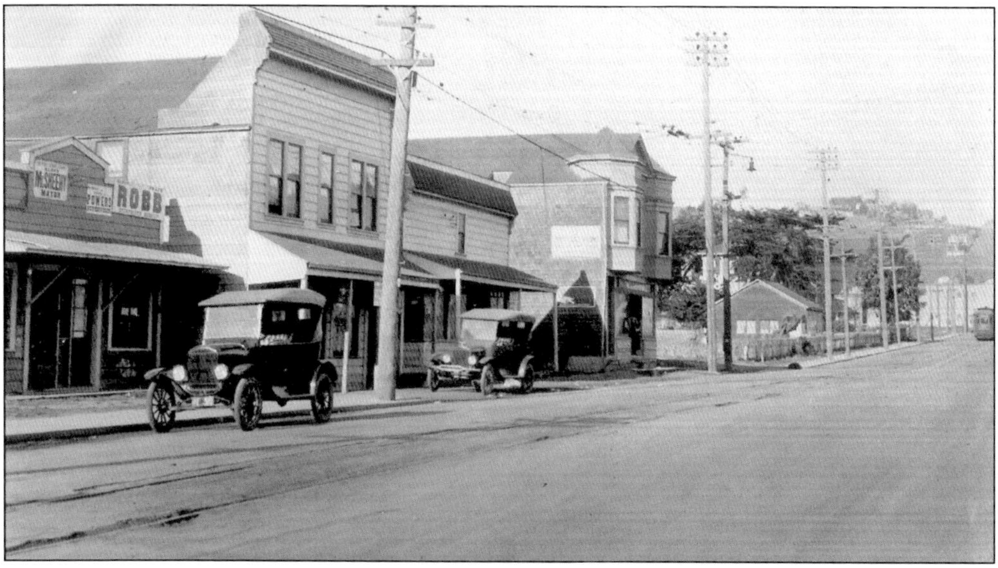

Another of Clarence Wikse's memories concerns the "streetcar line that ran on Railroad Avenue [now Third Street] out to the county line. The city newspapers were bundled up downtown and placed next to the motorman, and he would kick them off at Bayshore and Leland, where boys would pick them up and start their sales and deliveries." This 1924 photograph was taken on Bayshore, near the county line. (Courtesy a private collector.)

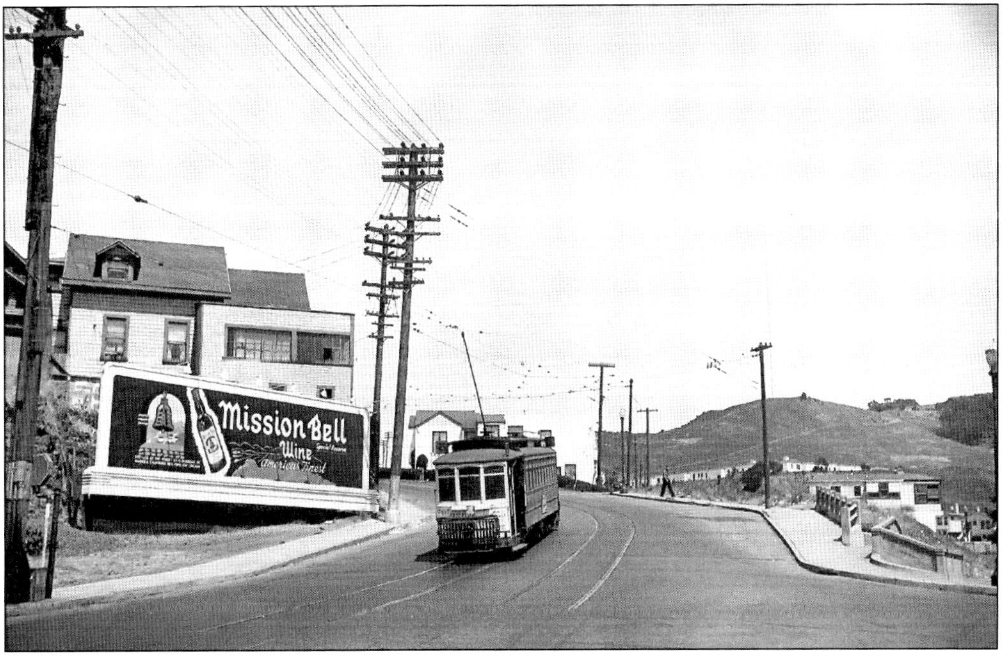

A streetcar rounds the curve where San Bruno still intersects with Bayshore. A "safety subway" was built to allow pedestrians to cross under the busy thoroughfare, but it eventually became so unsafe that residents preferred to risk crossing at street level instead. The underground passage no longer exists. (Courtesy a private collector.)

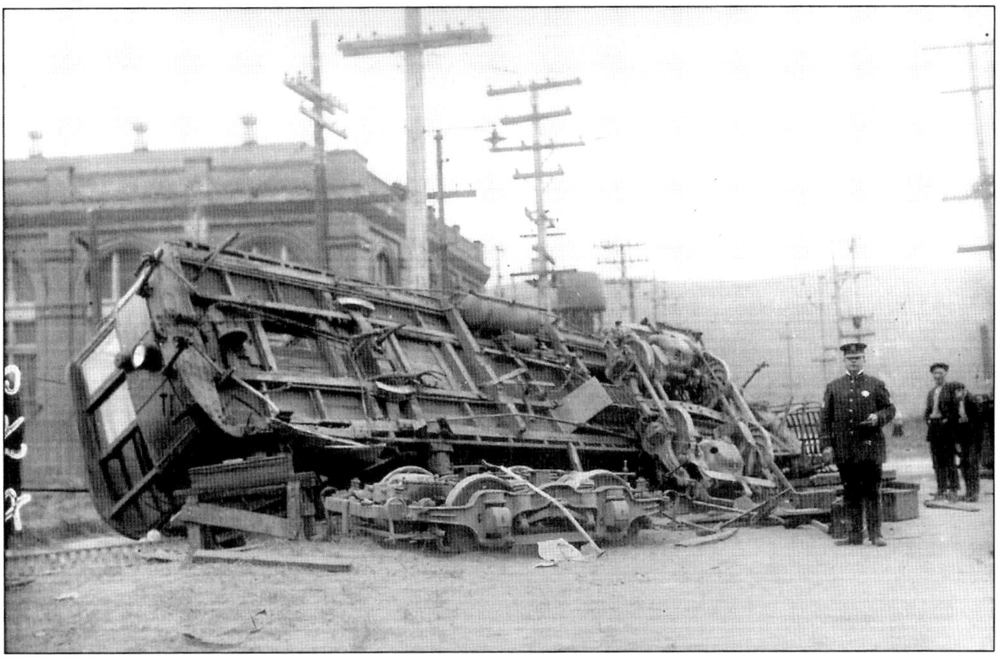

In July 1908, seven workers were killed and another 50 injured when a United Railroads car carrying passengers to the Schaw-Batcher shipyards in South San Francisco jumped the tracks. The crash occurred on a sharp curve at the foot of the Geneva Street hill, in front of the Pacific Gas and Electric Company's plant. (Courtesy a private collector.)

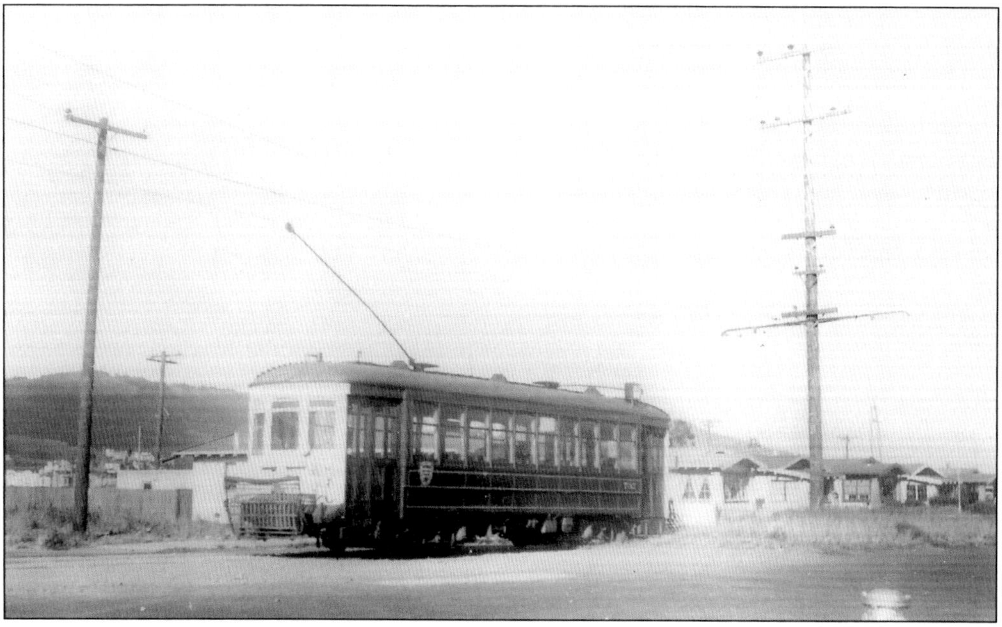

The Visitacion Valley Line operated for almost 30 years before service was suspended on July 31, 1937 so that the former Wallbridge Street could be widened as an eastern extension of Geneva Avenue. The following day, the No. 50 Crocker-Amazon bus took the streetcar's place. Within a few years of the end of World War II, all three of the Valley's original streetcar lines had been replaced by bus service. (Courtesy Tom Gray.)

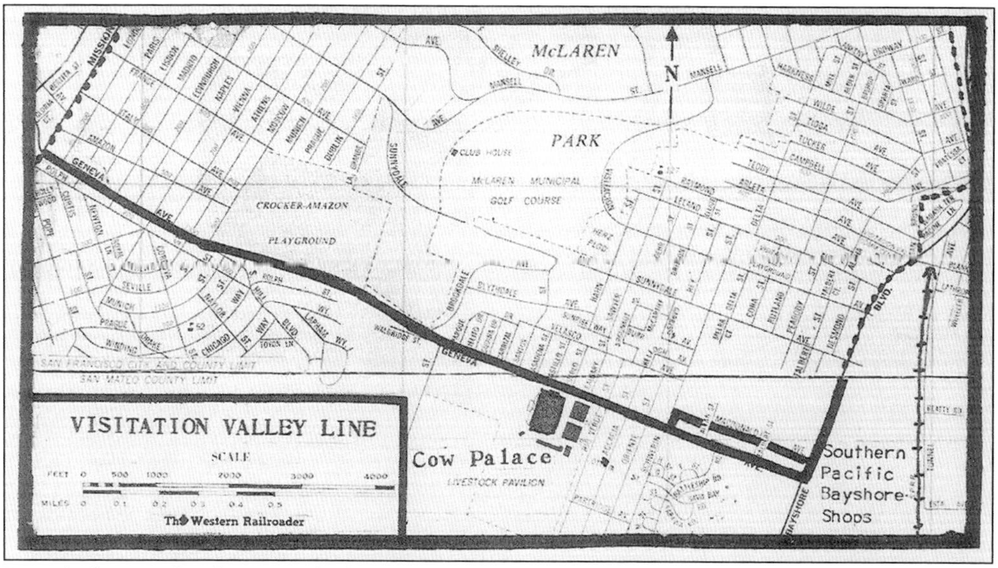

Years before any bus line stretched across the city, many residents rode the streetcar line between Geneva at Mission and the Six Mile House. Opened on October 25, 1909, to promote the sale of real estate in the Valley, the numberless line ran through tall grass and up dirt roads. A turnout allowed cars going in opposite directions to move simultaneously along the single track. (Courtesy *Western Railroader and Western Railfan*, May 1978.)

Over the years, transportation in the Valley has changed from horse-drawn wagons, to trolleys, to buses and cars. The lack of streetcar tracks and the lone boxcar crossing Bayshore Boulevard in this 1990s photograph recall a time when progress meant doing away with rail transport in favor of motor vehicles. (Courtesy Ron Gibson.)

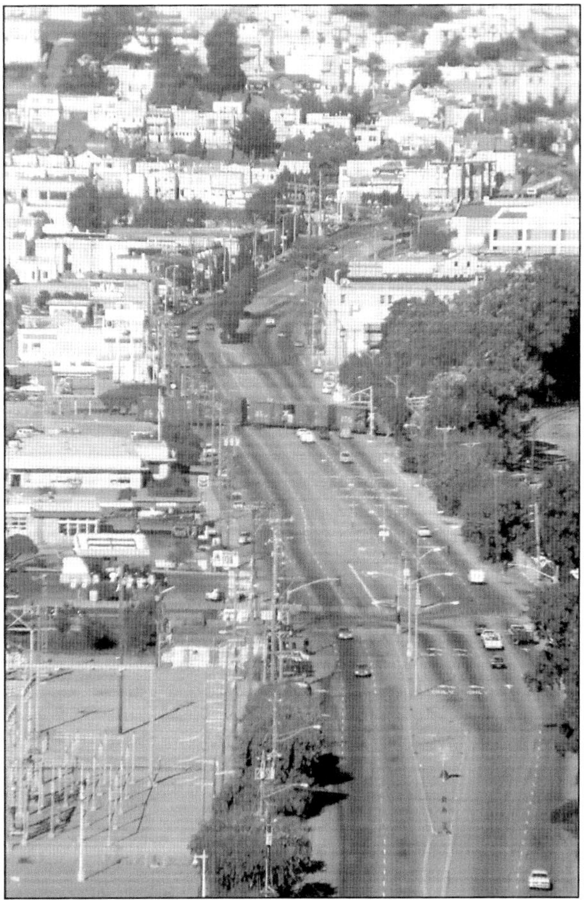

It has been a generation since streetcars ran on Bayshore Boulevard. Now residents await the opening of the Third Street Light Rail, scheduled for the spring or summer of 2006. This new line will run from the CalTrain station at Fourth and Townsend along Third Street, and terminate in the Valley. (Courtesy Edie Epps.)

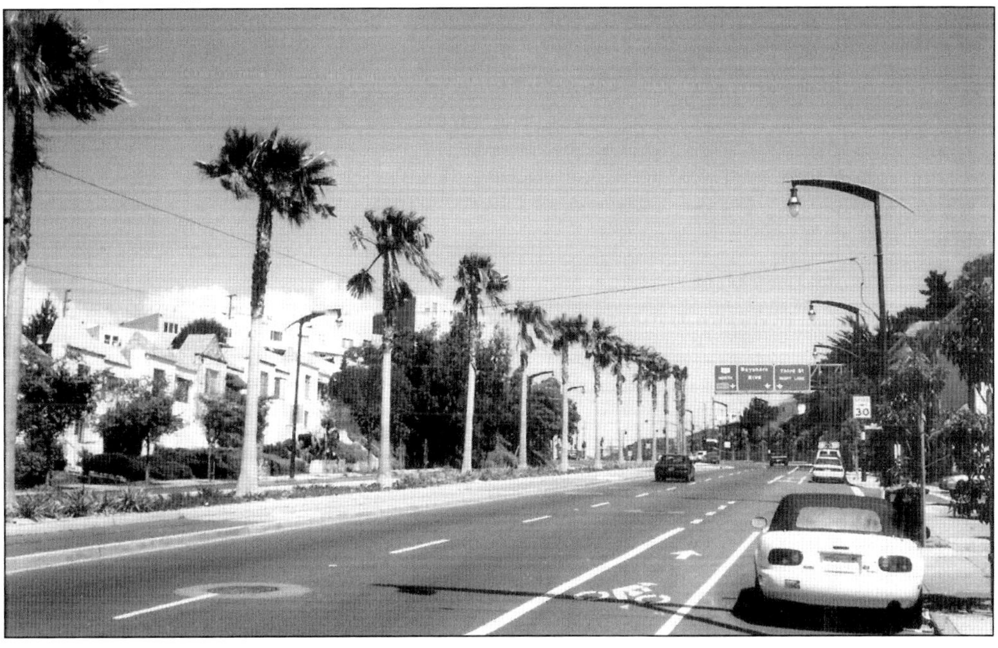

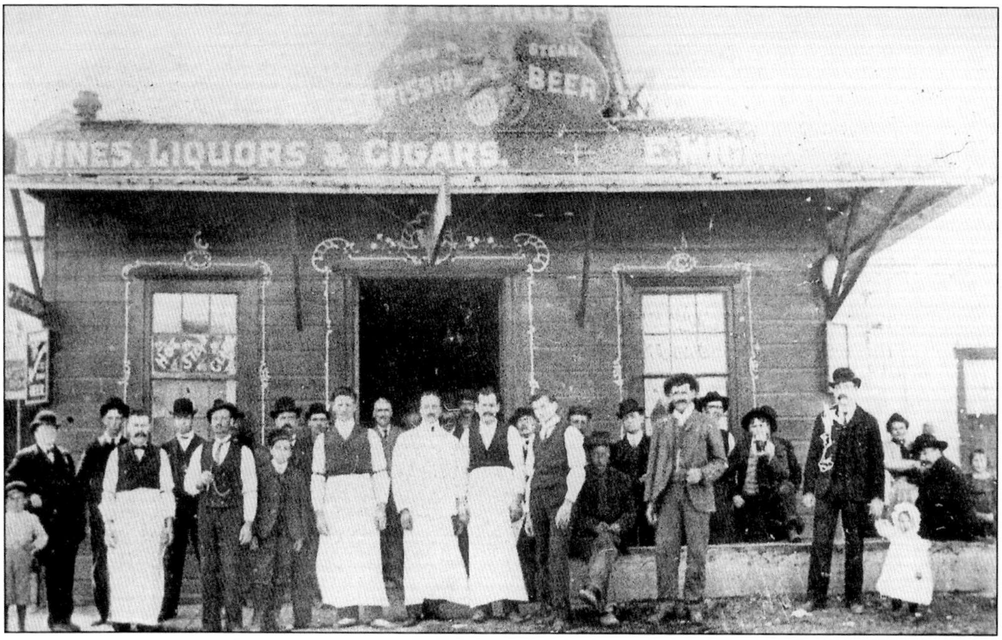

Since at least 1876, the Seven Mile House has been in business on Bayshore, just south of Geneva Avenue. Built alongside a toll road said to be so narrow that a driver had to pull his wagon into the deep grass to let another pass, the main traffic consisted of milkers who worked on dairy farms in Visitacion Valley, Brisbane, and South San Francisco. (Courtesy Vanessa Villacarlos, proprietor.)

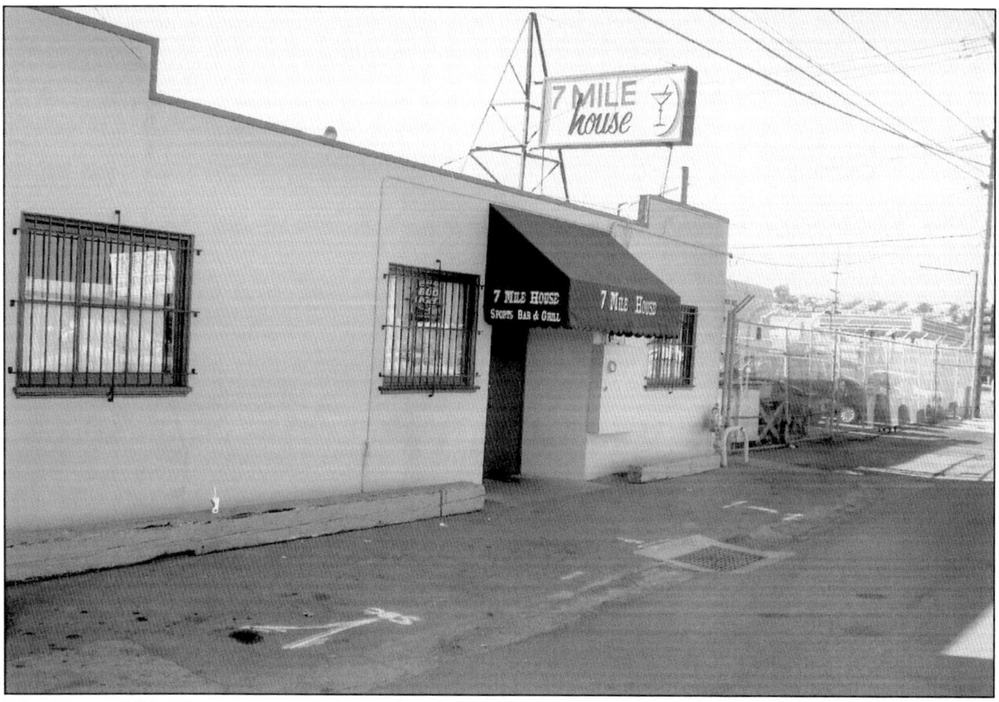

The Seven Mile House, recently remodeled, is still in operation as a bar and restaurant. (Courtesy Russel Morine.)

Three

Community Life

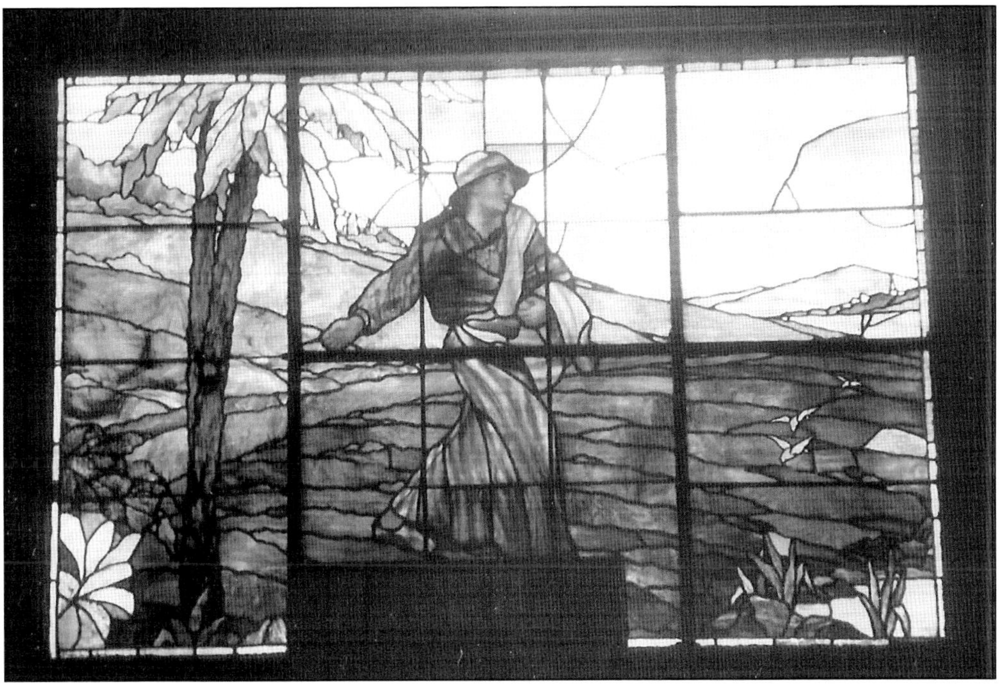

This stained-glass window of the parable of the sower was found in a Nevada ghost town and moved to St. James Presbyterian in 1923, when Julia Morgan designed the present church on Leland. (Courtesy Betty Parshall.)

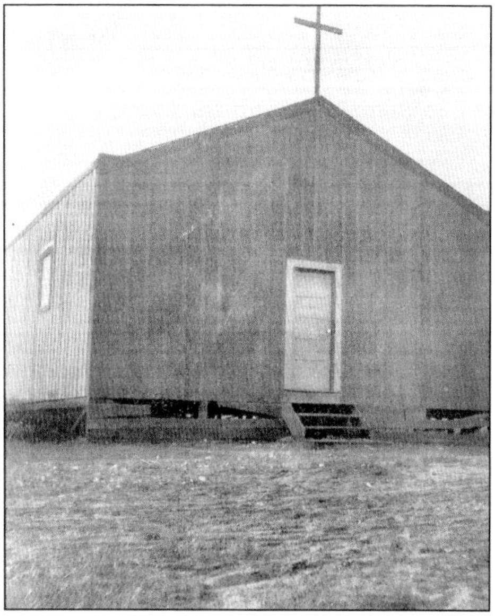

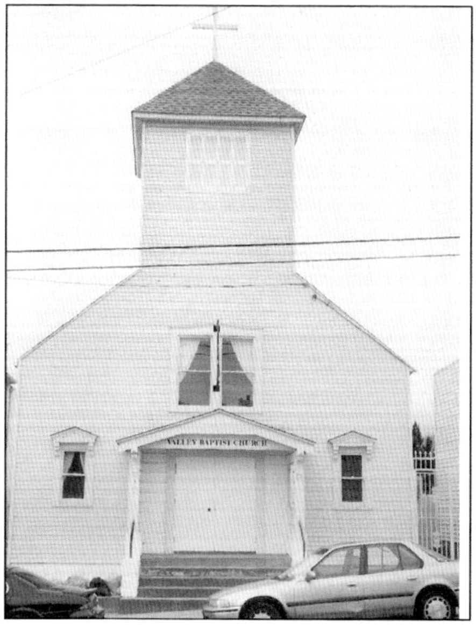

In March 1907, the Church of the Visitacion (above left) was established in the Valley. This small building was erected on Visitacion Avenue at Cora to serve the new Catholic congregation. From 1907 through 1919, a second church was built on Loehr Street (not pictured). Lumber from this church was recycled in the construction of the third Church of the Visitacion at Raymond and Delta, which served the Catholic community until 1952. Today the building is the home of Valley Baptist Church (above right.) (Above left photograph courtesy Church of the Visitacion; above right photograph courtesy Edie Epps.)

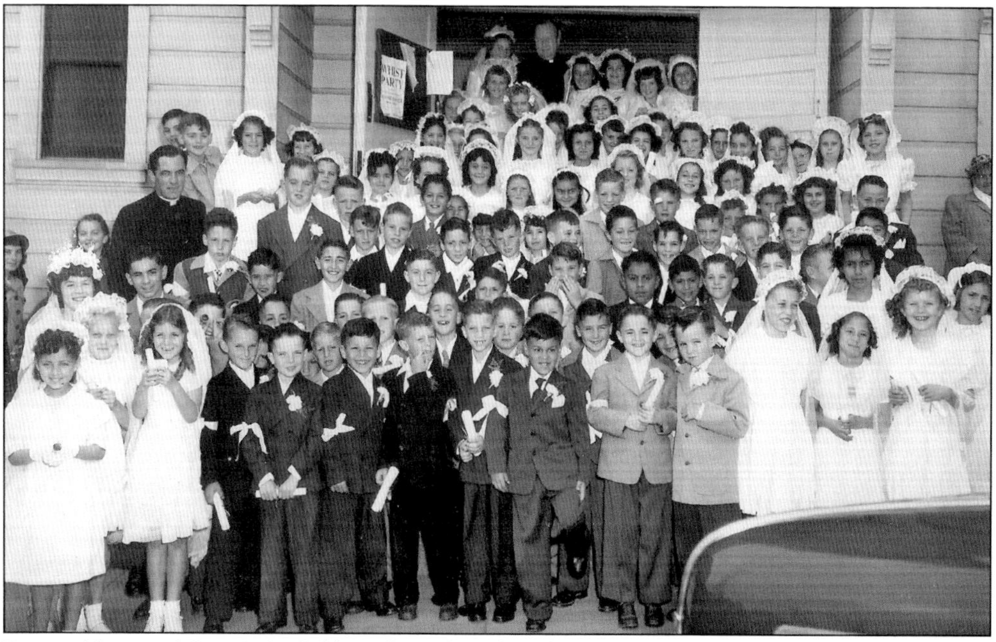

Pictured here in May 1949, children from the Church of the Visitacion's first-communion class pose with Fr. J. O'Malley on the steps of the church at Raymond and Delta. Father Krause stands behind the children in the doorway. The Sisters of the Holy Family, along with lay teachers, taught the religion classes. (Courtesy Linda Gookin.)

The fourth and current Church of the Visitacion, dedicated on April 20, 1952, along with the parish rectory and hall, stands on the same site as Governor Burnett's estate and the San Francisco Auto Camp. The parish hall is on the right. (Courtesy Edie Epps.)

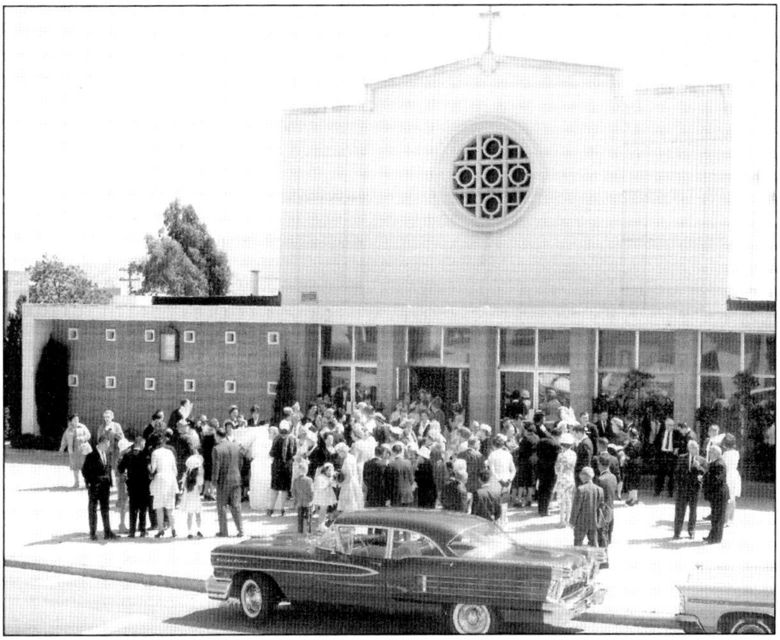

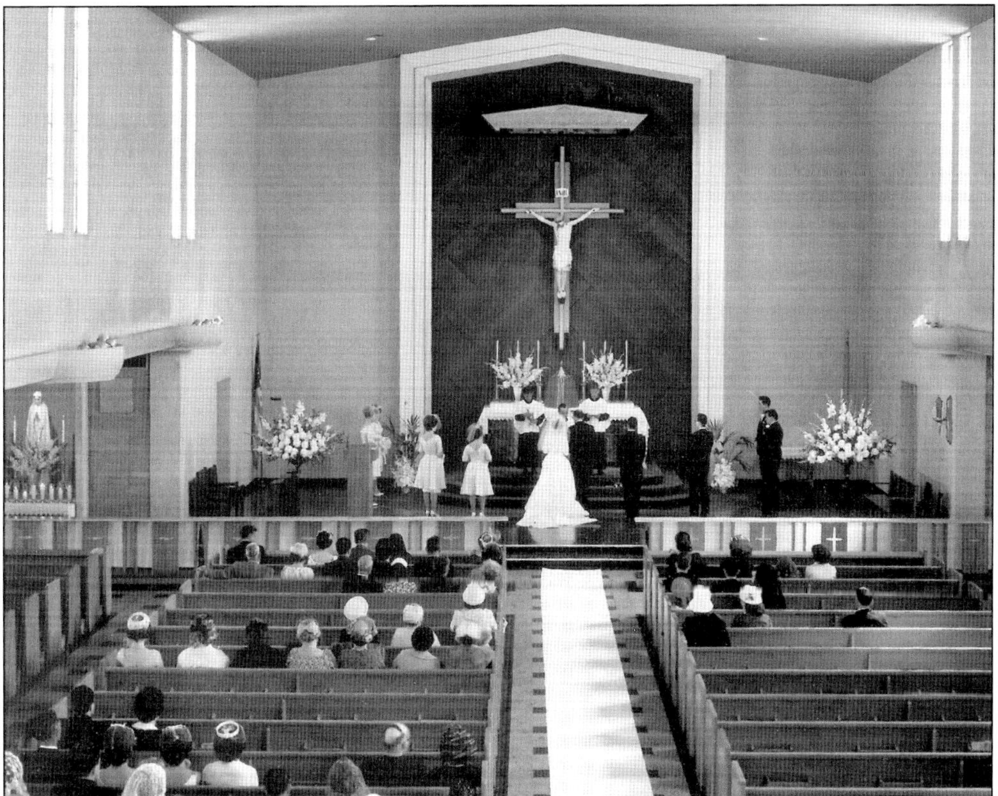

Pictured is the 1955 wedding of Celeste and Salvador Jimenez, still active parishioners at the Church of the Visitacion. The crucifix above the altar originally hung in the Raymond/Delta building. (Courtesy Jimenez family.)

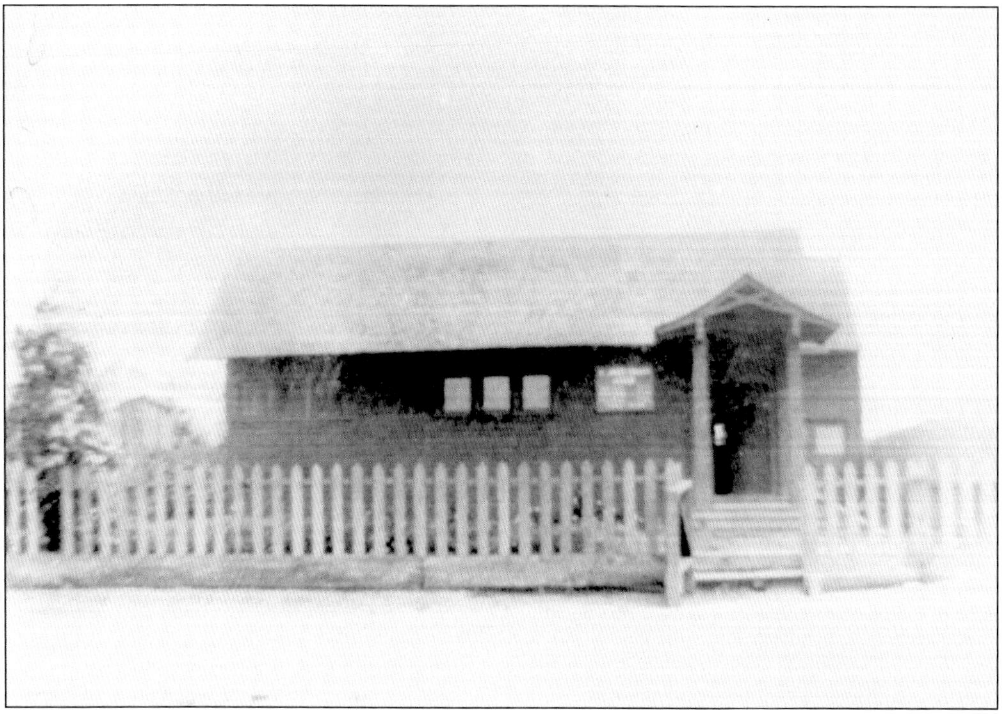

In February 1906, this small building was erected at 240 Leland as St. James Presbyterian. A gymnasium was added at the rear two years later, a source of irritation to neighbors whose gardens were now shaded more than they liked. (Courtesy St. James Presbyterian Church.)

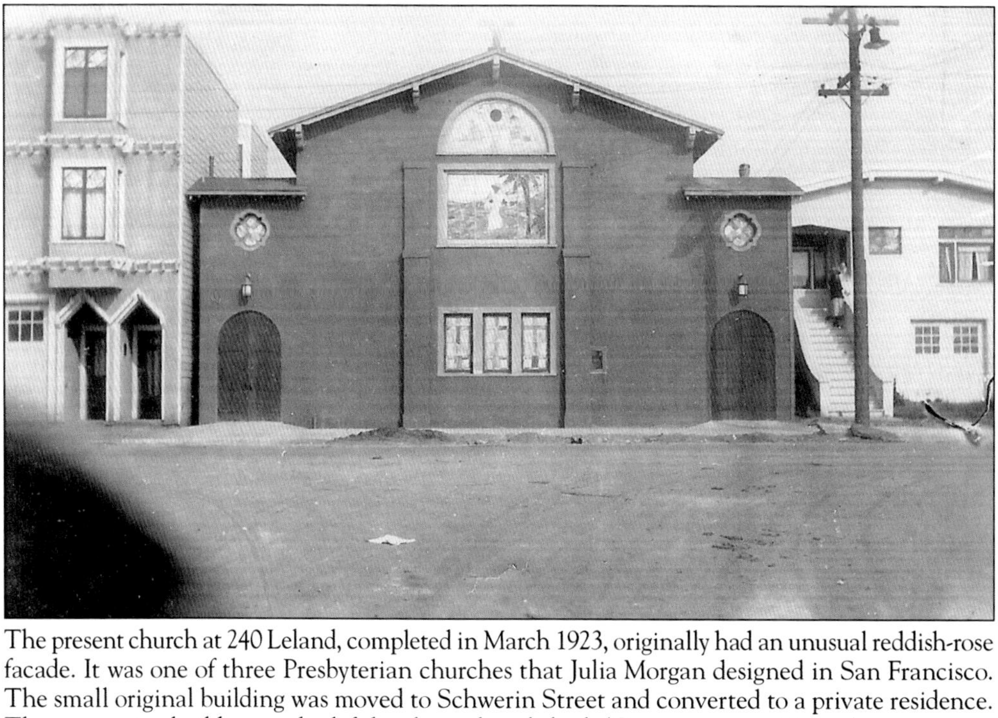

The present church at 240 Leland, completed in March 1923, originally had an unusual reddish-rose facade. It was one of three Presbyterian churches that Julia Morgan designed in San Francisco. The small original building was moved to Schwerin Street and converted to a private residence. The interesting building to the left has been demolished. (Courtesy Harry Pierce.)

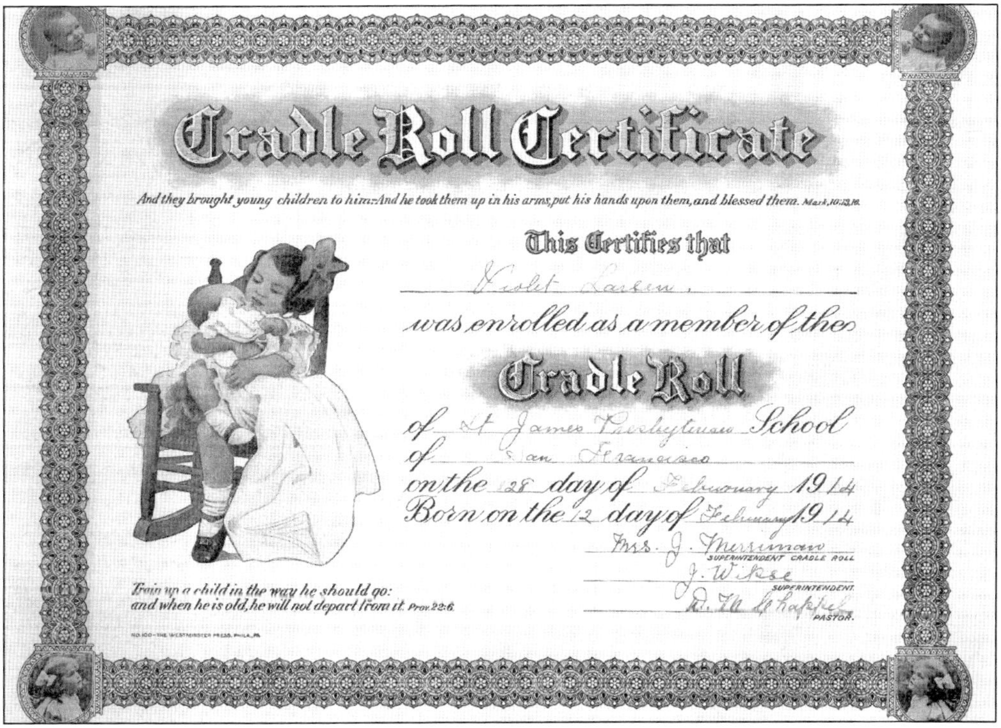
Cradle Roll Certificate

And they brought young children to him: And he took them up in his arms, put his hands upon them, and blessed them. Mark, 10:13,16.

This Certifies that

Violet Larsen.

was enrolled as a member of the

Cradle Roll

of St James Presbyterian School

of San Francisco

on the 28 day of February 1914

Born on the 12 day of February 1914

Mrs. J. Merriman
SUPERINTENDENT CRADLE ROLL

J. Wikse
SUPERINTENDENT

D. M. Schaffel
PASTOR.

Train up a child in the way he should go: and when he is old, he will not depart from it. Prov. 22:6.

NO. 100—THE WESTMINSTER PRESS, PHILA., PA.

Although her surname is misspelled on the certificate, Violet Larsson was enrolled in St. James' "Cradle Roll" just 16 days after her 1914 birth. (Courtesy Cynthia Cox.)

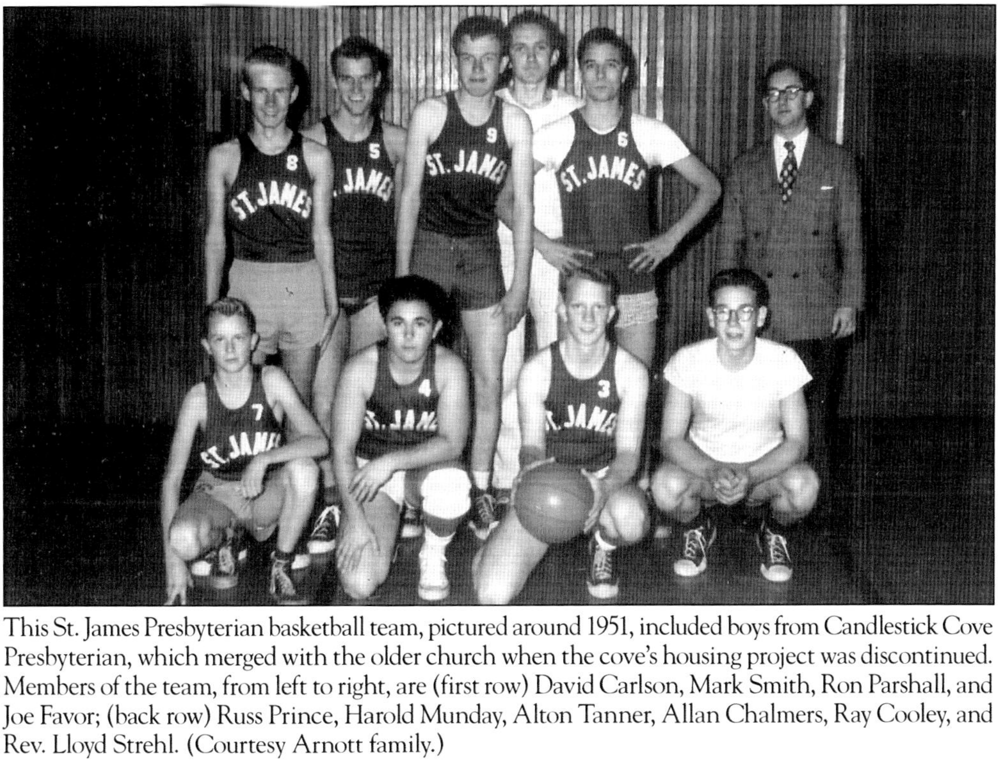

This St. James Presbyterian basketball team, pictured around 1951, included boys from Candlestick Cove Presbyterian, which merged with the older church when the cove's housing project was discontinued. Members of the team, from left to right, are (first row) David Carlson, Mark Smith, Ron Parshall, and Joe Favor; (back row) Russ Prince, Harold Munday, Alton Tanner, Allan Chalmers, Ray Cooley, and Rev. Lloyd Strehl. (Courtesy Arnott family.)

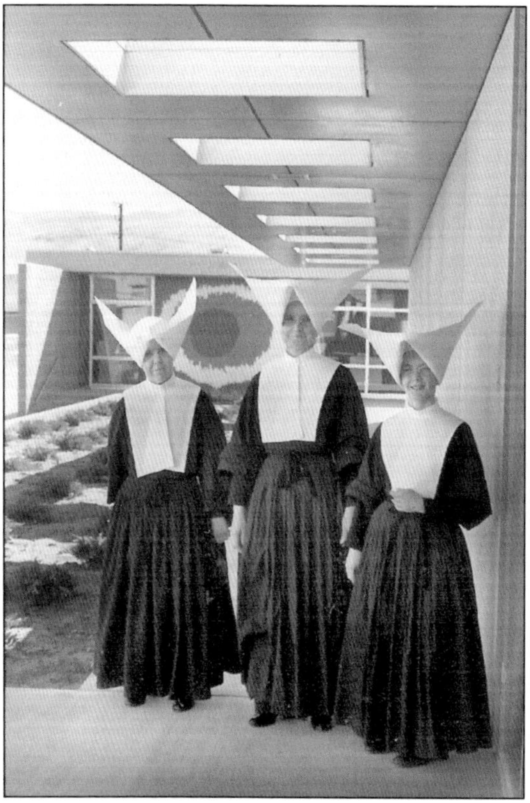

The Daughters of Charity came to the Valley in 1964 to teach the students at the new parish school, and continue to provide religious and academic education to the Valley students today. In this 1964 photograph, the sisters stand outside their new convent with Our Lady of the Visitacion School in the background. (Courtesy Church of the Visitacion.)

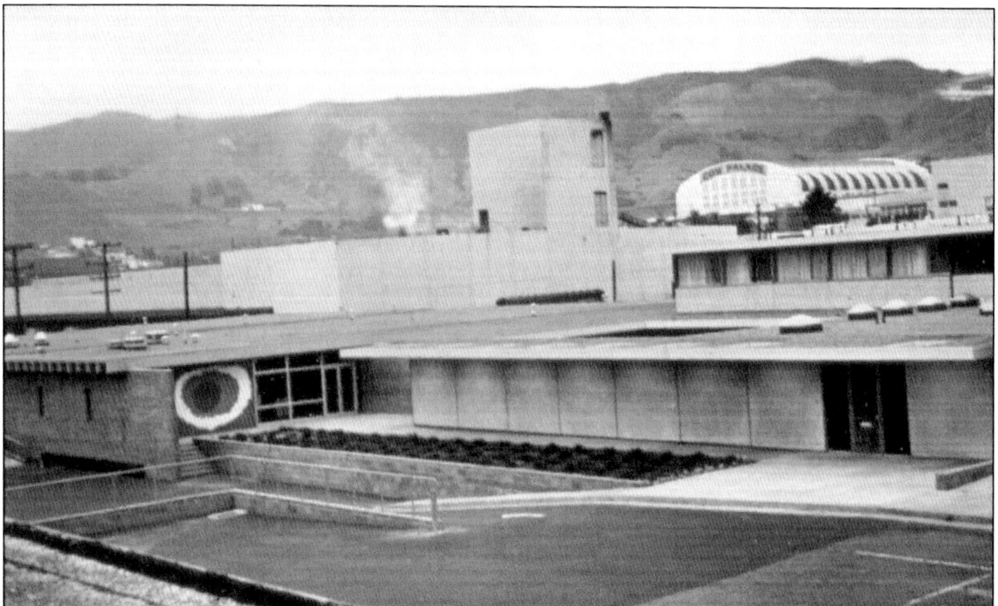

Our Lady of the Visitacion School, designed by Mario Ciampi, AIA, was dedicated April 4, 1965. The "Eye of God" mosaic can still be seen today. Note the S&W Foods building, the Cow Palace, and the lack of homes along the hillside in this 1965 postcard. (Courtesy Richard Brandi.)

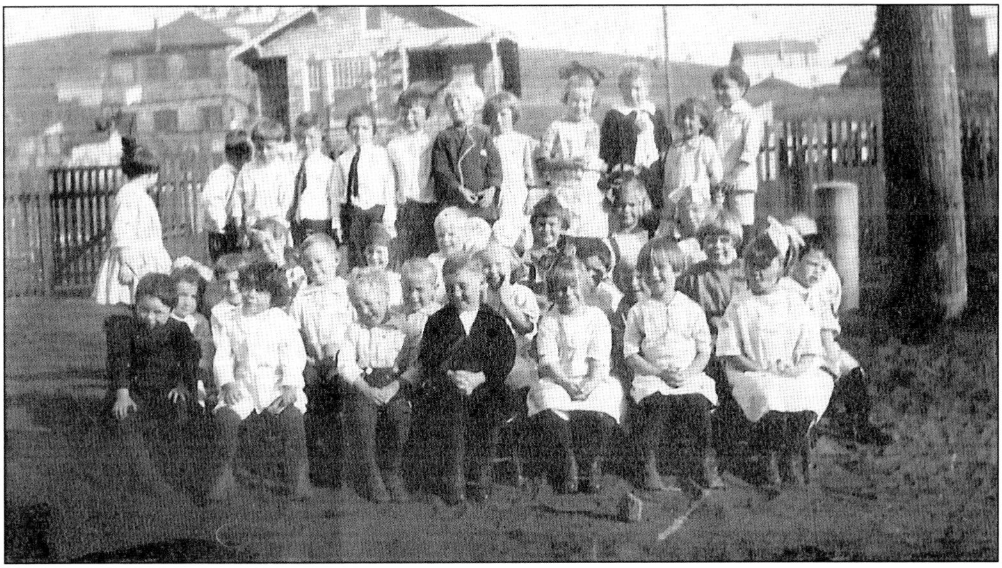

Anna Stuart Johnson recalls, "There was a lady who left money for a kindergarten [at 373 Wilde]. I only lived a little way so I could go out my back door and through the lot to school." In this c. 1915 photograph, the young students pose outside the building that was once a fire station and where a private home stands today. (Courtesy Taylor family.)

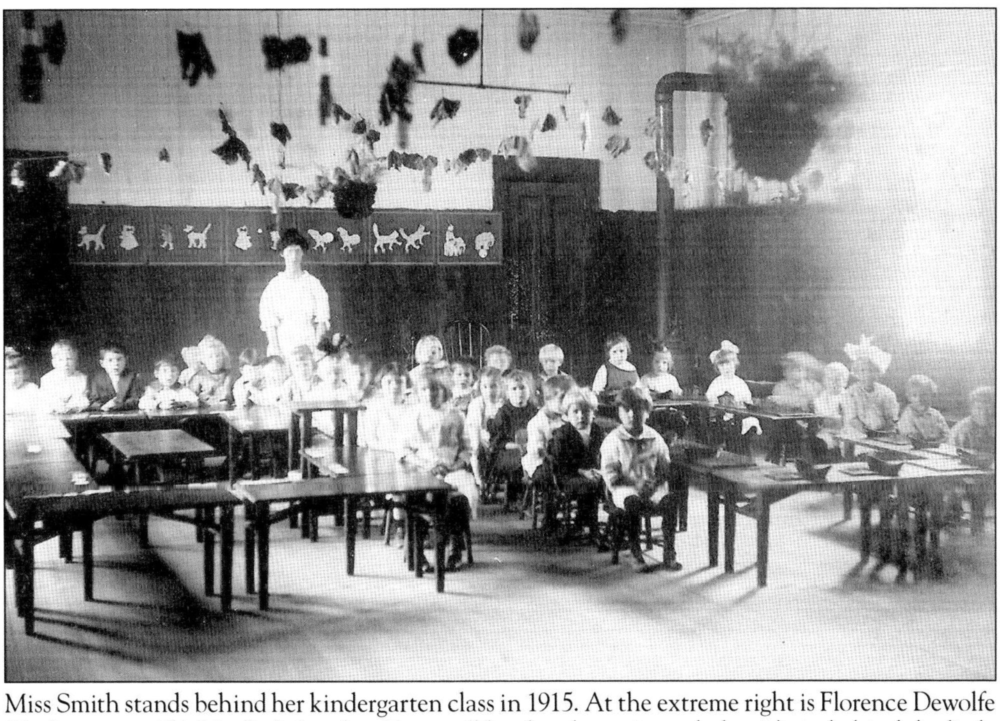

Miss Smith stands behind her kindergarten class in 1915. At the extreme right is Florence Dewolfe Chalmers, age 5½. Her little brother George (blond and wearing a dark suit) sits behind the little girl who is front center. We wonder how well the old stove heated this huge room in cold weather. (Courtesy Taylor family.)

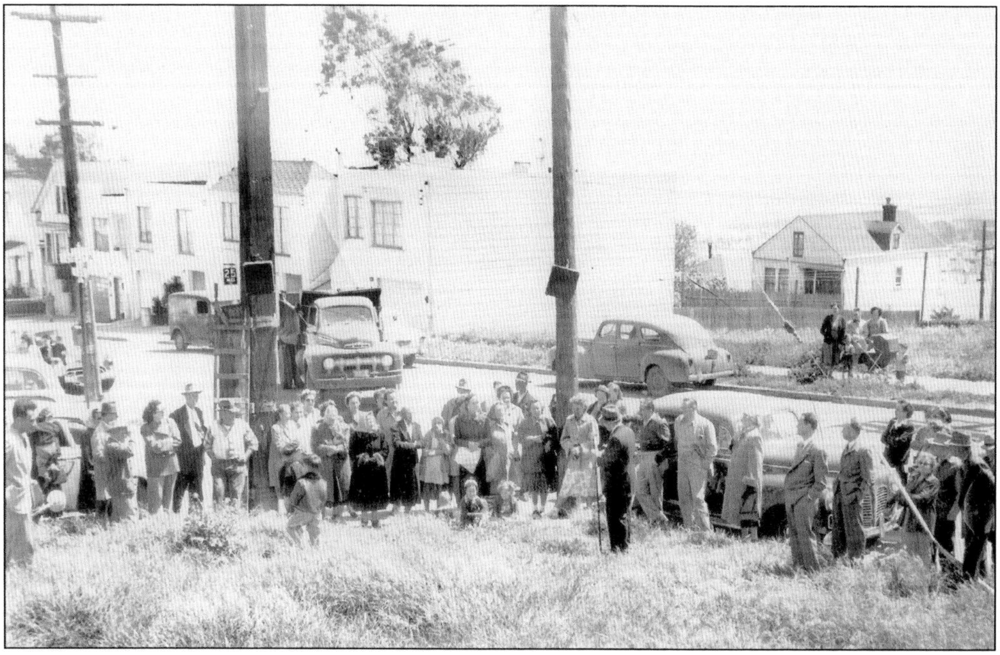

In May 1952, neighbors gathered on the former sandlot at Delta and Wilde to break ground for El Dorado, originally conceived as a school for kindergarten to third grade. (Courtesy Taylor family.)

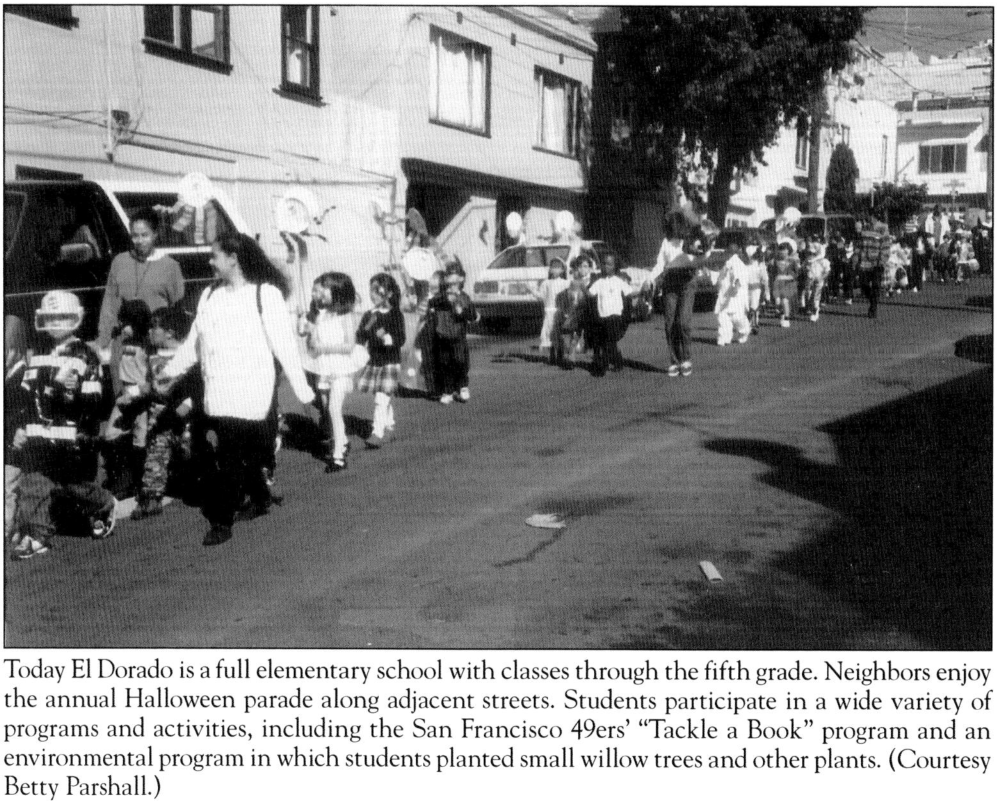

Today El Dorado is a full elementary school with classes through the fifth grade. Neighbors enjoy the annual Halloween parade along adjacent streets. Students participate in a wide variety of programs and activities, including the San Francisco 49ers' "Tackle a Book" program and an environmental program in which students planted small willow trees and other plants. (Courtesy Betty Parshall.)

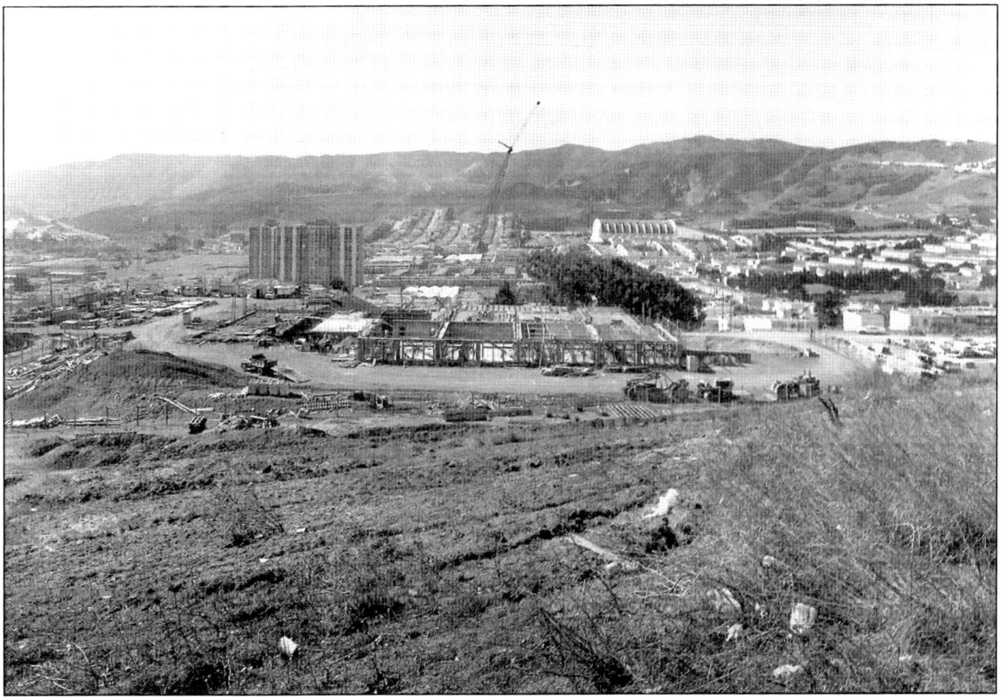

Construction began on the Visitacion Valley Middle School at 450 Raymond in the late 1960s and was completed in 1971. Perched on a steep hillside adjacent to McLaren Park, the school overlooks the entire Valley. Currently over 800 students attend the school. (Courtesy Principal James Dierke.)

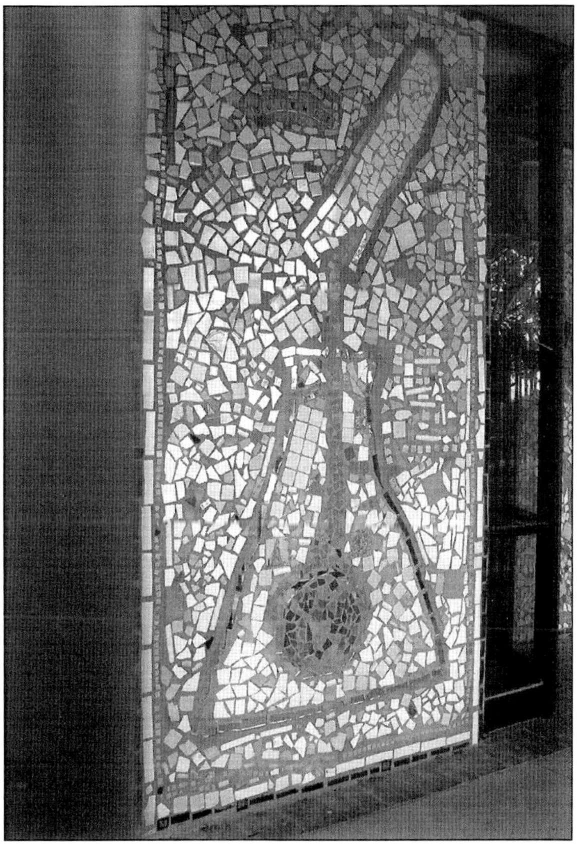

A striking addition to the Valley's middle school are five mosaic murals of ceramic tile, painted glass, colored grout, and paint, designed by the sixth-grade class of 2004 and representing major academic subjects studied. A coat of two-toned blue paint adds to the middle school's already imposing presence on the hillside. (Courtesy Edie Epps.)

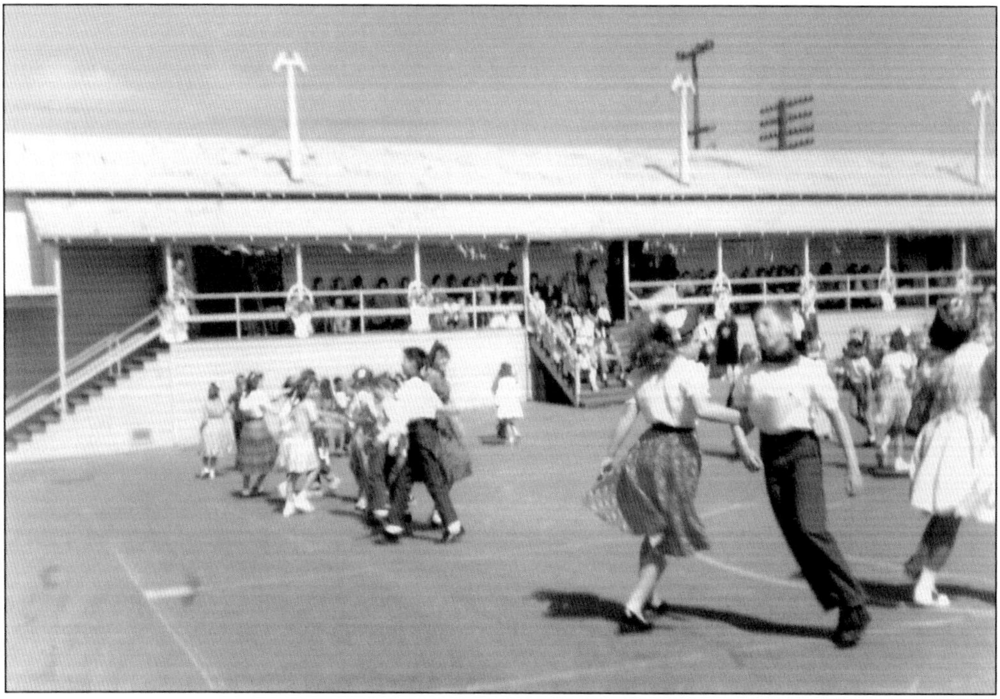

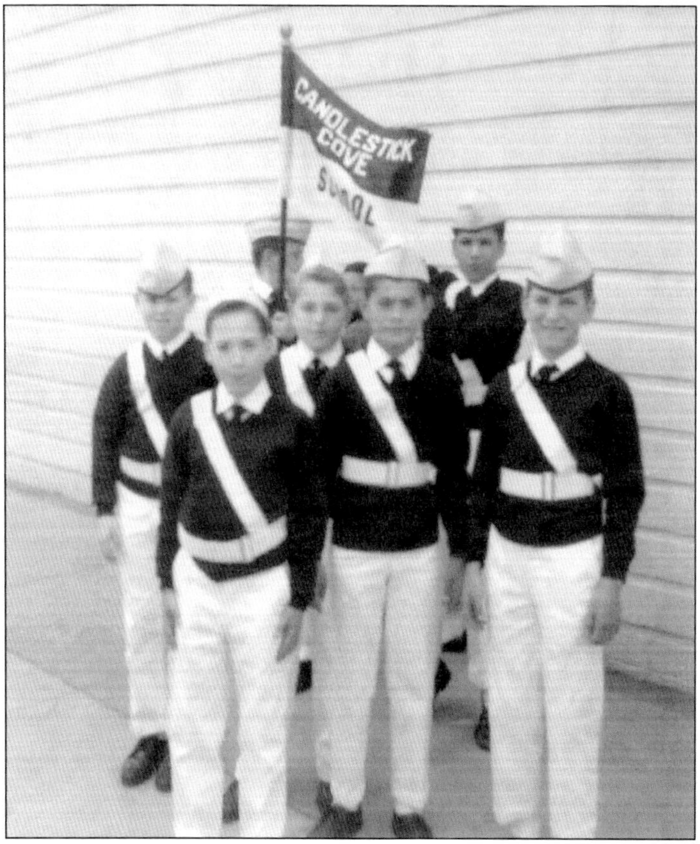

The Candlestick Cove School opened in the mid-1940s to educate the children of Little Hollywood. Graduates' memories include "theme days" where the students dressed accordingly and the PTA served sandwiches and cupcakes. There were also schoolyard dances, as depicted in this 1950s photograph. (Courtesy Arnold Salinas.)

The Candlestick Cove Safety Patrol of 1961 included, from left to right, (first row) Scott Jordan, Steven Lewis, Steve O'Brien, Bobby McCoy, and Gary Camelleri; (second row) Jerry Snell and Arnold Salinas. (Courtesy Arnold Salinas.)

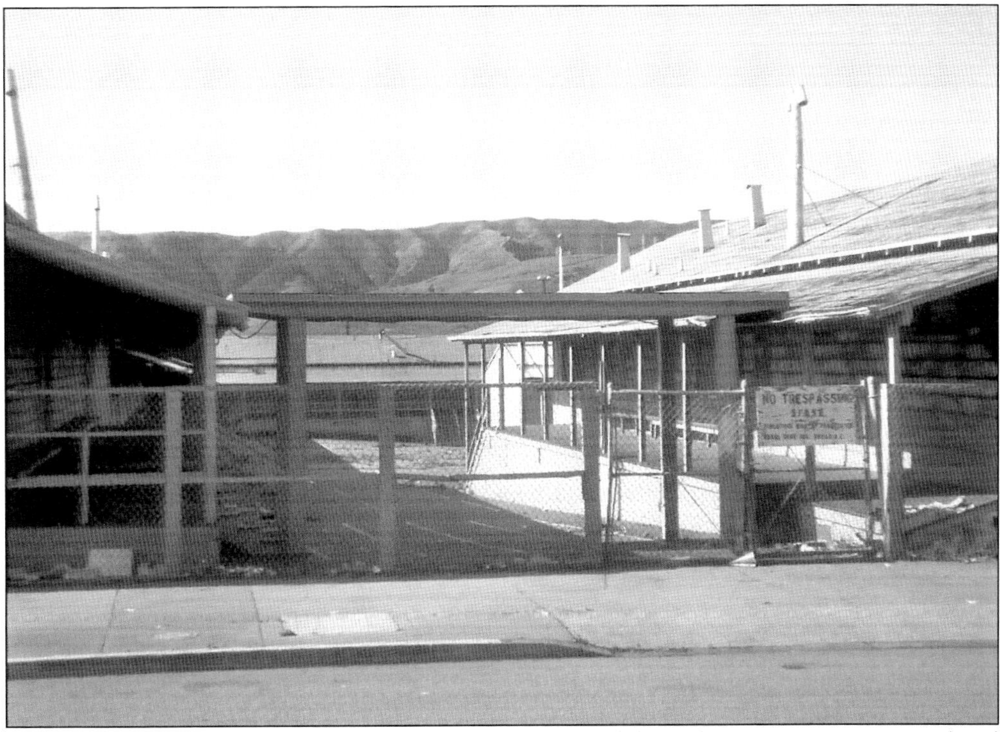

The Candlestick Cove School, pictured here against the backdrop of San Bruno Mountain, closed in the 1960s. (Courtesy Ron Gibson.)

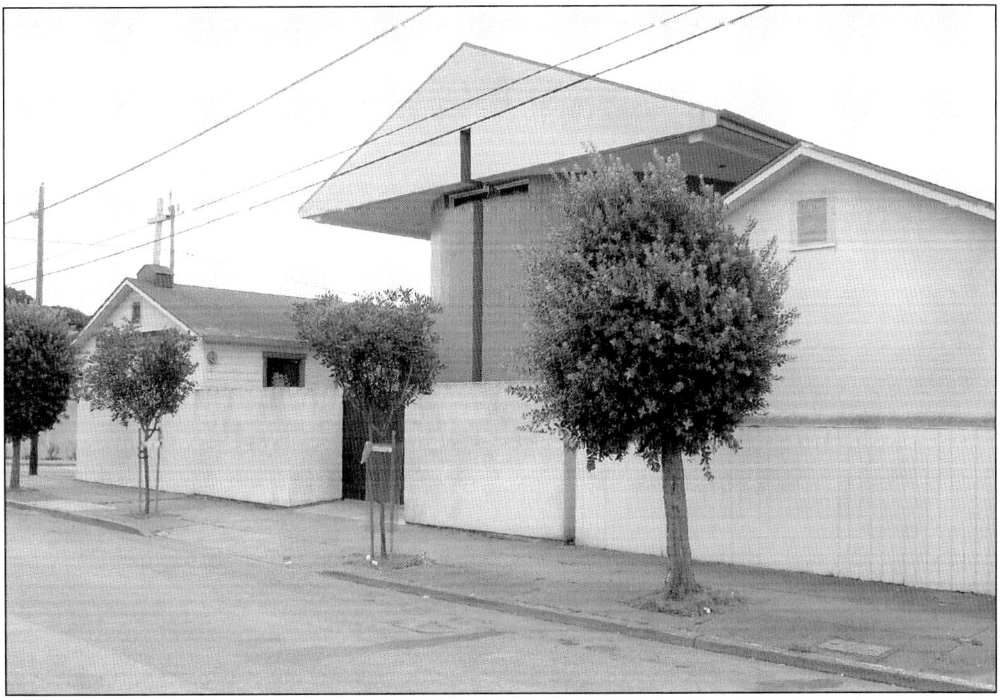

Today the buildings that were Candlestick Cove School at Tunnel and Lathrop Streets are the home of the Korean First Presbyterian Church. (Courtesy Russel Morine.)

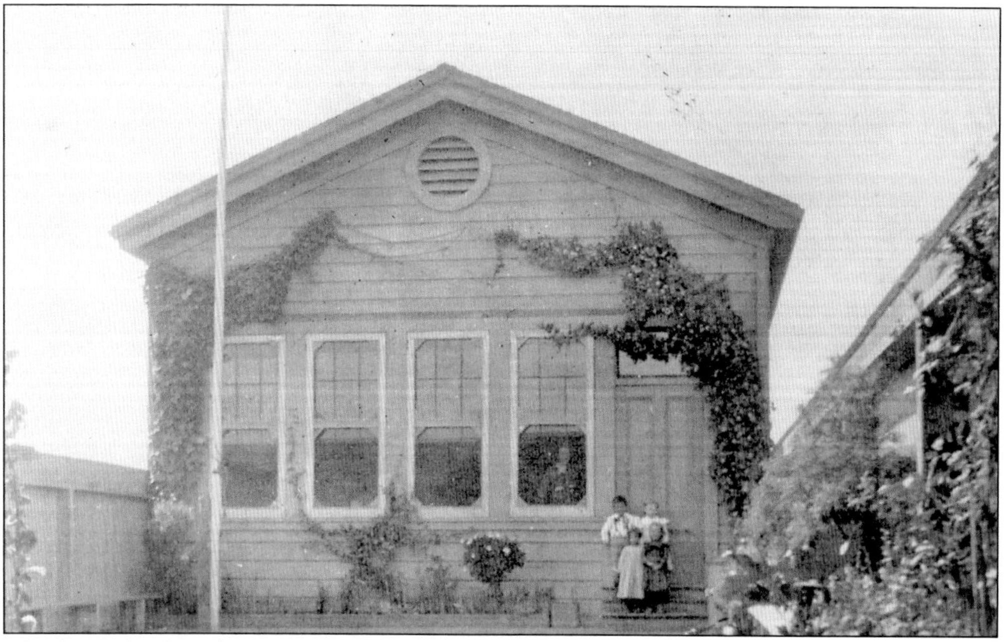

The first school in the Sunny Vale Public School District opened in September 1896 and was subsequently given the name of the Visitacion Valley School. Although it had been decided that the Spanish spelling should be retained, the board of education misspelled the name as "Visitation" on the new sign, provoking much local laughter. (Courtesy San Francisco History Center, San Francisco Public Library.)

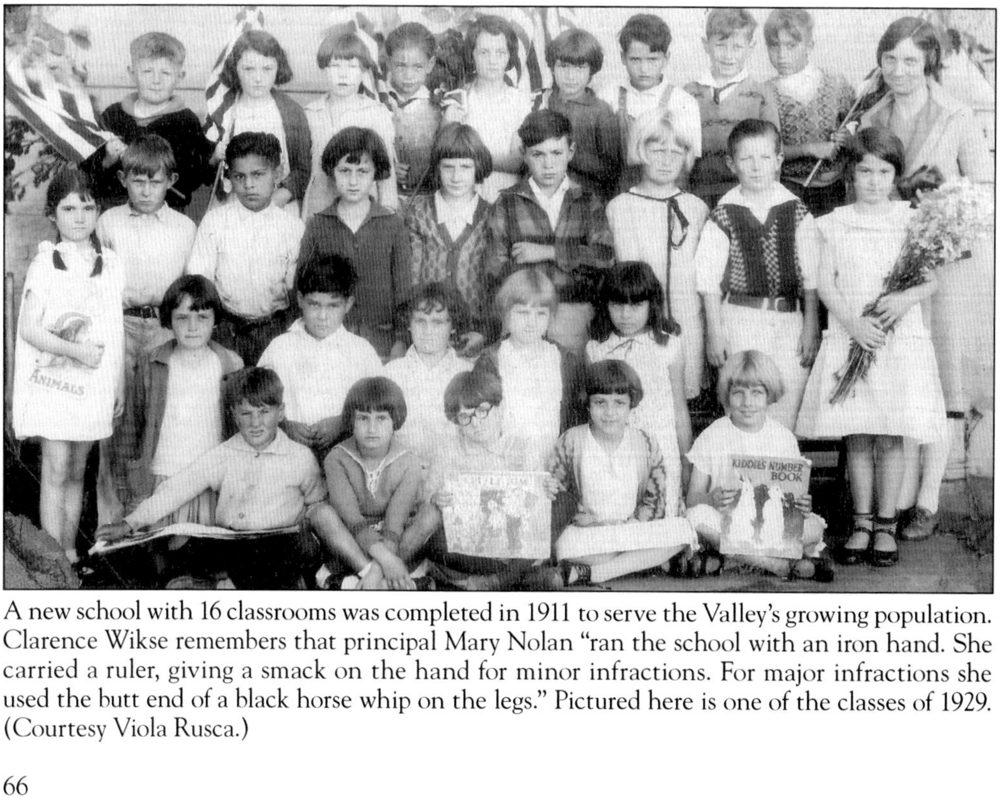

A new school with 16 classrooms was completed in 1911 to serve the Valley's growing population. Clarence Wikse remembers that principal Mary Nolan "ran the school with an iron hand. She carried a ruler, giving a smack on the hand for minor infractions. For major infractions she used the butt end of a black horse whip on the legs." Pictured here is one of the classes of 1929. (Courtesy Viola Rusca.)

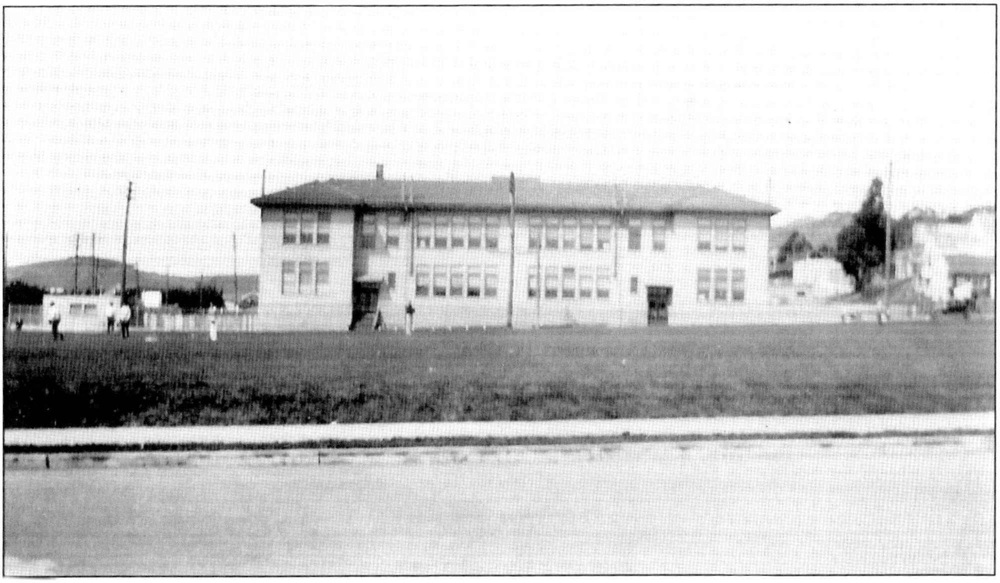

The 1911 school faced Schwerin Street with a huge play area in front. While the new building was under construction on this open space in 1936–1937, the students continued to attend classes in the old school.

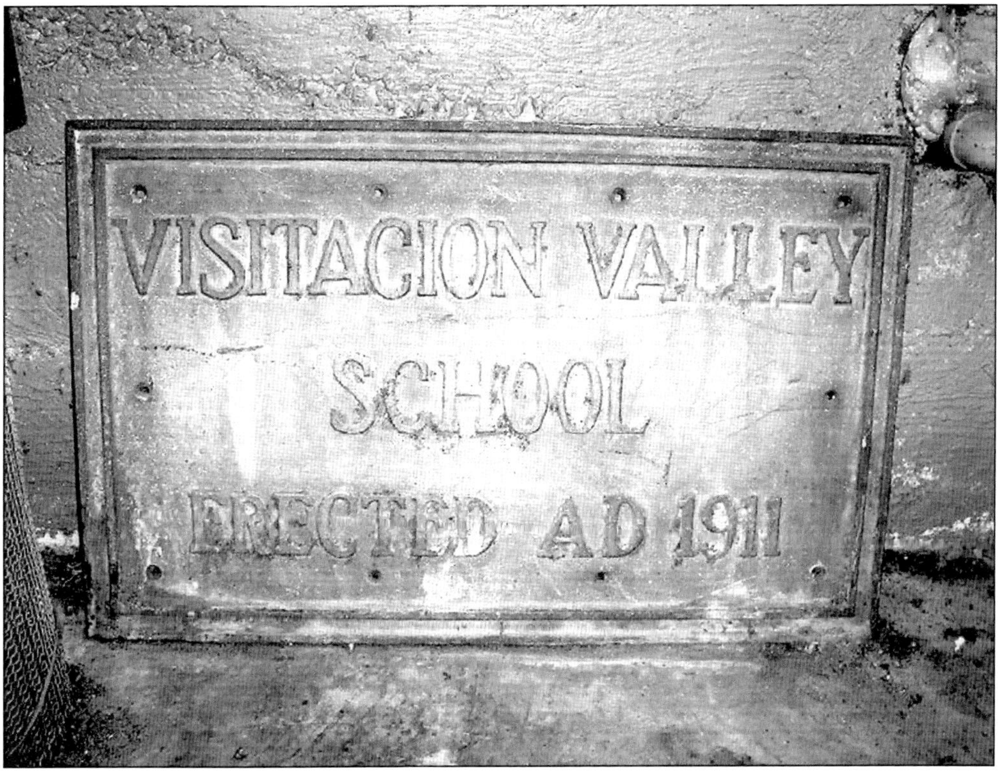

This cast-iron plaque from the school's 1911 dedication was tucked away in the "new" Visitacion Valley Elementary's boiler room and almost forgotten until the custodian brought it out for inspection in 2005. (Courtesy Edie Epps.)

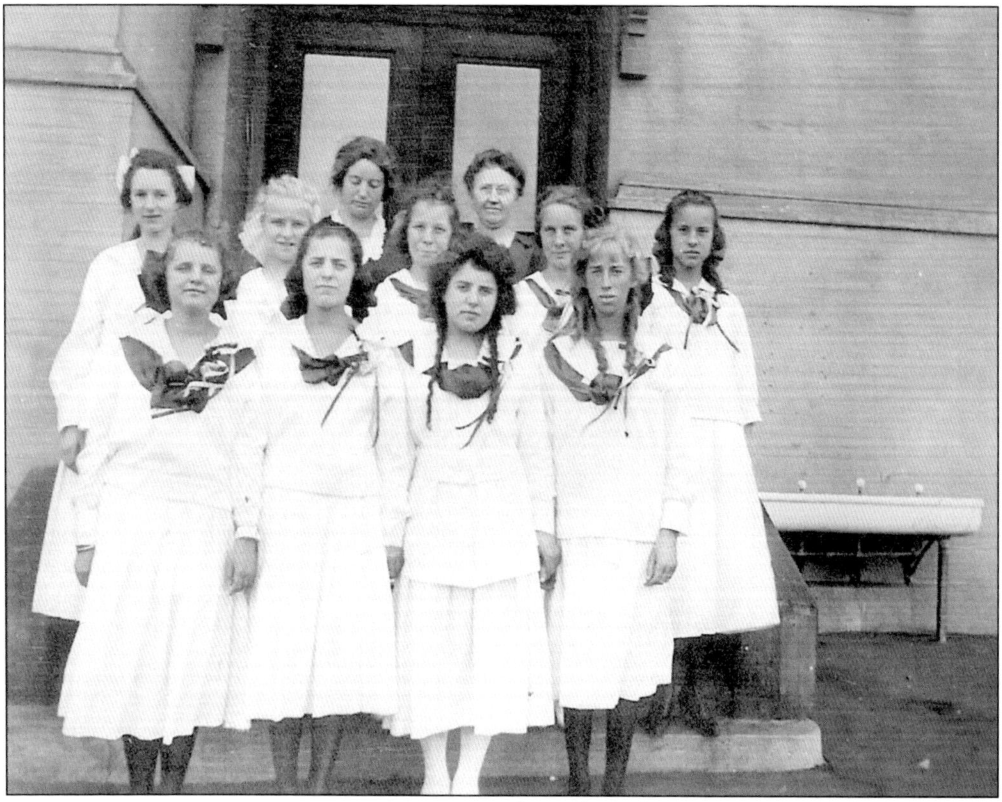

The girls in this 1919 photograph took sewing and cooking classes at the local community center after school twice a week. One of the outcomes of these lessons was the girls' making their own graduation dresses, remembered by Mary Schwartz as being of "chiffon in light blue, green or pink." (Courtesy Taylor family.)

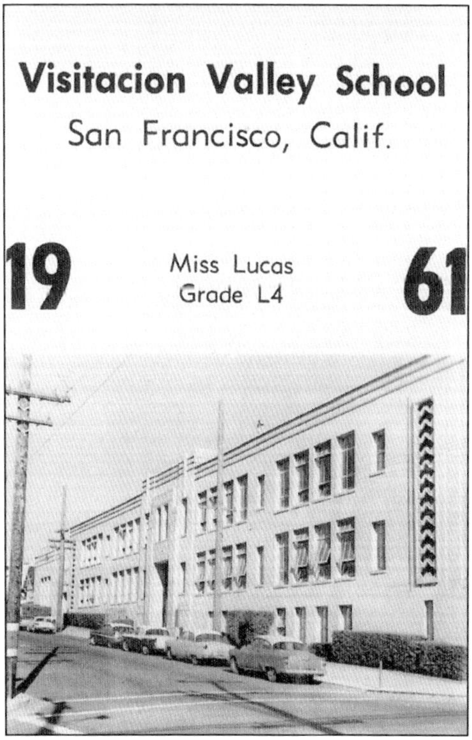

The Art Deco-inspired building that still serves the Valley's children was completed in 1937 as part of a public works project. The construction cost was $162,000. Today over 800 children attend classes K-5. Vincent Chao has been the school's principal for over 10 years. (Courtesy Parshall family.)

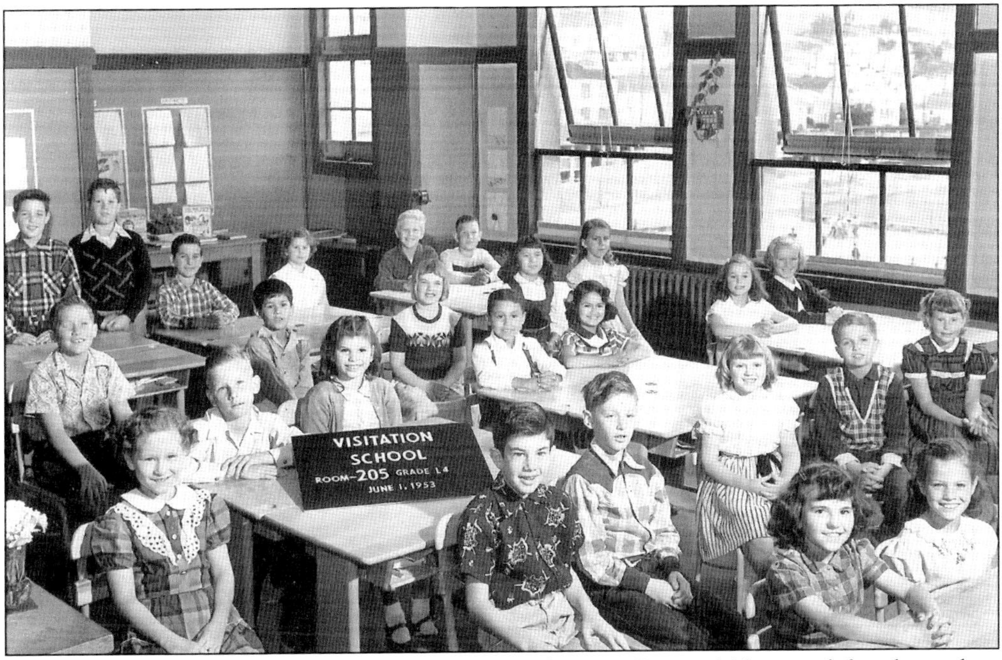

In June 1953, Visitacion Valley's fourth-grade class, in Room 205, posed for their class picture. Whoever prepared the sign, must not have been a resident of Visitacion Valley. (Courtesy Taylor family.)

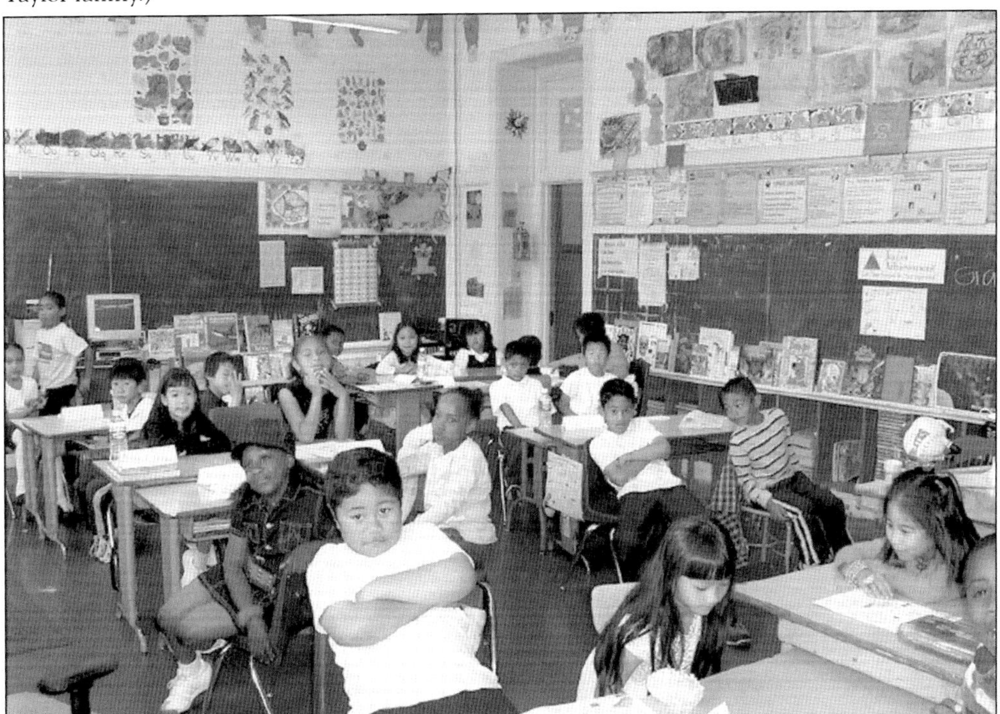

The students of Room 205 at the same school had this candid class photograph taken in Spring 2005. (Courtesy Edie Epps.)

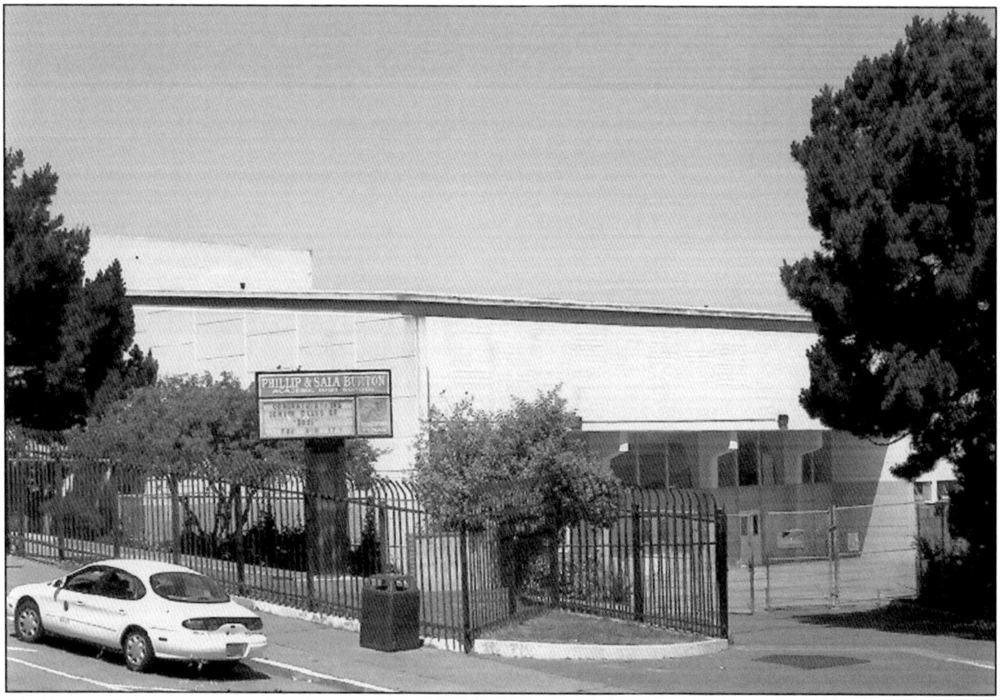

Phillip and Sala Burton Academic, formerly Woodrow Wilson High, on Mansell at the very top of the Valley, has a multicultural student body of 1,600. The school's Touch of Class Choir has a world-famous reputation throughout the musical community. (Courtesy Edie Epps.)

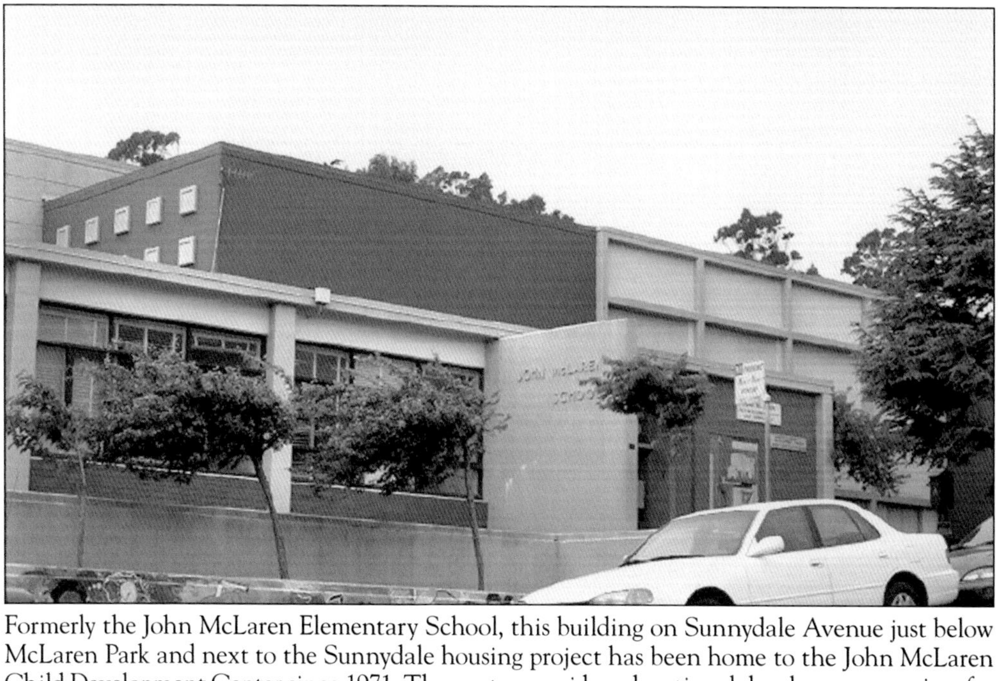

Formerly the John McLaren Elementary School, this building on Sunnydale Avenue just below McLaren Park and next to the Sunnydale housing project has been home to the John McLaren Child Development Center since 1971. The center provides educational development services for both preschool and school-aged children. Of note is the fact that English, Cambodian, Cantonese, Spanish, and Vietnamese are all spoken here. (Courtesy Edie Epps.)

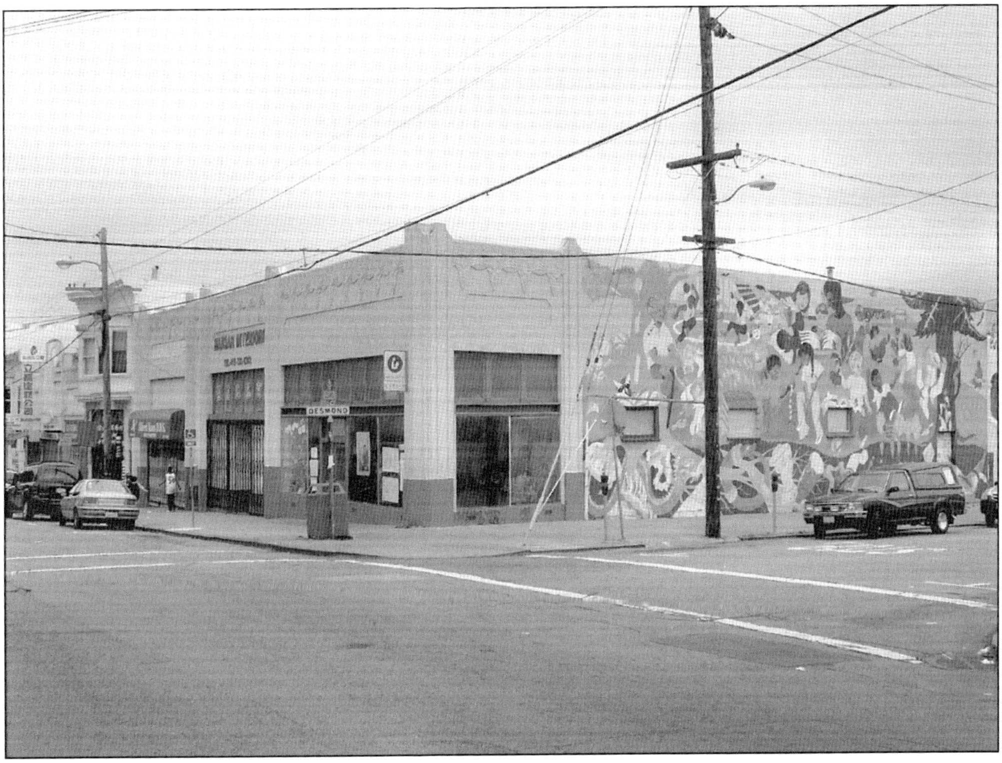

Visitacion Valley's one-room library is on Leland at Desmond. Residents eagerly anticipate the new branch four blocks further along Leland, promised as part of a bond measure passed by San Francisco's voters in November 2000. (Courtesy Russel Morine.)

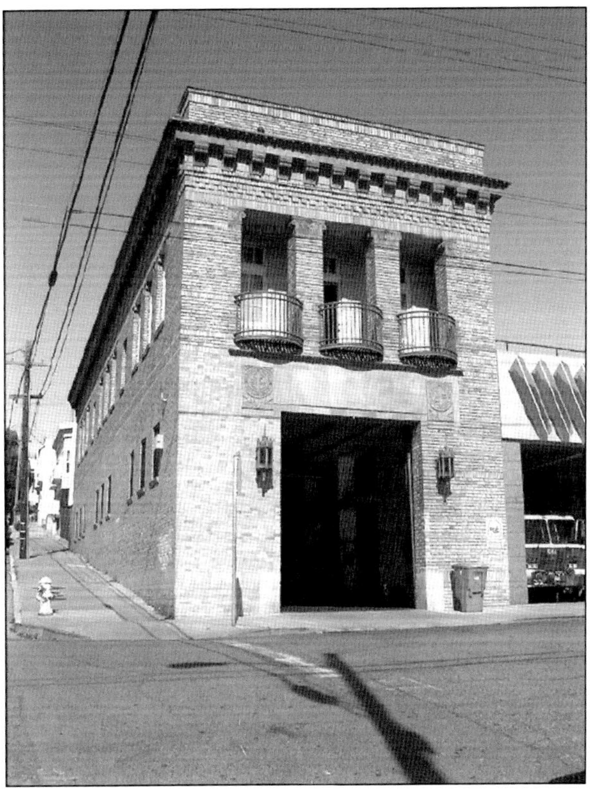

Engine Company No. 47, later redesignated No. 44, occupies this building at 1298 Girard, one of the oldest firehouses still in active service in San Francisco. Although the station was completed in 1913, it could not be used until the arrival of the "motor driven apparatus" from the east. Designed by John Reid Jr., the two-story brick structure has "SFFD" and "No. 47" embossed in terra cotta medallions on either side of the main door. Originally the Valley was protected by a volunteer fire company housed at 373 Wilde Avenue. (Courtesy Edie Epps.)

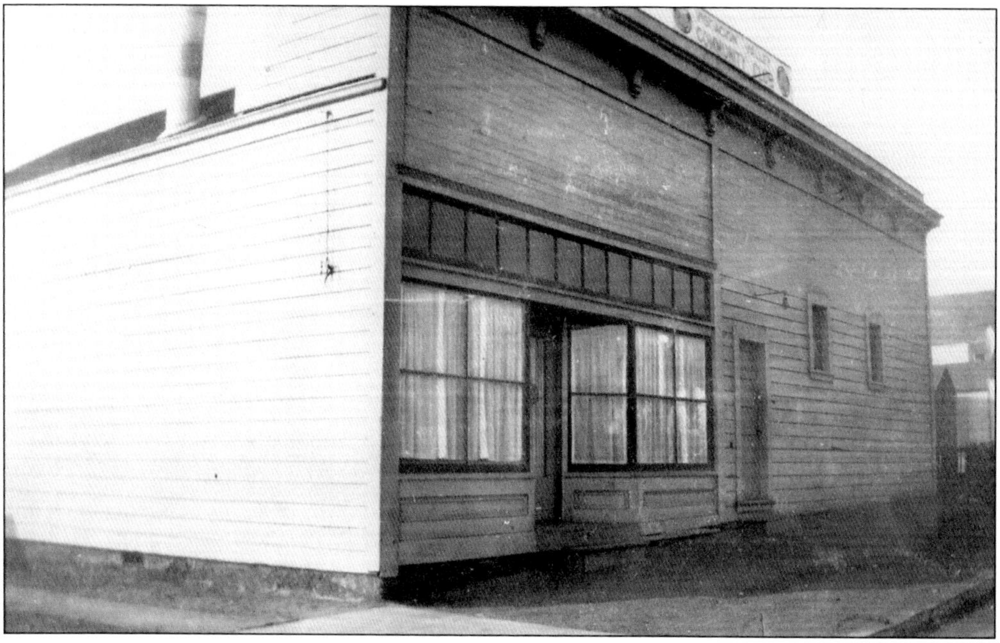

In 1918, Florence Friedman, one of the first teachers at the Visitacion Valley Elementary School, volunteered to operate the War Camp Community Center in this building at the corner of Raymond and Alpha. Serving military personnel from the nearby camp on Southern Pacific property, neighbors pitched in to provide potluck dinners and social activities. Miss Friedman, who had a telephone, invited servicemen to her own home to call home on holidays. (Courtesy Visitacion Valley Community Center.)

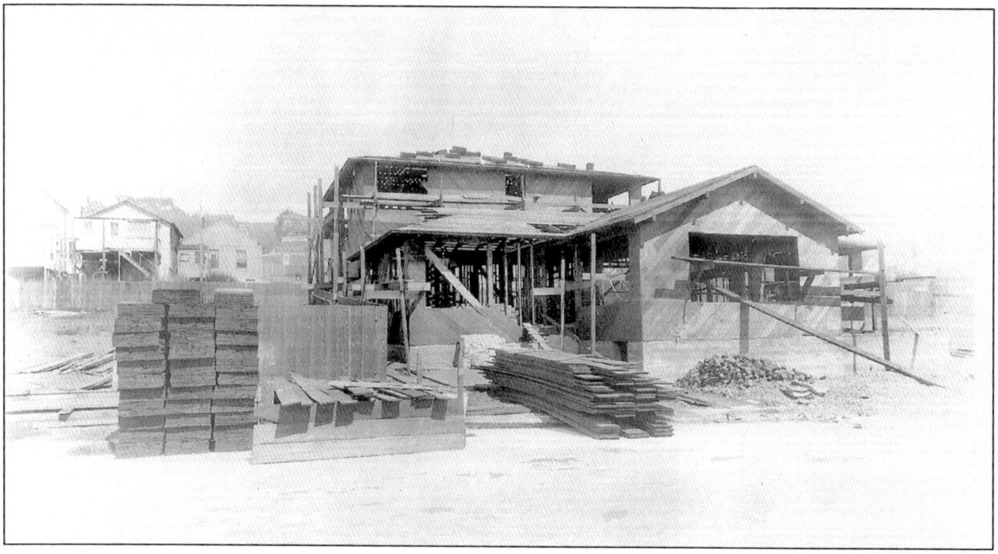

When World War I ended, the need for a continuing community center was apparent. In 1922, a new building was erected by community volunteers, organized by neighborhood contractor Charles Eisenhut after a vigorous and successful fund-raising campaign by founder and director Florence Friedman. Justine Baron Marcelli recalls, "My father worked on the building; he was a carpenter. . . . My mother did volunteer work; she'd teach people how to sew. She was a beautiful seamstress." (Courtesy Visitacion Valley Community Center.)

Although Miss Friedman founded the community center to serve all the Valley's residents, her first priority was always the young people. The free well baby clinic—the first in San Francisco—and nursery school were two such services. (Courtesy Visitacion Valley Community Center.)

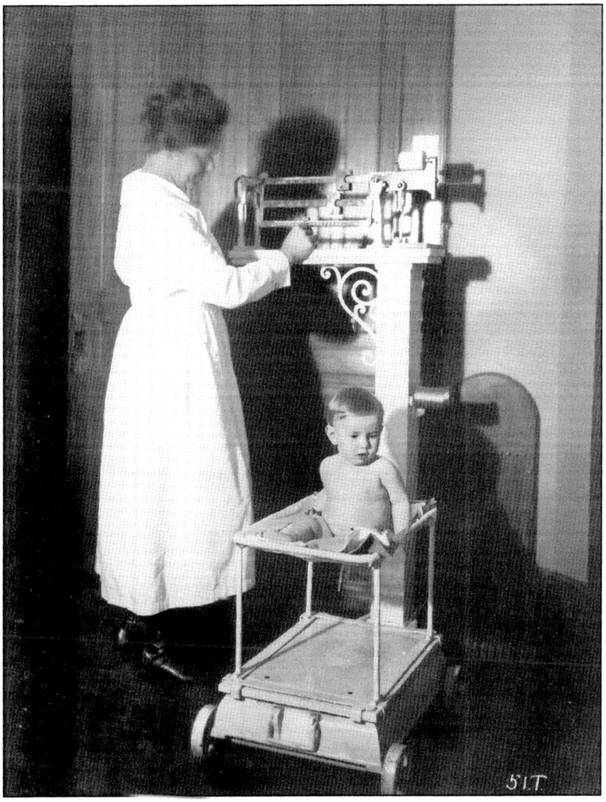

The community center sponsored Boy Scout Troop 78. This 1919 photograph illustrates the boys' support of the war effort. (Courtesy Visitacion Valley Community Center.)

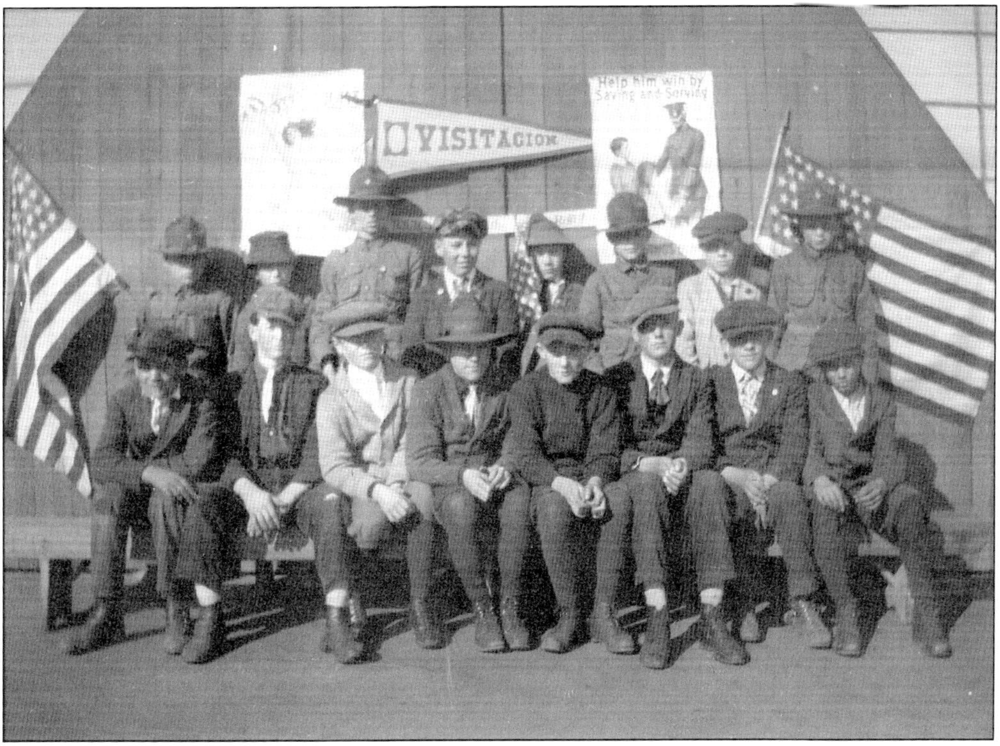

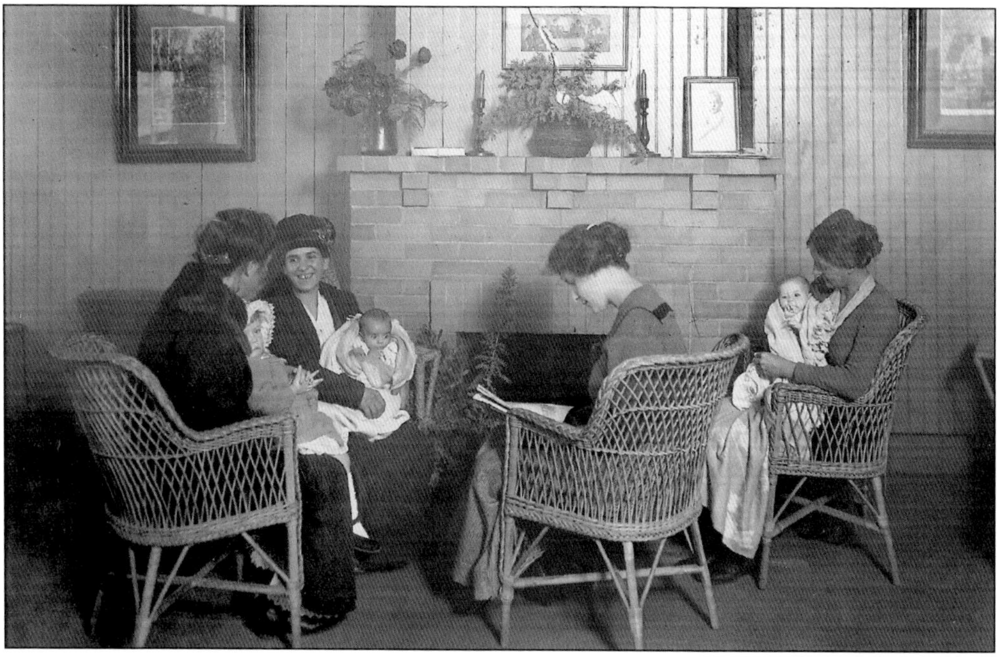

As this 1918 photograph of mothers and babies demonstrates, Visitacion Valley families needed expanded services as the population grew. (Courtesy Visitacion Valley Community Center.)

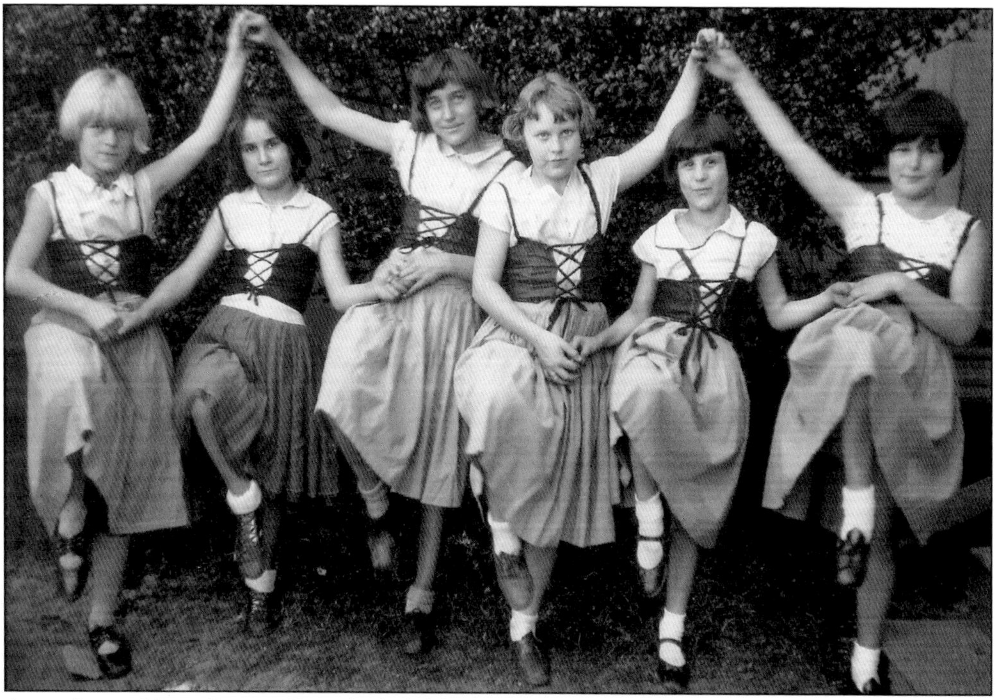

According to Harry Pierce, "See, the kids liked to dance and Florence Friedman had good dances. My brother went to the folk dancing class at the center, and that's where he met Gladys Casey [his future wife]. There was a good group down there. They put on good plays too." (Courtesy Visitacion Valley Community Center.)

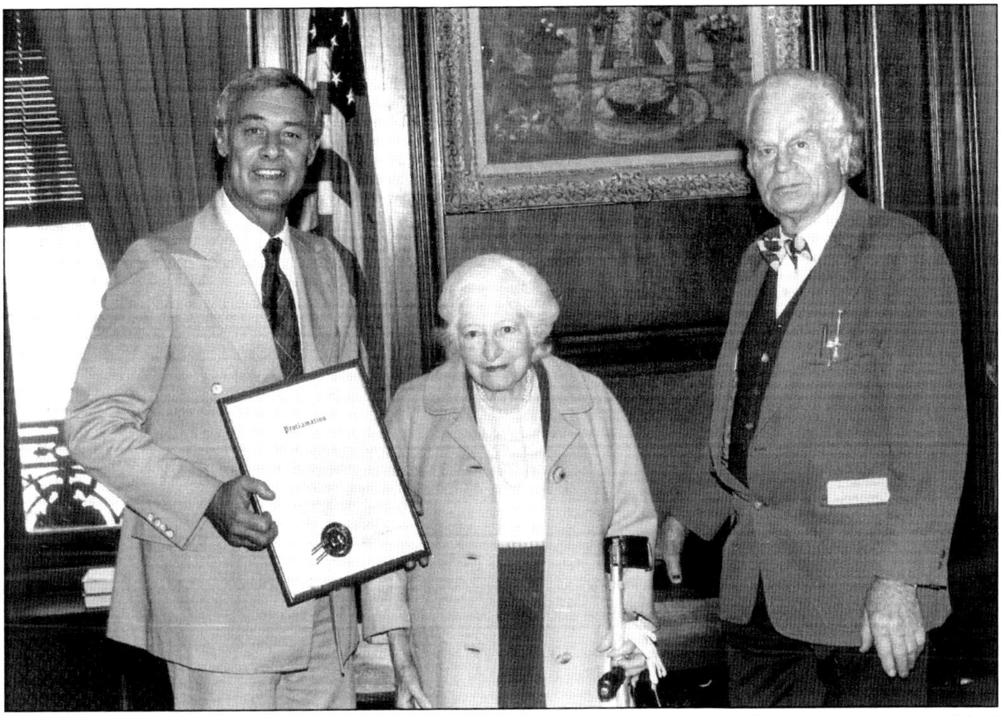

In addition to her many community activities, Florence Friedman fostered children from troubled families. Only 22 when she arrived in 1909, she never ceased efforts to bring benefits to her beloved "Valley of the Good Neighbor" throughout her 95 years. In this photograph, Mayor George Moscone and civic leader Henry Schindel honor her many achievements. (Courtesy Harriet Schindel Newhart.)

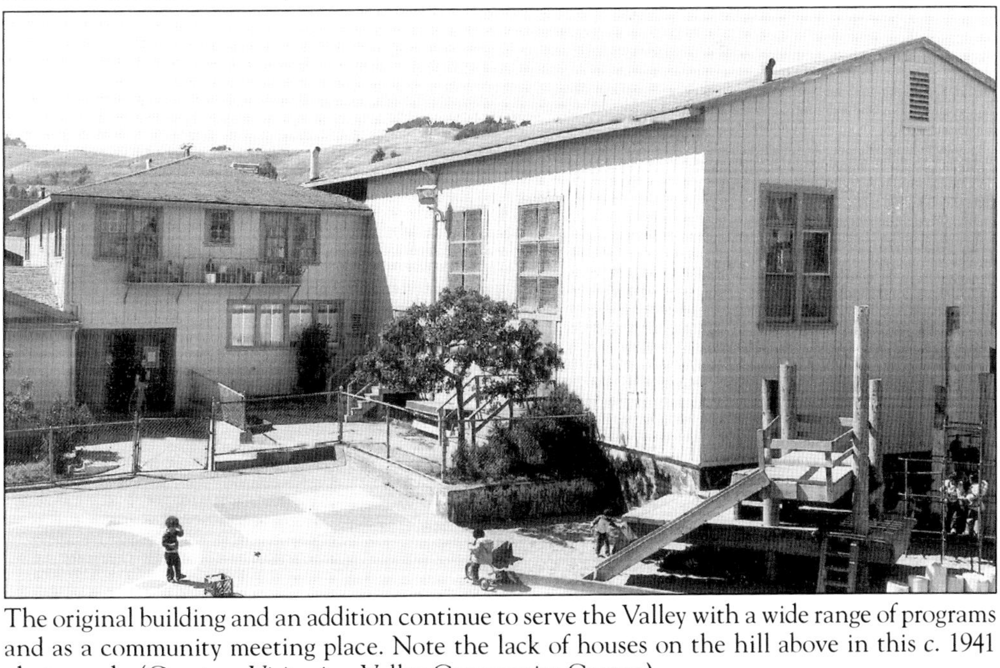

The original building and an addition continue to serve the Valley with a wide range of programs and as a community meeting place. Note the lack of houses on the hill above in this c. 1941 photograph. (Courtesy Visitacion Valley Community Center.)

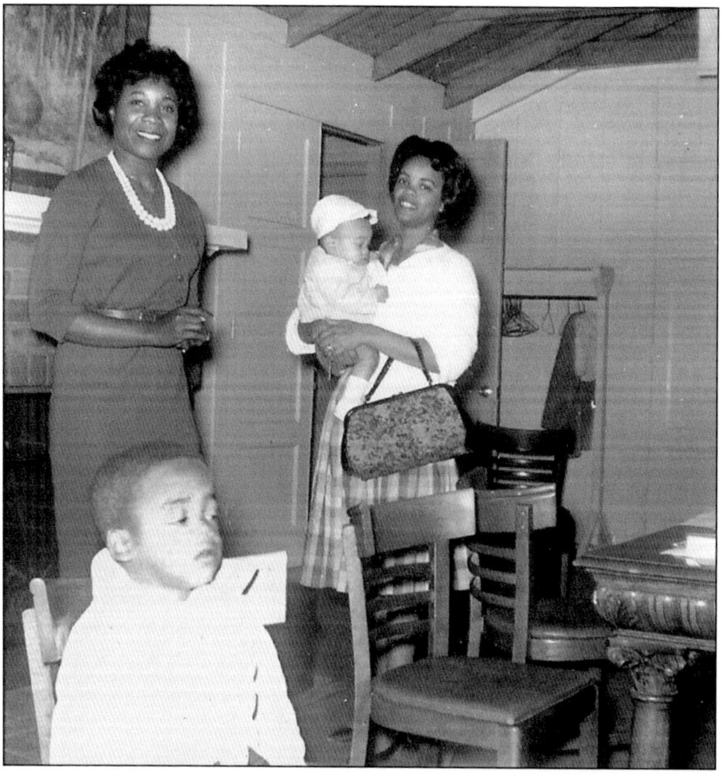

The community center continues to provide programs for children and adults. The center currently offers infant childcare, preschool and after-school programs, ESL classes, activities, assistance and counseling for seniors, and many more services. (Courtesy Visitacion Valley Community Center.)

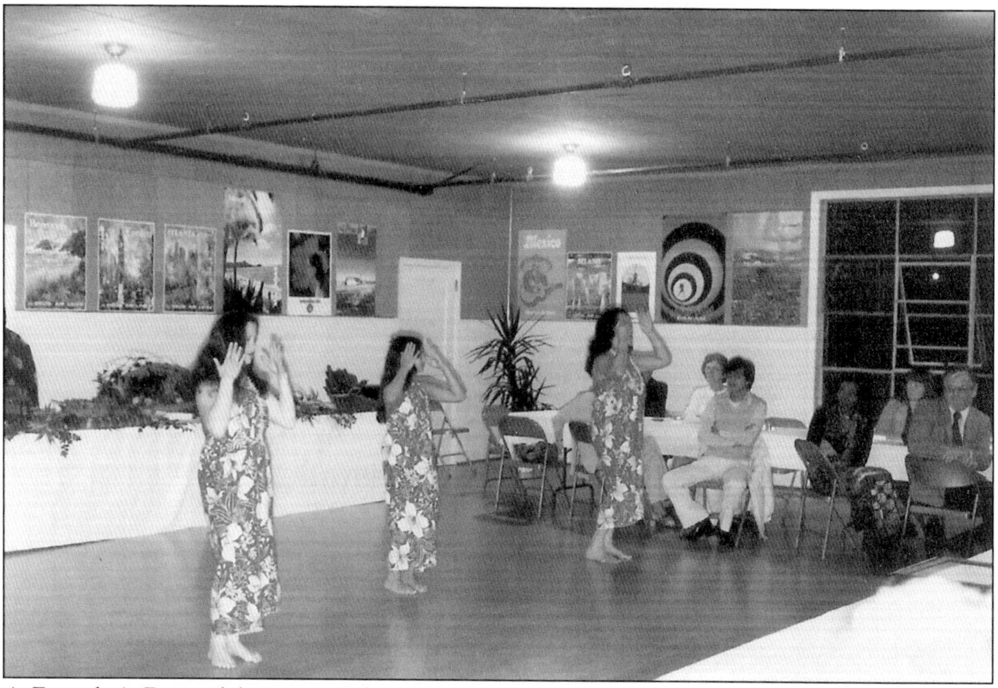

A Founder's Day celebration at the community center featured entertainment by various neighborhood groups, including this group that performed a hula for the crowd in the 1980s. (Courtesy Visitacion Valley Community Center.)

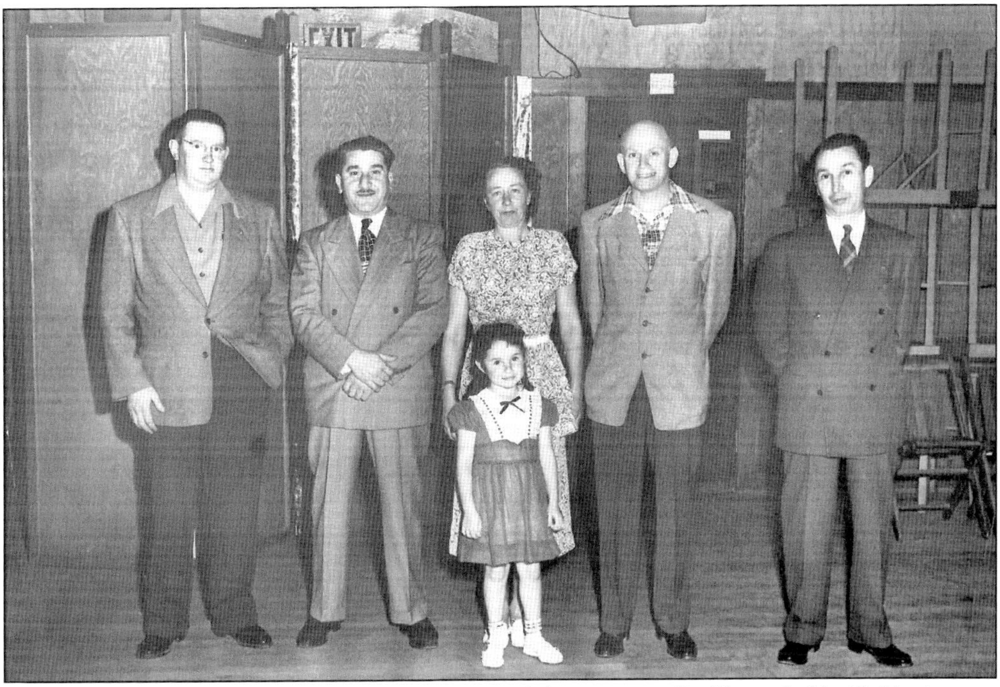

The Reis-Paul Tract Improvement Club represented the "upper valley" bounded by Teddy Avenue to the top of the hill (Mansell today). In this photograph, from left to right, are officers Clarence Guttner, Joe Cimino, Vera Holmes, Leo Hammer, and Harold Shapiro. Margaret Shapiro was one of the youngest members of the club. (Courtesy Taylor family.)

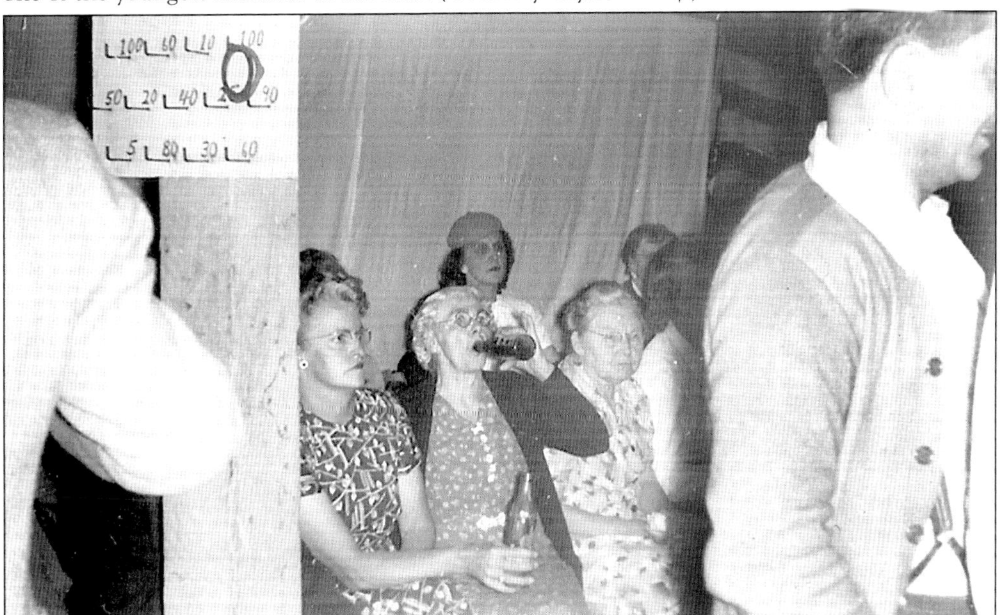

Among the Reis-Paul Tract Club's achievements were instituting the first bus service for the "hill folks," building the swimming pool at Sunnydale and Hahn, starting El Dorado School, and preserving the property that later became the site for Visitacion Valley Middle School. The club also had some great cioppino dinners in Mrs. Reid's basement. (Courtesy Taylor family.)

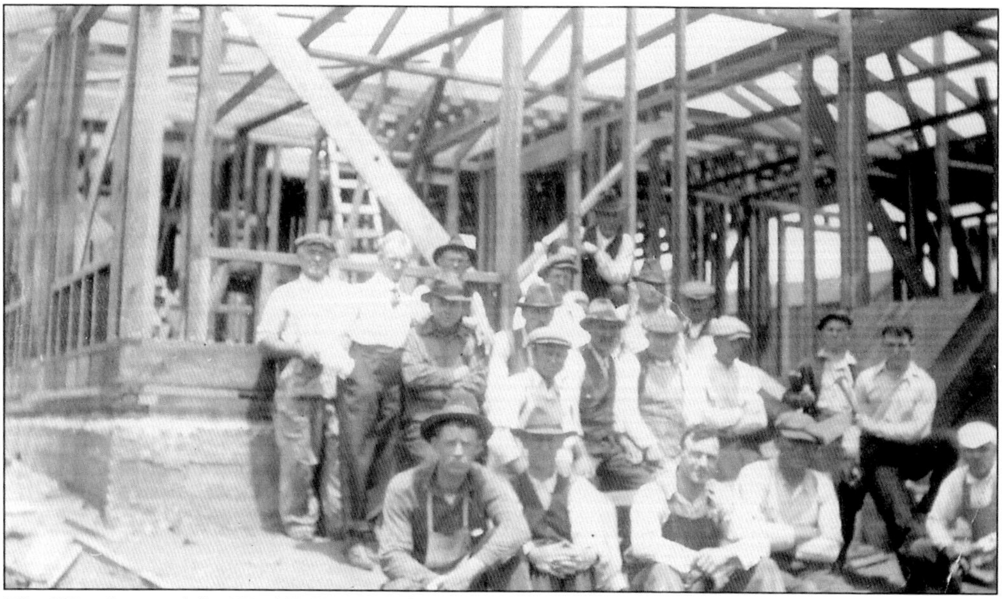

The Woodmen of the World's Fern Leaf Camp No. 808, active volunteers for social improvement, was organized in Visitacion Valley on September 26, 1906. Members had built their own hall at Raymond and San Bruno by 1914, and by 1927 the membership reached 400. The ladies' branch was known as Fern Leaf Circle No. 659, Neighbors of Woodcraft. (Courtesy Taylor family.)

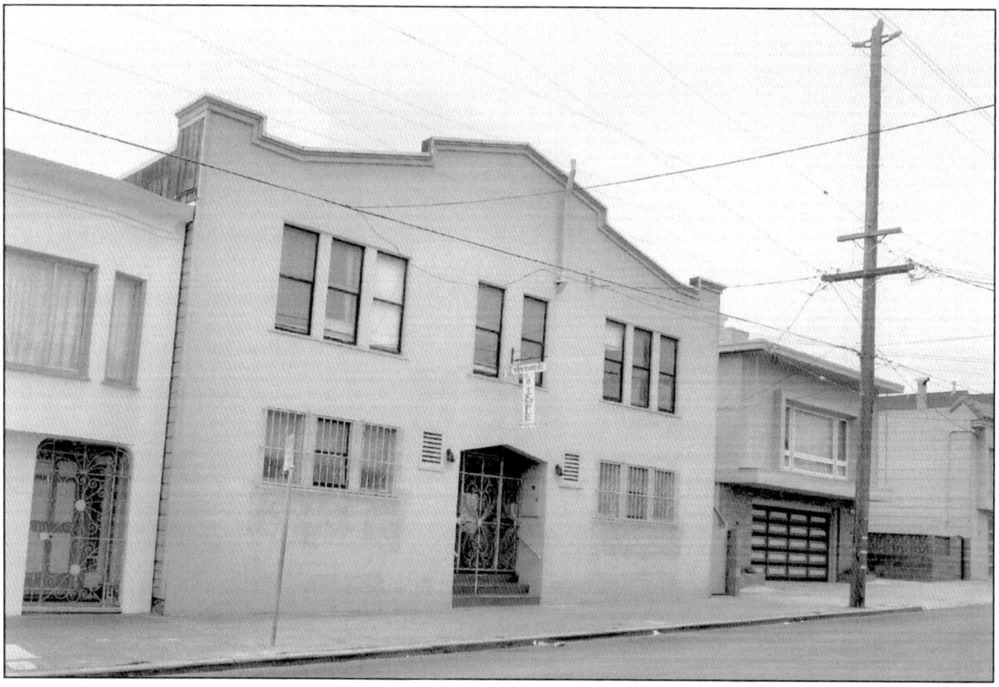

The Visitacion Valley Athletic Association, organized on October 17, 1907, incorporated in 1920 and built a large gymnasium on Raymond—one of the largest in the city—where many exciting basketball games were held. In later years, the hall served as the headquarters of the Bonvitas social improvement club and was owned by its shareholders. Since 1975, it has been a Masonic lodge, Thutmose Temple No. 74. (Courtesy Russel Morine.)

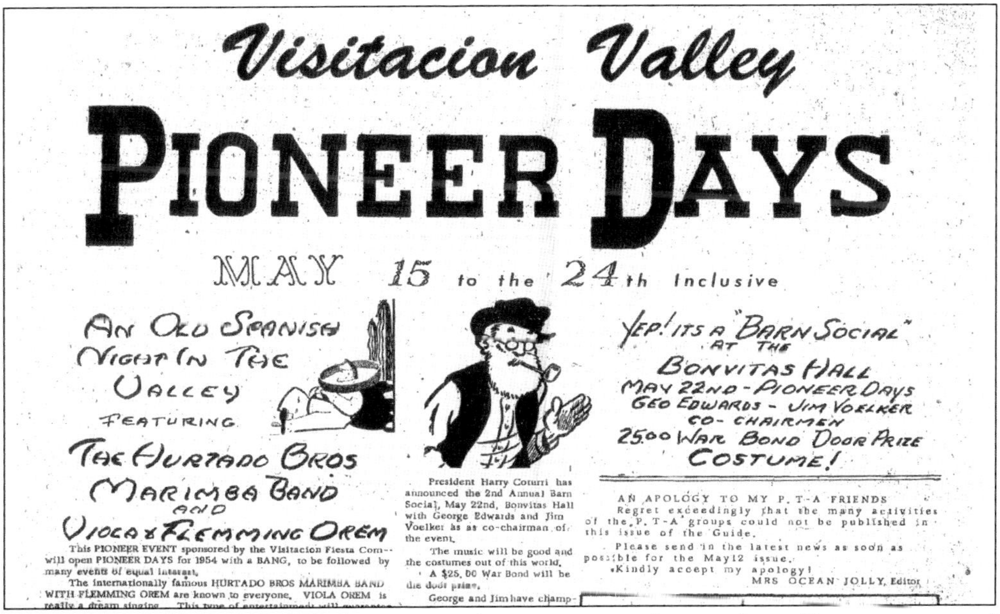

Visitacion Valley PIONEER DAYS

MAY 15 to the 24th Inclusive

AN OLD SPANISH NIGHT IN THE VALLEY
FEATURING
THE HURTADO BROS MARIMBA BAND
AND
VIOLA & FLEMMING OREM

This PIONEER EVENT sponsored by the Visitacion Fiesta Com-- will open PIONEER DAYS for 1954 with a BANG, to be followed by many events of equal interest.

The internationally famous HURTADO BROS MARIMBA BAND WITH FLEMMING OREM are known to everyone. VIOLA OREM is really a dream singing ...

President Harry Coturri has announced the 2nd Annual Barn Social, May 22nd, Bonvitas Hall with George Edwards and Jim Voelker as as co-chairman of the event.

The music will be good and the costumes out of this world.

A $25.00 War Bond will be the door prize.

George and Jim have champ-

YEP! ITS A "BARN SOCIAL" AT THE BONVITAS HALL
MAY 22ND - PIONEER DAYS
GEO EDWARDS - JIM VOELKER
CO- CHAIRMEN
25.00 WAR BOND DOOR PRIZE
COSTUME!

AN APOLOGY TO MY P. T-A FRIENDS

Regret exceedingly that the many activities of the P. T-A groups could not be published in this issue of the Guide.

Please send in the latest news as soon as possible for the May12 issue.

Kindly accept my apology!

MRS OCEAN JOLLY, Editor

Valley entertainment included whist parties, dances, amateur theatricals, and bazaars sponsored by various clubs, churches, and service organizations. Venues included the community center, the Bay Shore Hall above Anderson's Coal Yard on Leland, the Fireman's Hall on Wilde, and the Six Mile House gymnasium. In 1954, the Bonvitas Hall on Raymond was the place to be for a week-long Pioneer Days celebration. (Courtesy *Visitacion Guide*, April 14, 1954.)

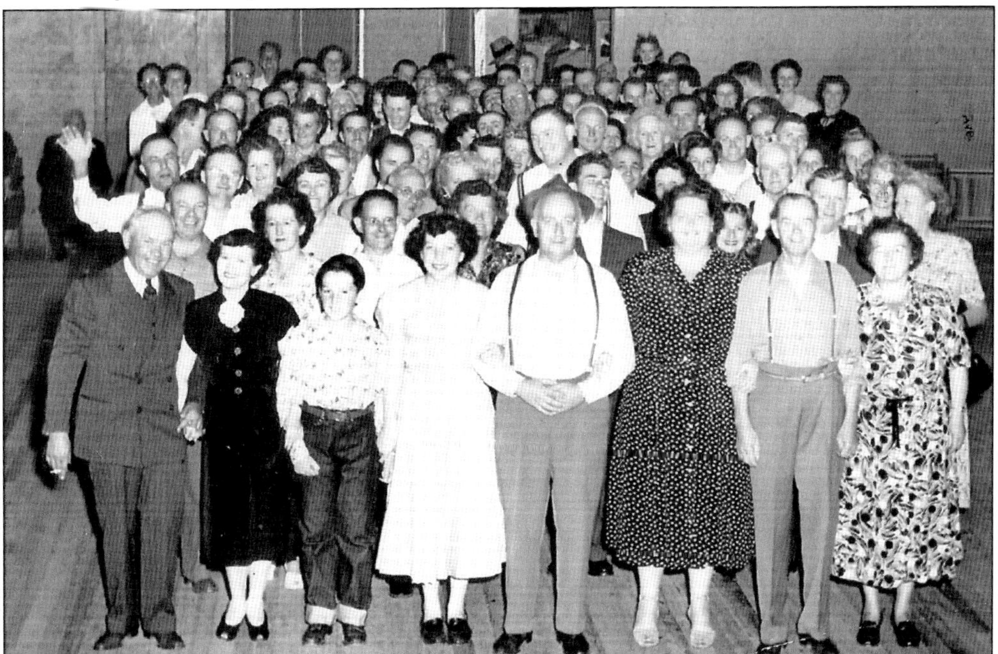

Valley improvement clubs often joined forces on issues to benefit the neighborhood and combined good times and fund-raising with dinners and dances at the Bonvitas Hall on Raymond. Here attendees of a 1949 Bonvitas dance line up for the Grand March. (Courtesy Taylor family.)

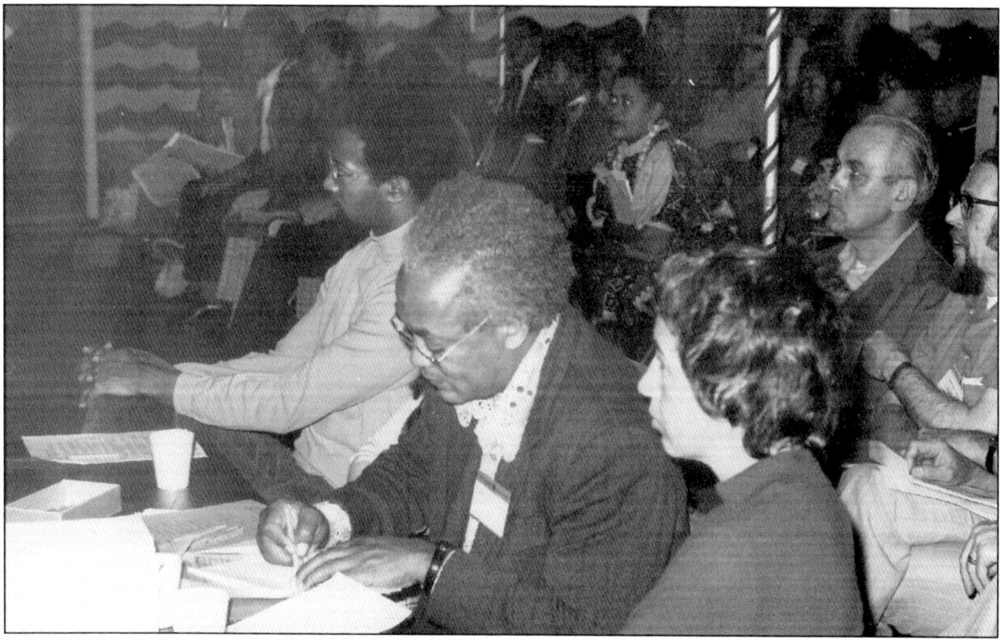

The All Peoples' Coalition (APC) consisted of existing and newly formed organizations, under the guidance of organizer Mike Miller, to bring improvements to the Valley through negotiations and action by a united community. The first Community Congress of the APC was held at Visitacion Valley Elementary School on December 1, 1972. (Courtesy John Arnott.)

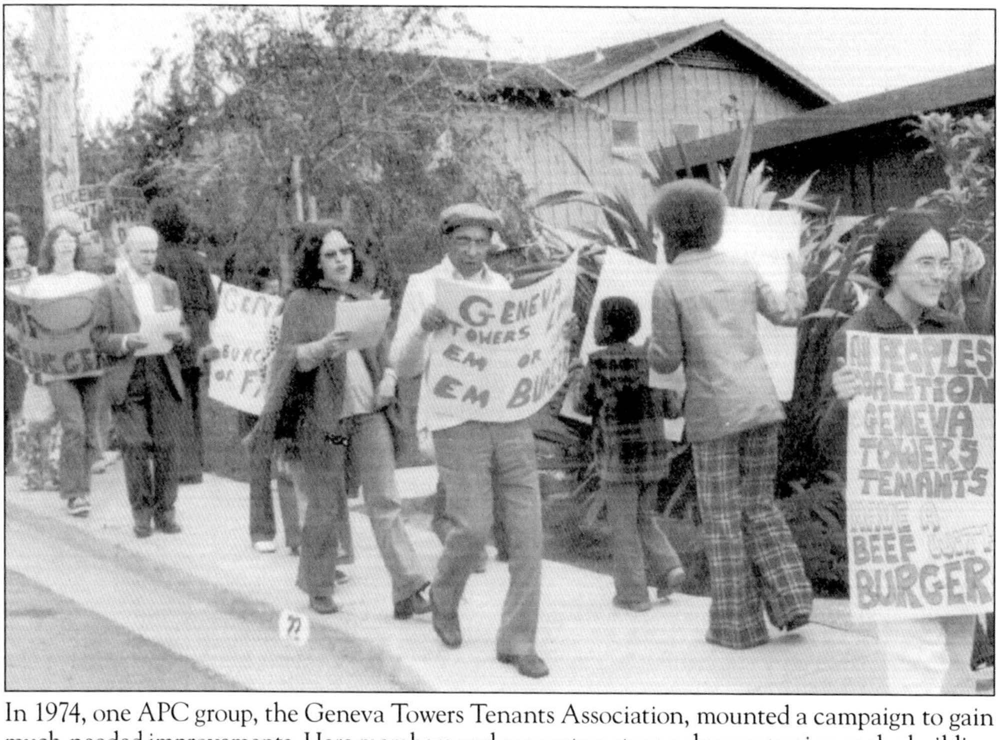

In 1974, one APC group, the Geneva Towers Tenants Association, mounted a campaign to gain much-needed improvements. Here members and supporters stage a demonstration at the building manager's Marin County home. (Courtesy Mike Miller.)

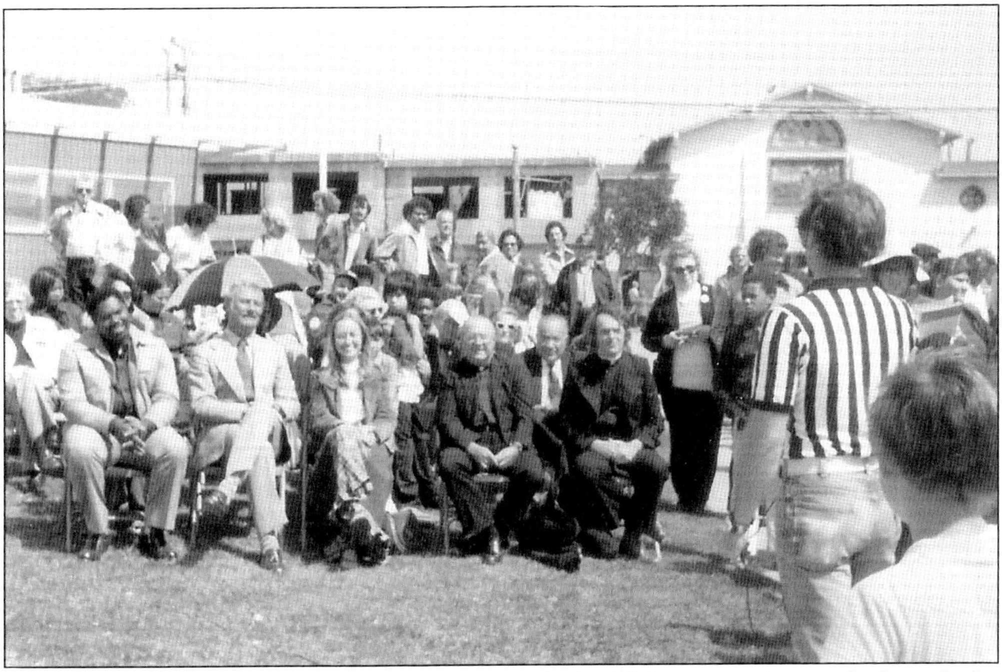

On September 4, 1976, to celebrate the bicentennial, the APC sponsored a parade through the neighborhood and a community fair at a local park. APC president John Haug (in a striped shirt) addressed the crowd. (Courtesy Betty Parshall.)

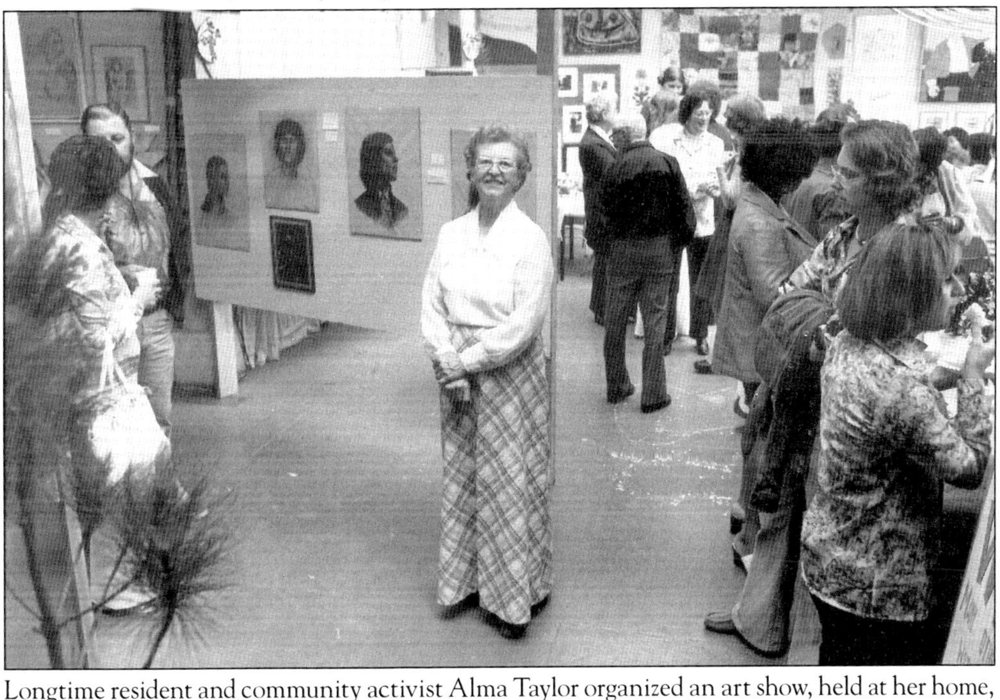

Longtime resident and community activist Alma Taylor organized an art show, held at her home, for the benefit of APC and to highlight the many artistic talents of her Valley neighbors. Visitors to the art show enjoyed the wide variety of works on display, as well as good food and company. (Courtesy Taylor family.)

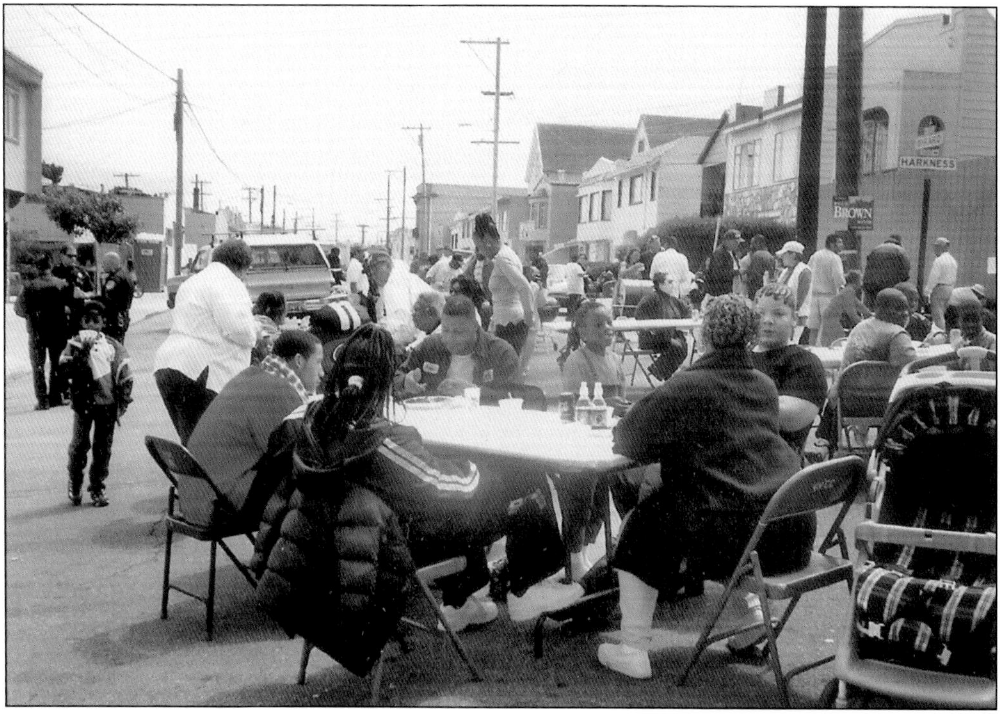

The El Dorado Neighborhood Betterment Association works to build unity among residents. Their annual barbeque each fall, with both good food and a positive purpose, is always a popular and well-attended event. (Courtesy Betty Parshall.)

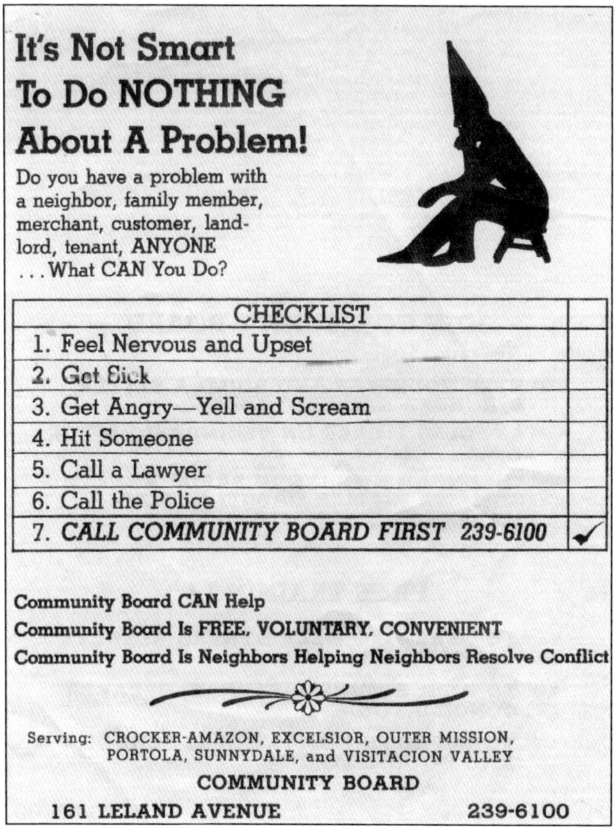

Community boards, designed to give neighbors the ability to resolve disputes in a safe, fair, informal, and free manner, originated in Visitacion Valley in 1976. Paid staff trained volunteers in mediation techniques in a storefront office on Leland. In turn, these volunteers trained others in the neighborhood. Today the Valley office is gone, but Community Boards still provides the same conflict resolution service to San Francisco residents, plus offers programs in schools, businesses, and public and social organizations. (Courtesy Rita Adrian.)

Street memorials, such as this one pictured on a Sunnydale corner, are a sad reminder of the thoughtless violence that too often affects individuals, families, and the community as a whole. (Courtesy Judith Williams Sandoval.)

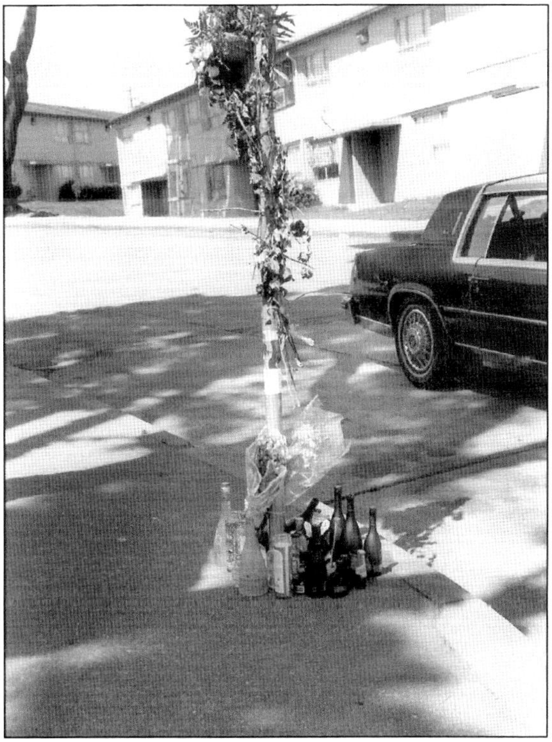

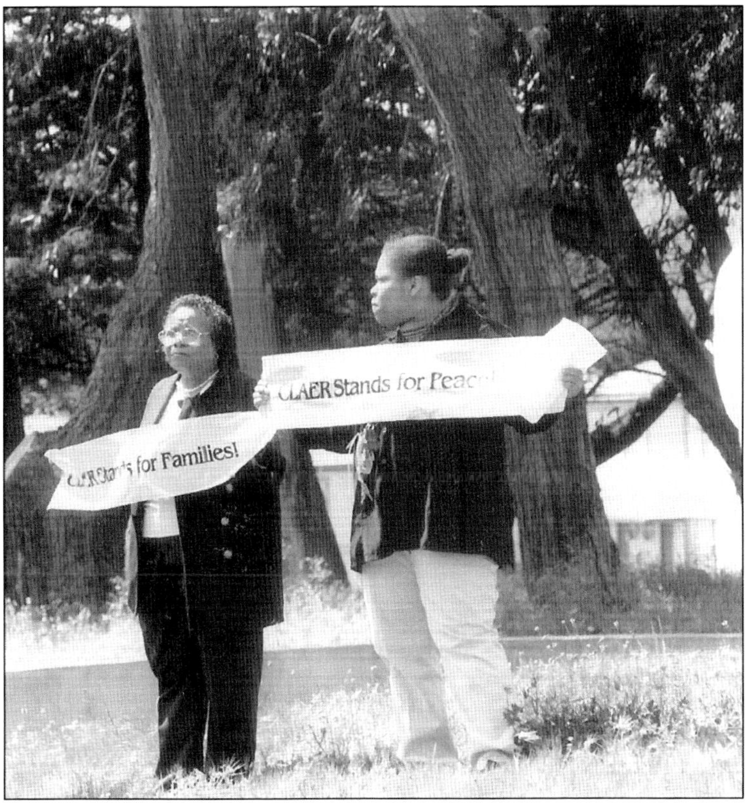

The modern-day CLAER—the Community Leadership Academy Emergency Response—was formed to bring comfort and practical support to residents whose relatives and friends became victims of violence. CLAER also works to improve the lives of people in many ways, including teaching children to resist hostility and join together for a safer community. (Courtesy Judith Williams Sandoval.)

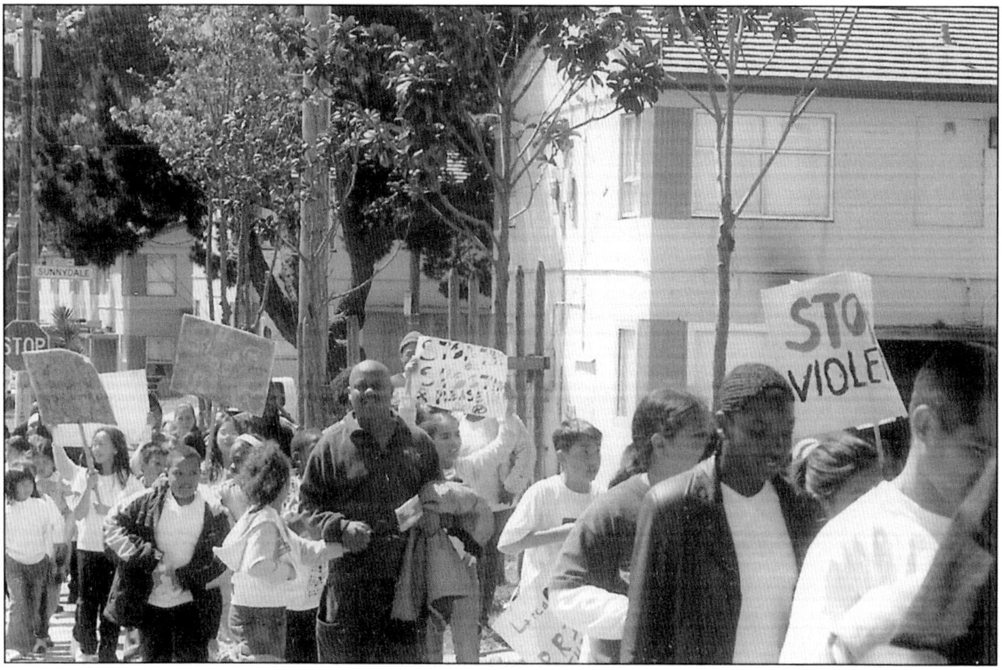

On April 8, 2004, children and adults set out from Sunnydale to walk the neighborhood in a demonstration against violence. (Courtesy Judith Williams Sandoval.)

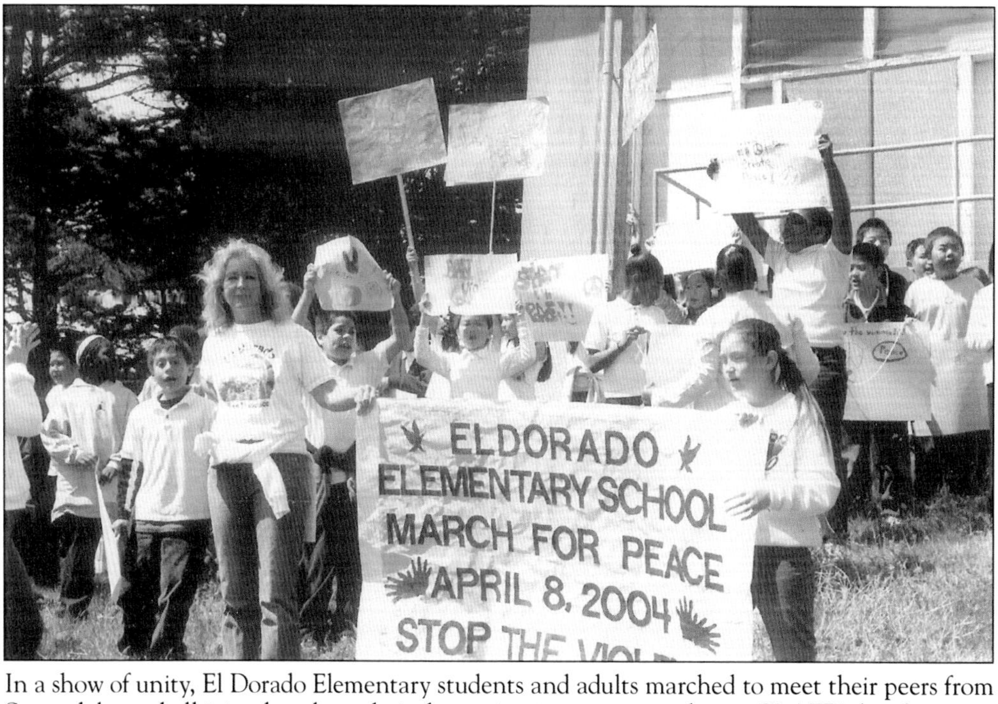

In a show of unity, El Dorado Elementary students and adults marched to meet their peers from Sunnydale, and all joined to show their determination to stop violence. CLAER's headquarters are on Sunnydale Avenue in the heart of the Valley. (Courtesy Judith Williams Sandoval.)

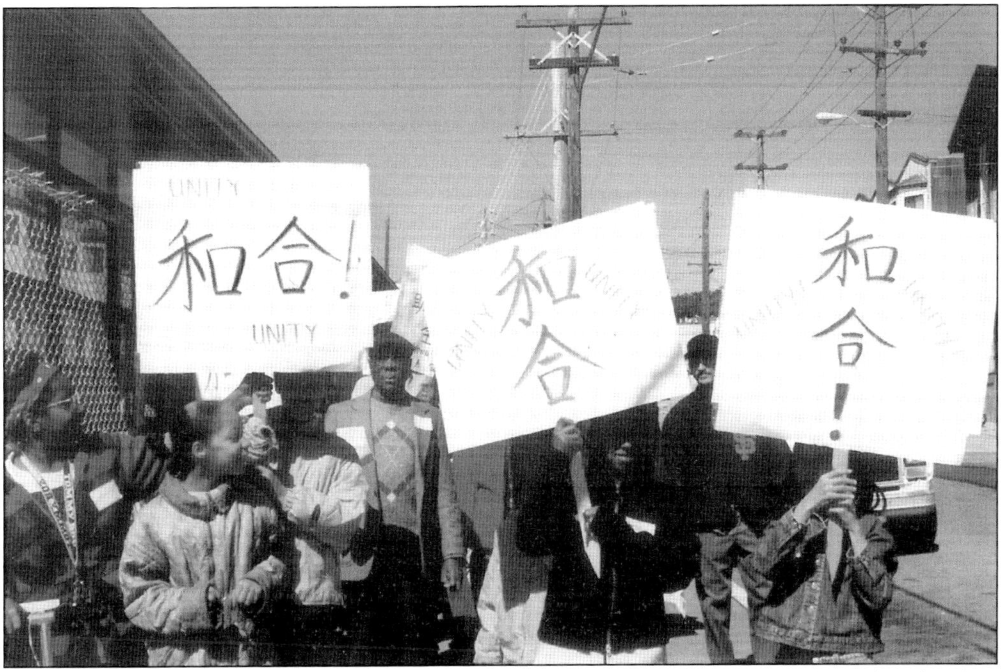

Neighborhood children carried their signs written in Chinese. Asians and Pacific Islanders now comprise more than 50 percent of the population of Visitacion Valley. (Courtesy Judith Williams Sandoval.)

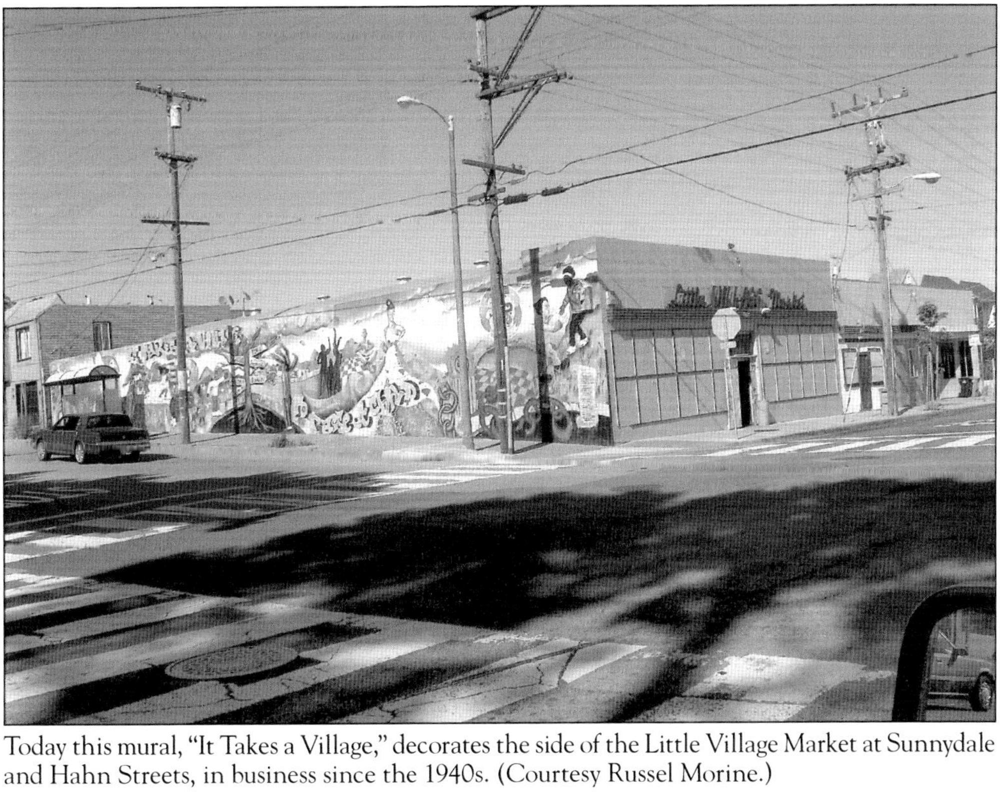

Today this mural, "It Takes a Village," decorates the side of the Little Village Market at Sunnydale and Hahn Streets, in business since the 1940s. (Courtesy Russel Morine.)

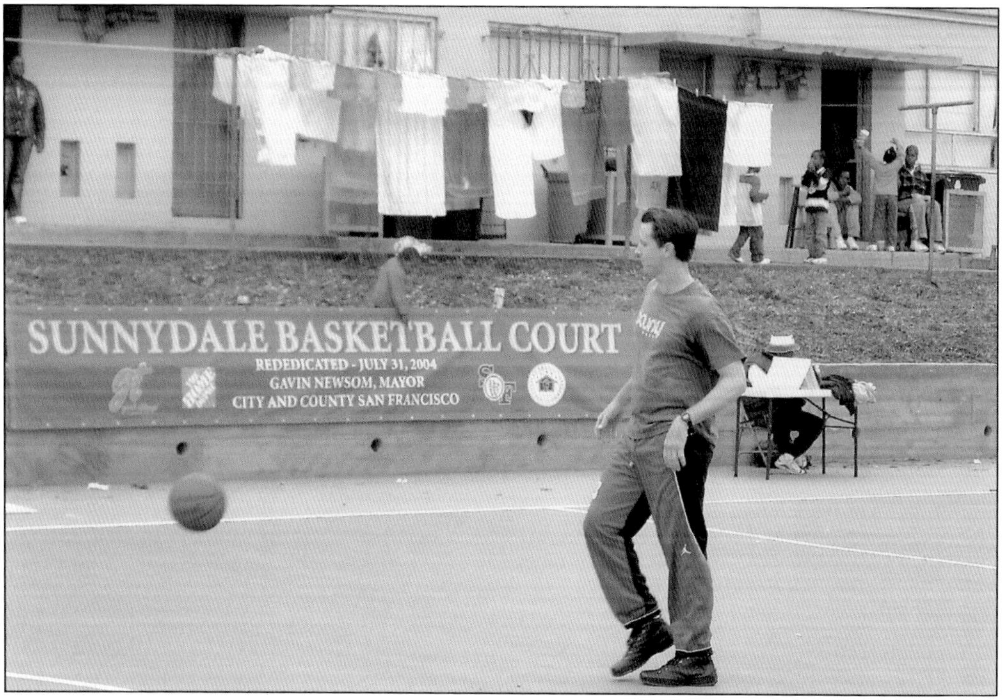

Mayor Gavin Newsom, elected in 2004, has made improving safety and health at the city's underserved neighborhoods one of the priorities of his administration. Here he prepares to shoot a few hoops on the new basketball court now installed at the Sunnydale housing project. (Courtesy Russel Morine.)

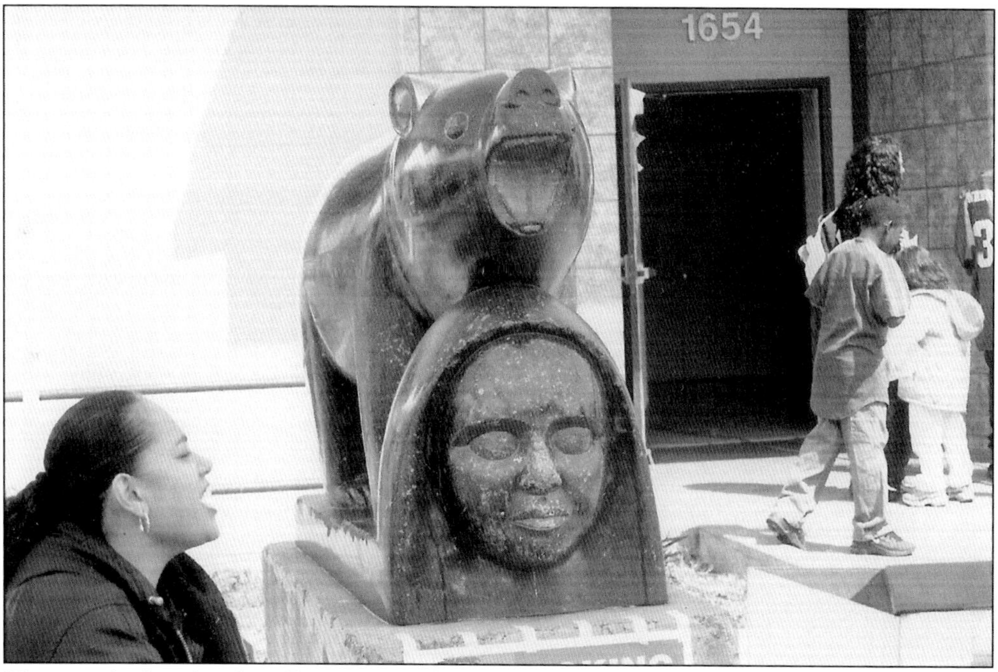

This piece by famed sculptor Beniamino Bufano, entitled "California Bear," stands at the community center at the Sunnydale housing project. (Courtesy Judith Williams Sandoval.)

Four

THE VALLEY AT PLAY

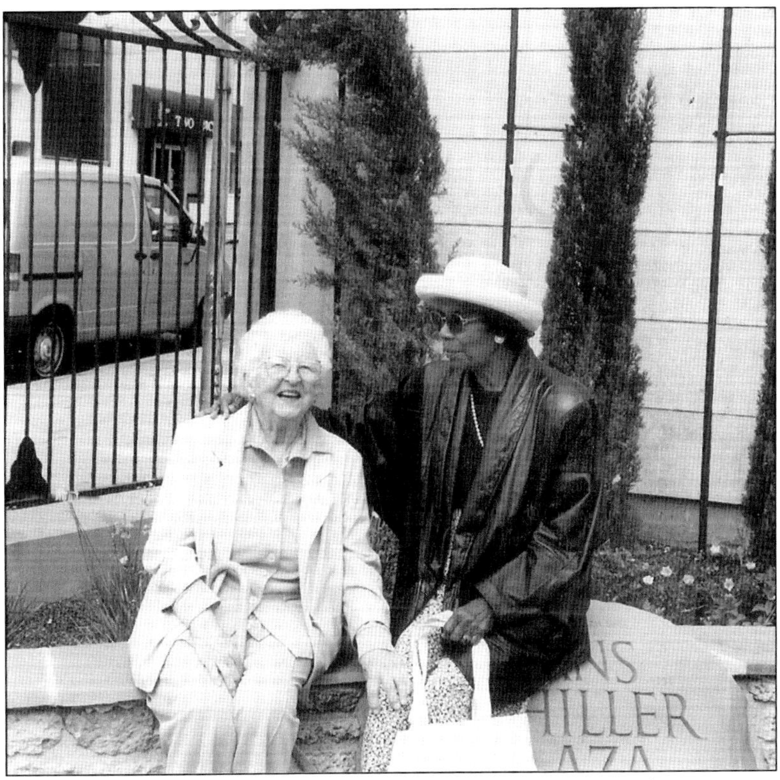

Circle of Elders participants Alma Taylor (left) and Rose Mary Watson share impressions at the grand opening of the first Greenway Project garden in March 2001. (Courtesy Edie Epps.)

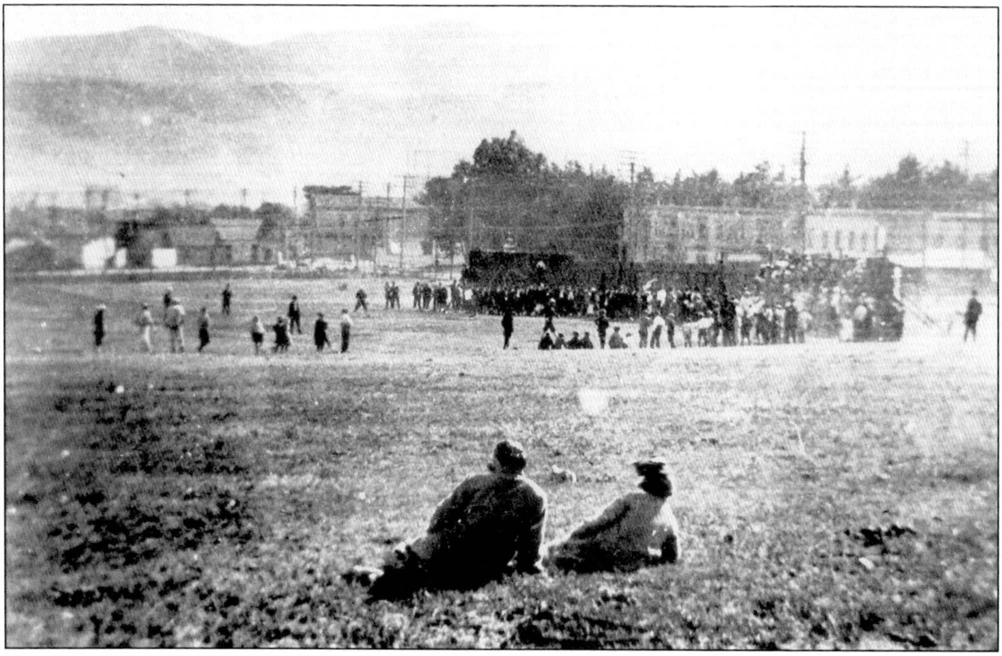

The Visitacion Valley Athletic Association sponsored baseball games like this one played on the field that would later become the home of Schlage Lock. The first club rooms were in the old training quarters at Blanken's Six Mile House. (Courtesy Taylor family.)

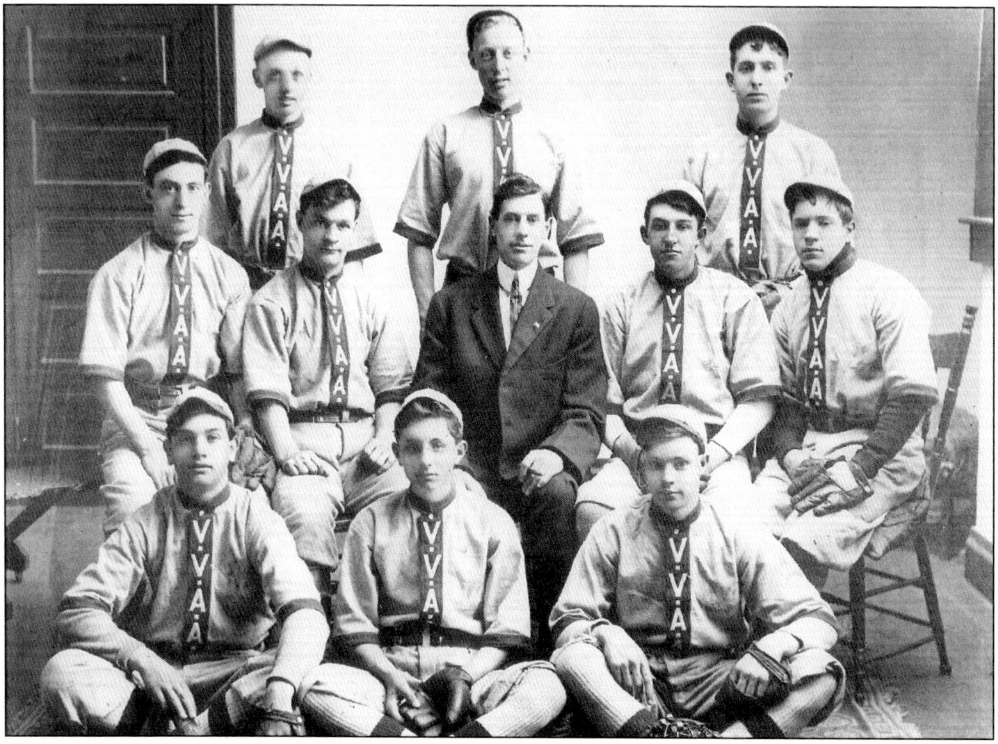

One of the Valley's early baseball teams poses with their coach. Their uniform denote their sponsorship by the association. (Courtesy Visitacion Valley Community Center.)

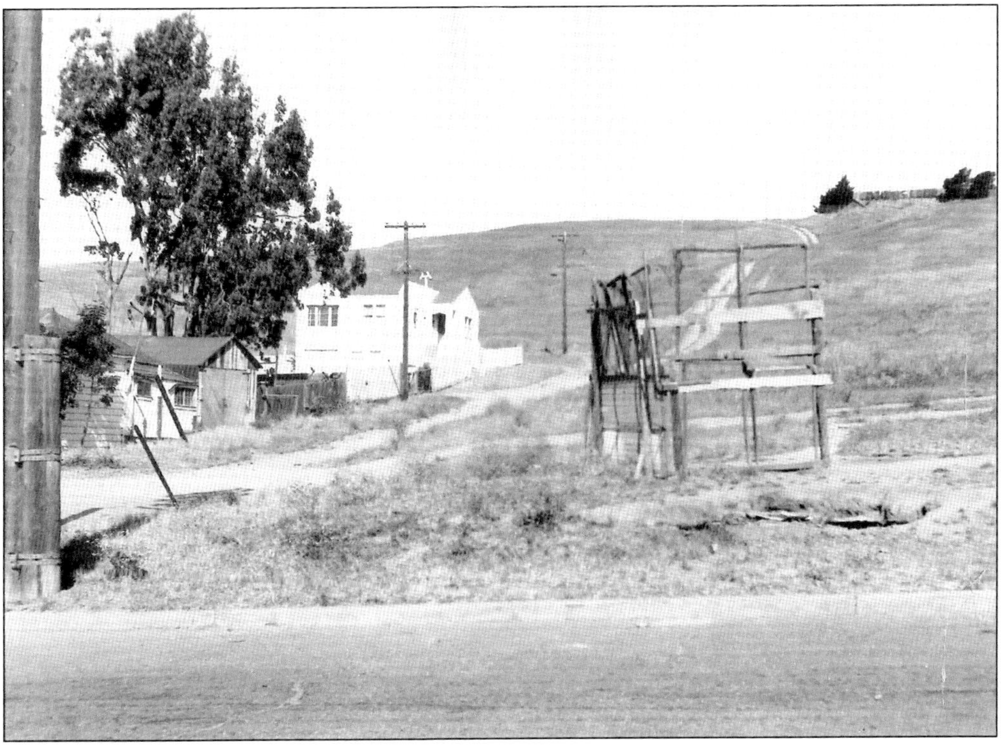

The vacant land at the corner of Delta and Wilde became a baseball diamond for the neighborhood kids when Tom Taylor built a backstop, around 1945. Wilde Avenue was paved only to Delta, but a dirt road continued up the hill into McLaren Park. (Courtesy Taylor family.)

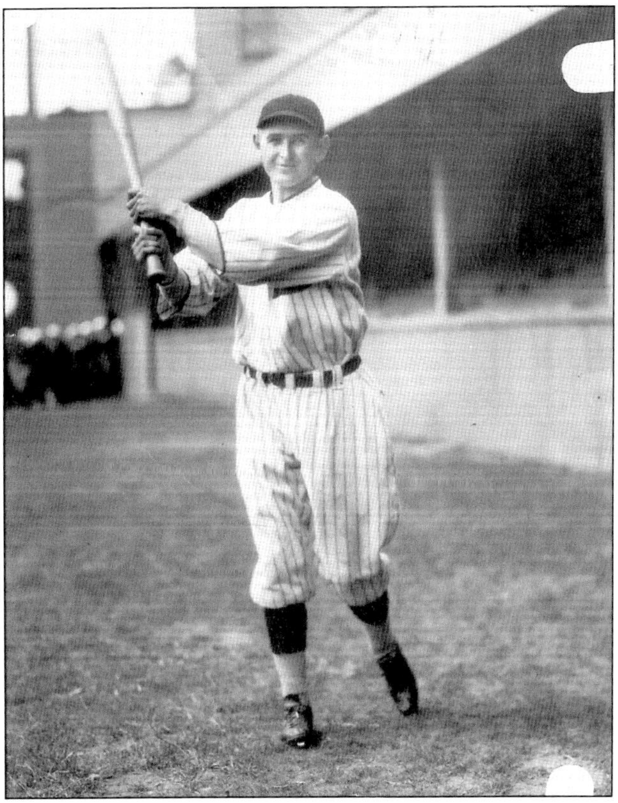

Walter Lister Sr., who grew up on Wilde Avenue, was a fireball right-hander who pitched for the Seals and the Oaks of the Pacific Coast League and holds the record for being a member of more championship semipro teams—29 of them between 1924 and 1949—than any other player in California history. Although he received major league offers, he always refused, since he had a family to support and did better financially with his job at American Can Company. (Courtesy Phoebe Adams.)

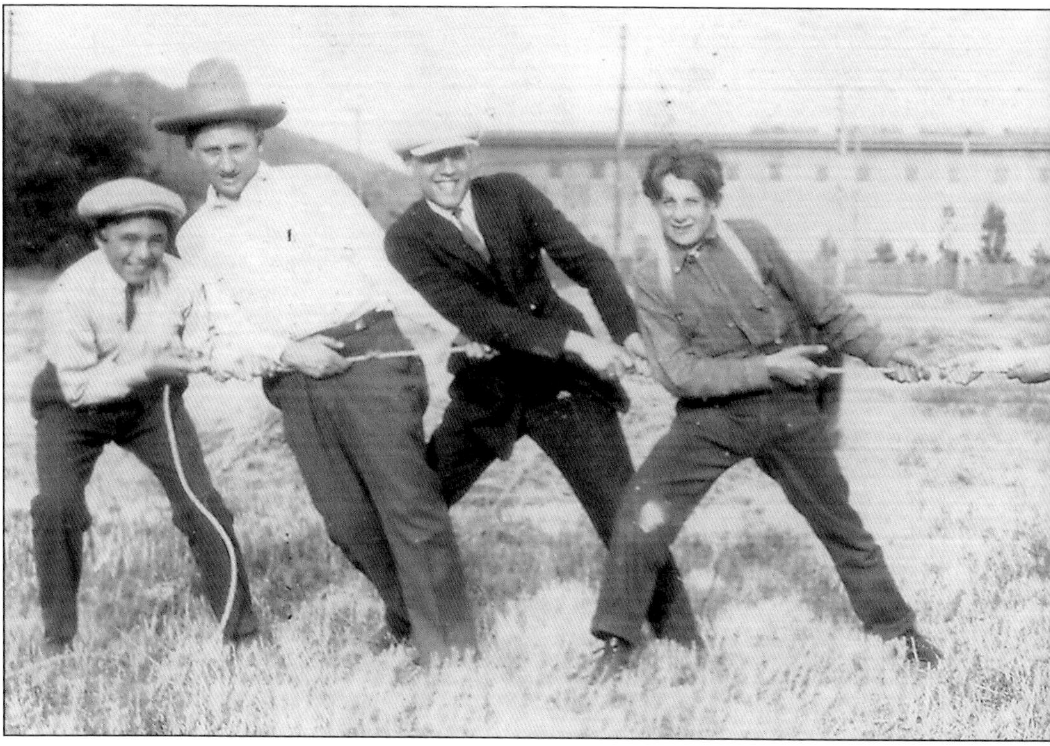

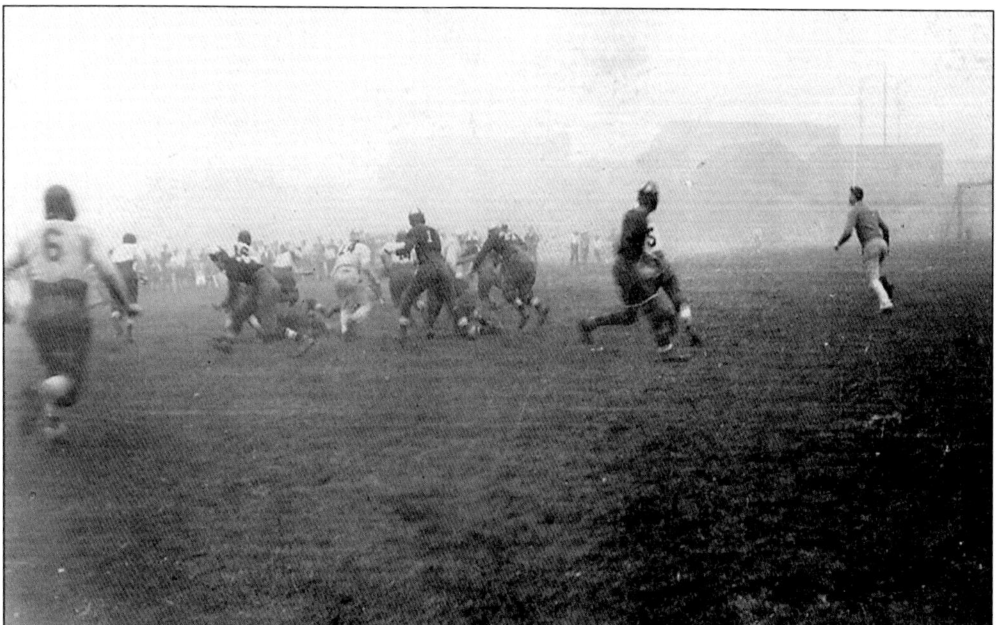

The Visitacion Valley Athletic Association sponsored football teams as well. Here the local team plays Bay View on a foggy day in 1925. (Courtesy Mary Schwartz.)

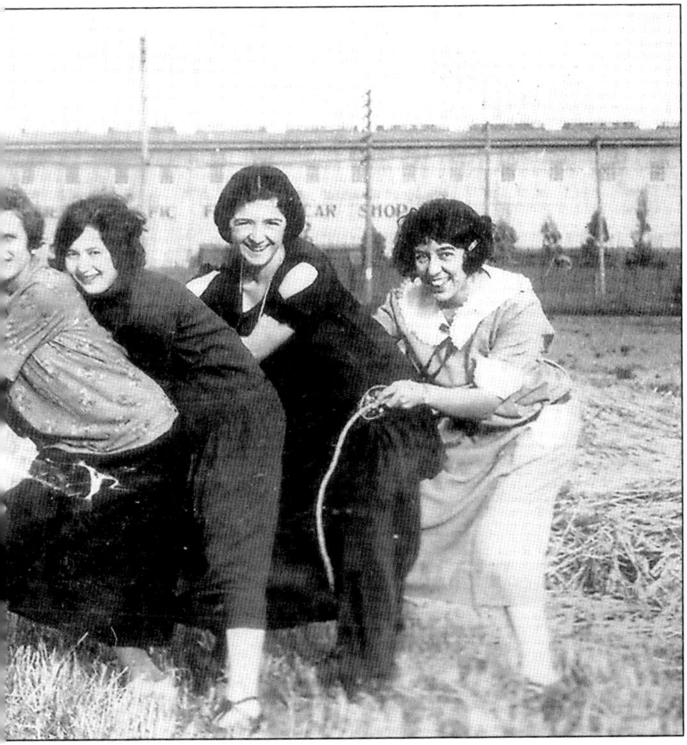

This tug-of-war took place on the Sechini ranch in June 1924. Pictured here, from left to right, are Frank Callero, Albert Armanino, Raymond Garassino, Ed (Bill) Armanino, Edna Armanino, Eileen Sechini, Argentina (Orri) Sechini, and Anna Bazzuro. The Southern Pacific Car Shop can be seen in the background. (Courtesy Richard Brandi.)

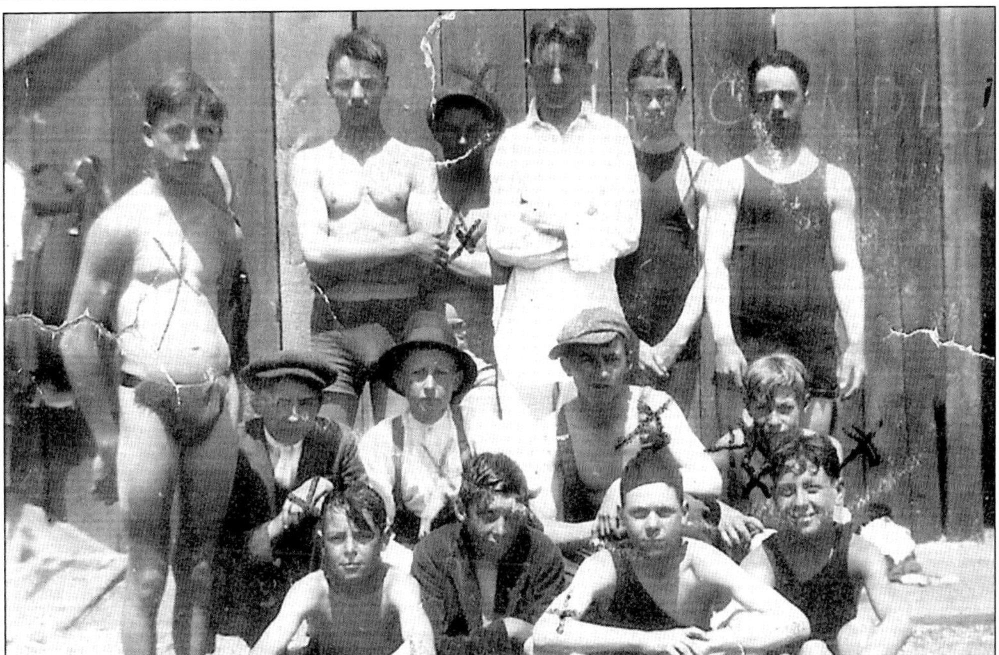

Swimming in the bay off Candlestick Cove was very popular. This 1917 photograph was taken on the Johnson and Brown wharf. From left to right are (first row) C. Stagnaro, W. Douglas, G. Wilson, and Ab. Shesky; (second row) M. Lister, H. Rossbach, F. Schrerts, and E. Burman; (third row) E. Edelman, Bill Schwartz, John Johnson, N. Metz, and W. Opitz. (Courtesy Mary Schwartz.)

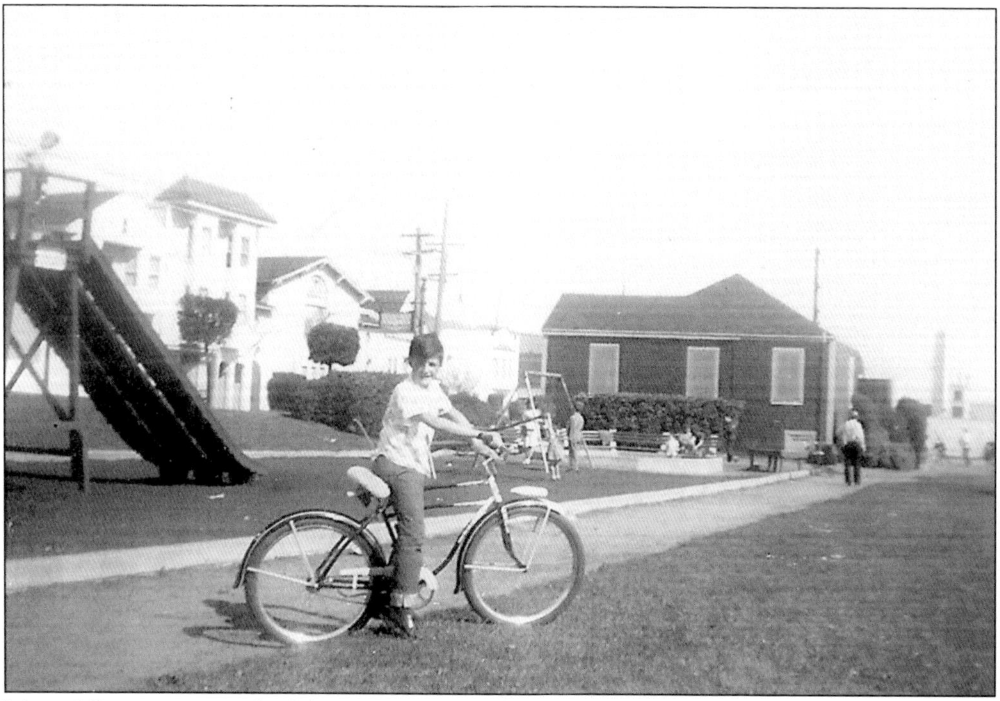

Manuel Serano poses on his bike at Visitacion Valley Park, around 1945. The old clubhouse, which had a dark green shingle finish, can be seen in the background. (Courtesy Betty Parshall.)

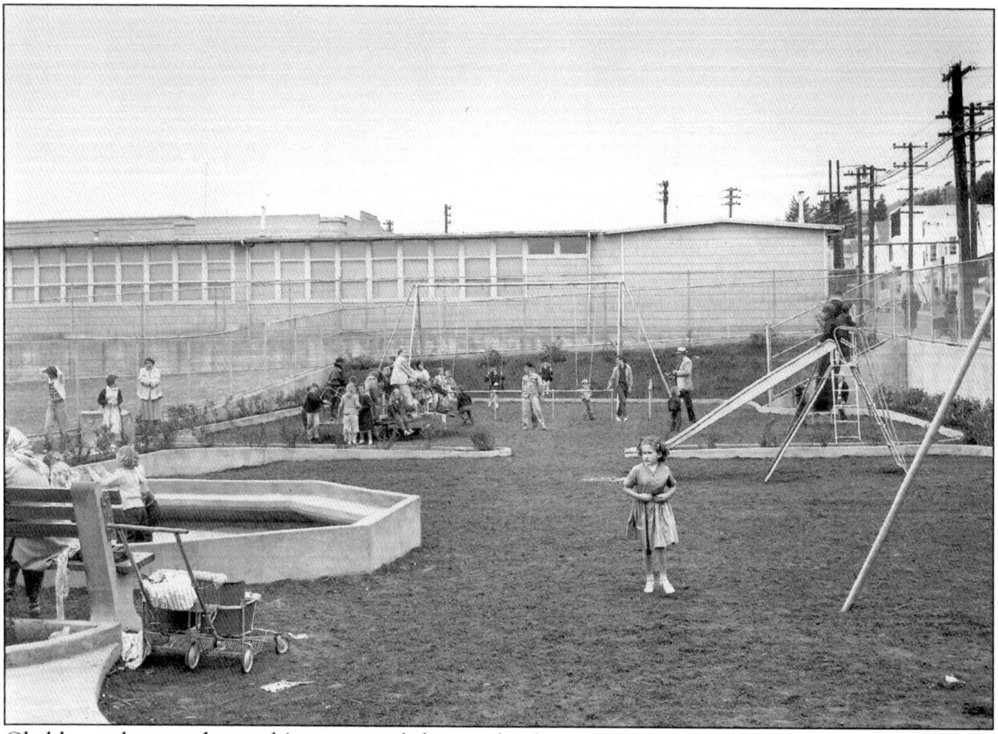

Children play on the park's swings, slides, and other equipment in this *c.* 1950 photograph. (Courtesy Harriet Schindel Newhart.)

In October 2003, the newest clubhouse at Cora and Leland opened with a celebratory fair on the park green. The building, designed by San Francisco's Bureau of Architects/ Department of Public Works and already honored by San Francisco Beautiful, has "green building" features such as energy-efficient lighting, skylights, and south-facing windows for natural daylight and passive solar heating, and water-efficient fixtures. (Courtesy Russel Morine.)

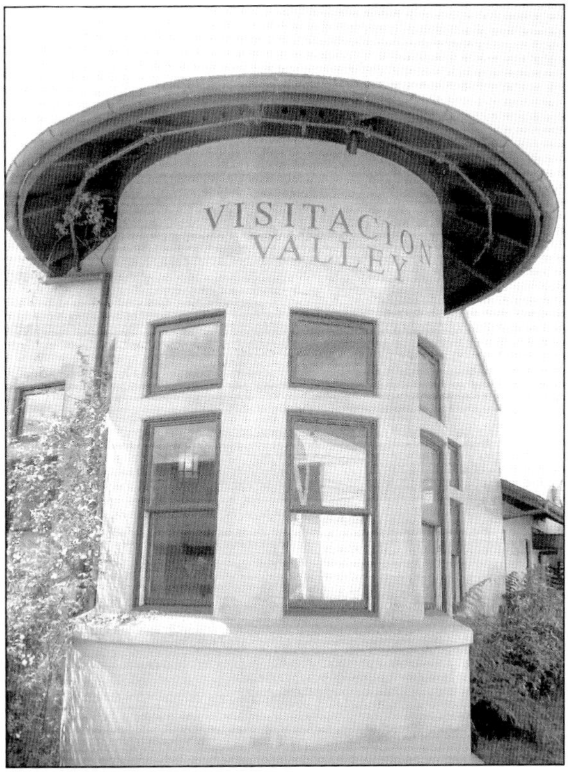

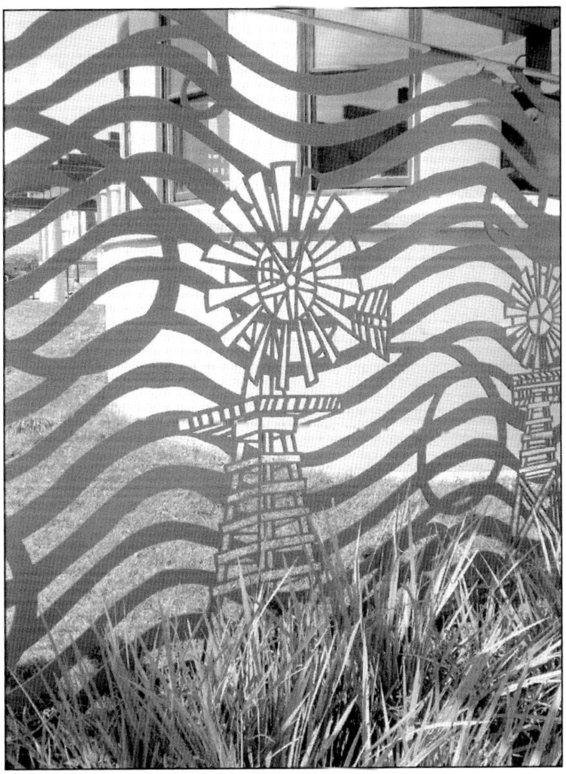

Artist Victor Mario Zaballa designed the bright blue fence and gates that protect the clubhouse and adjacent playground. The windmill motif references the nickname of the Valley, where evenings can become filled with strong gusts. (Courtesy Russel Morine.)

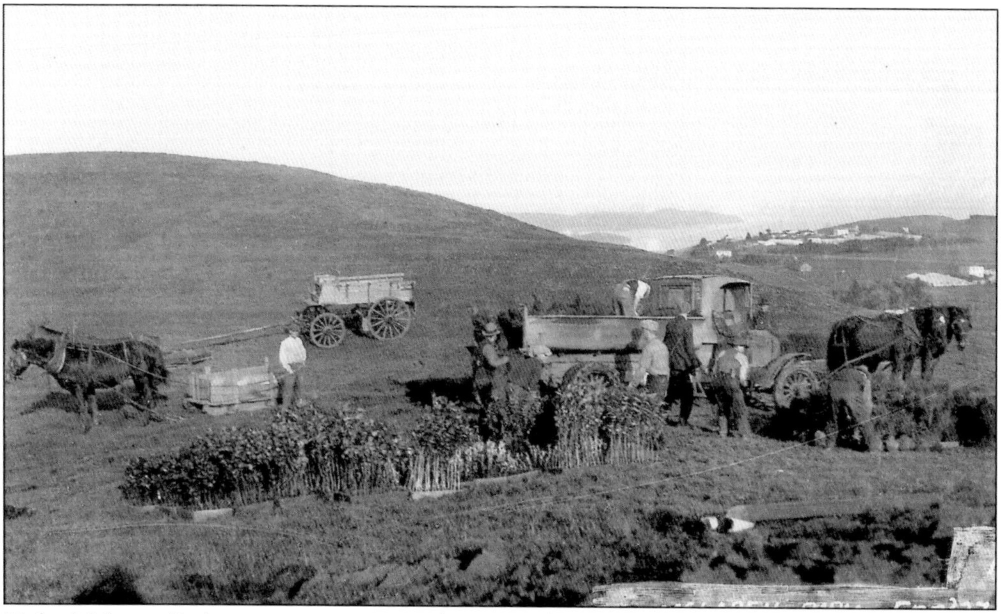

Today McLaren Park is a major recreational resource for Visitacion Valley residents and the entire city. Its 317 acres include natural areas rich in native plants and animals, as well as gardens, play fields, picnic areas, and children's playgrounds. Long ago, Ohlone natives coexisted with the rich diversity of plants and animals found here. In 1927, truckloads of seedling eucalyptus trees were delivered for planting in the newly designated park. (Courtesy a private collector.)

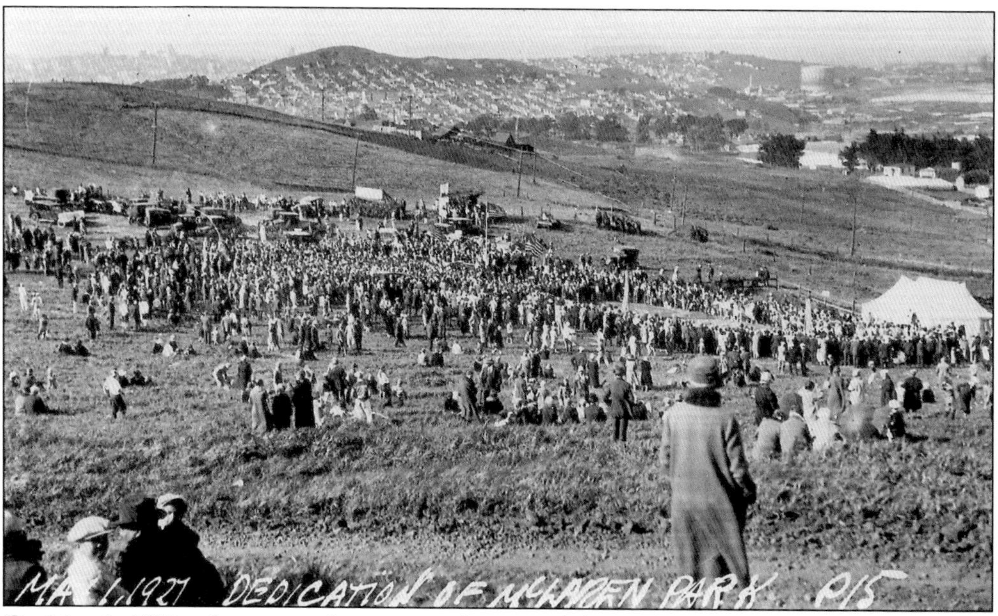

On May 1, 1927, a large crowd came together to celebrate the dedication of the park. The lack of trees is very noticeable, when compared to what the park looks like today. (Courtesy a private collector.)

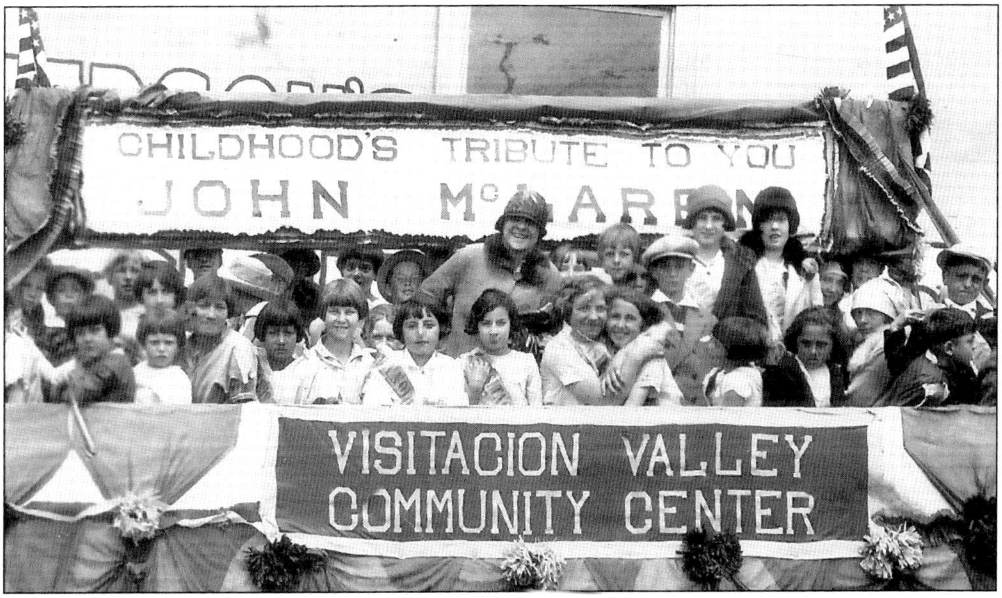

At the dedication in 1927, Elizabeth Stagnaro, a lifelong Valley resident, presided over the ceremonies as the queen of McLaren Park. Anna Stuart Johnson remembers, "I was about nine or 10. And my friend Violet [Larsson] and I were taking violin lessons and so we were on a float, posed with our violins. I don't remember much else, but I do remember that . . . We had a parade. There might be some pictures of it, as they made a big thing of it." (Courtesy Visitacion Valley Community Center.)

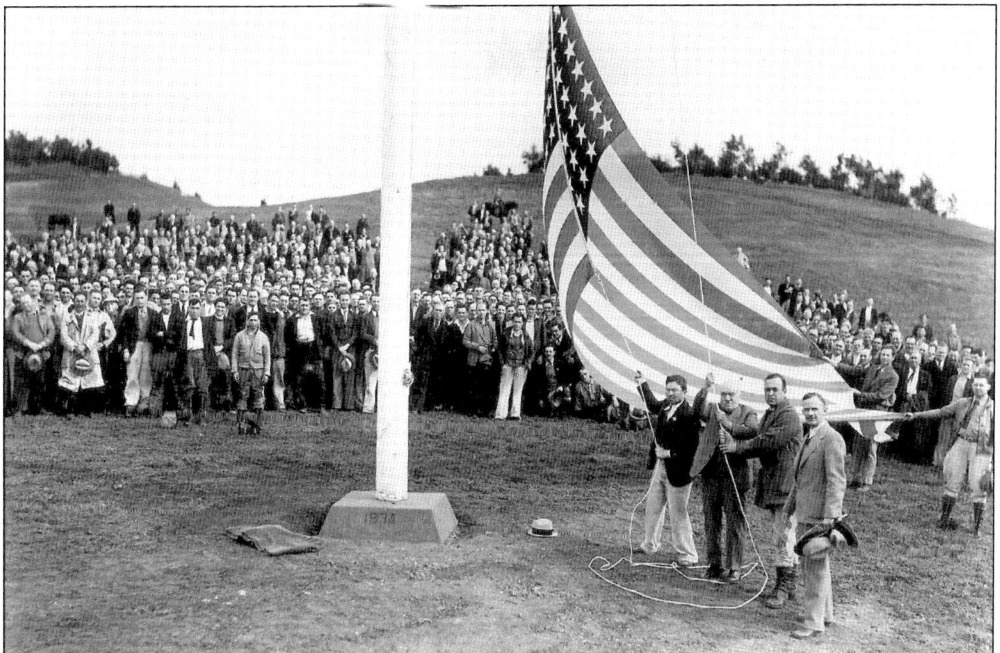

A flag presented to John McLaren in honor and appreciation of his work is raised in McLaren Park on February 25, 1934. The location of the base of the flagpole is an ongoing quest for park visitors. (Courtesy a private collector.)

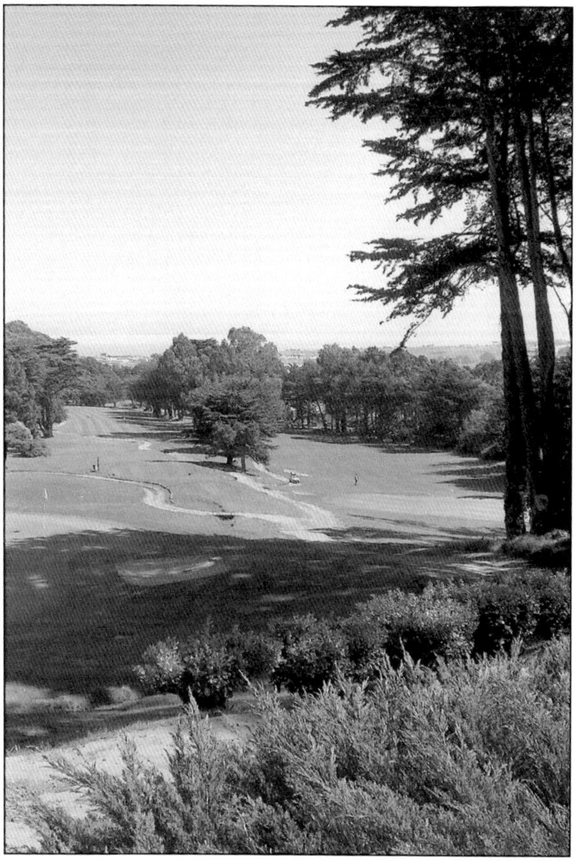

Gleneagles International Golf Course in McLaren Park is a hidden jewel, with beautiful vistas and one of the most challenging courses in the Bay Area—tight fairways and hilly and often windy conditions. Champion golfer Lee Trevino played this nine-hole course several times and couldn't break par. The course was redesigned in 1982 by Robert Muir Graves. (Courtesy Russel Morine.)

The new Visitacion Valley Greenway is composed of six publicly owned parcels cutting across the hillside from Tioga to Leland. Developed by the members of the Greenway Project in partnership with the San Francisco Recreation and Park Department, the Greenway is designed to serve as a classroom and recreation area for all. The first and southernmost lot, Hans Schiller Plaza, dedicated in 2001, was named for a Bay Area architect and environmental activist and has received a San Francisco Beautiful award. (Courtesy Edie Epps.)

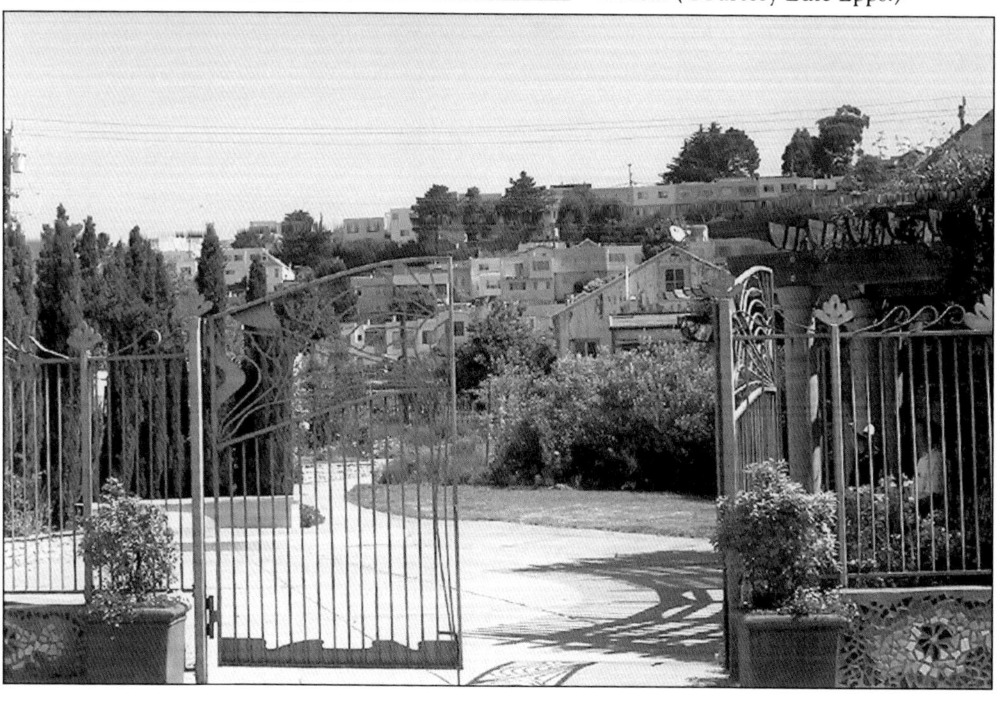

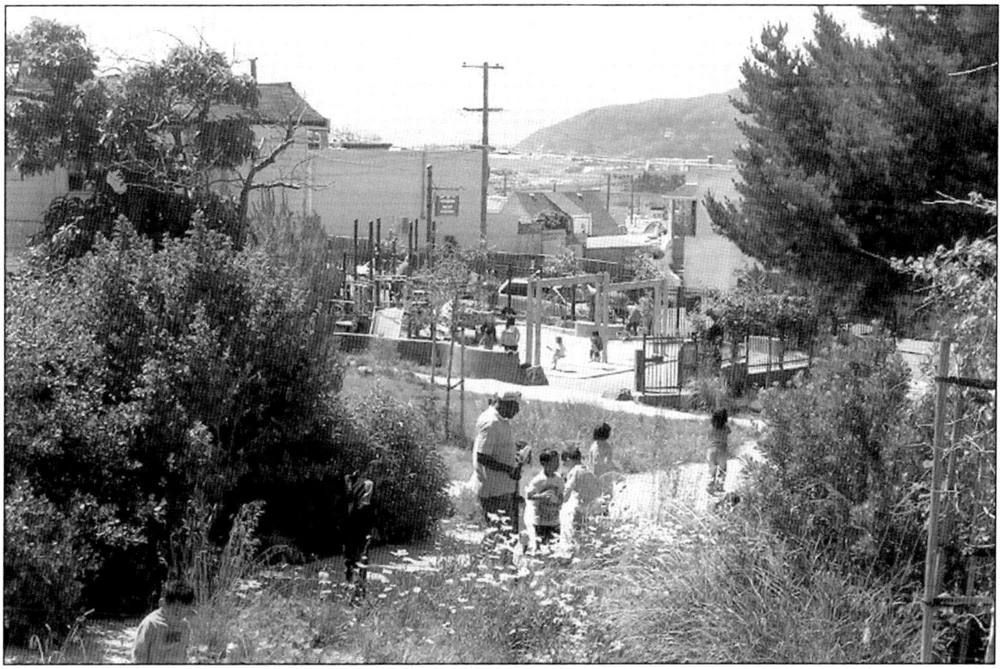

The Children's Play Garden between Campbell and Teddy, opened in September 2004, includes an "enchanted forest," a butterfly garden, a playground, and an area where children are supplied with tools and instructions for gardening. Adults and youngsters alike enjoy the "magic meadow" and the beautiful view of the Valley (Courtesy Edie Epps.)

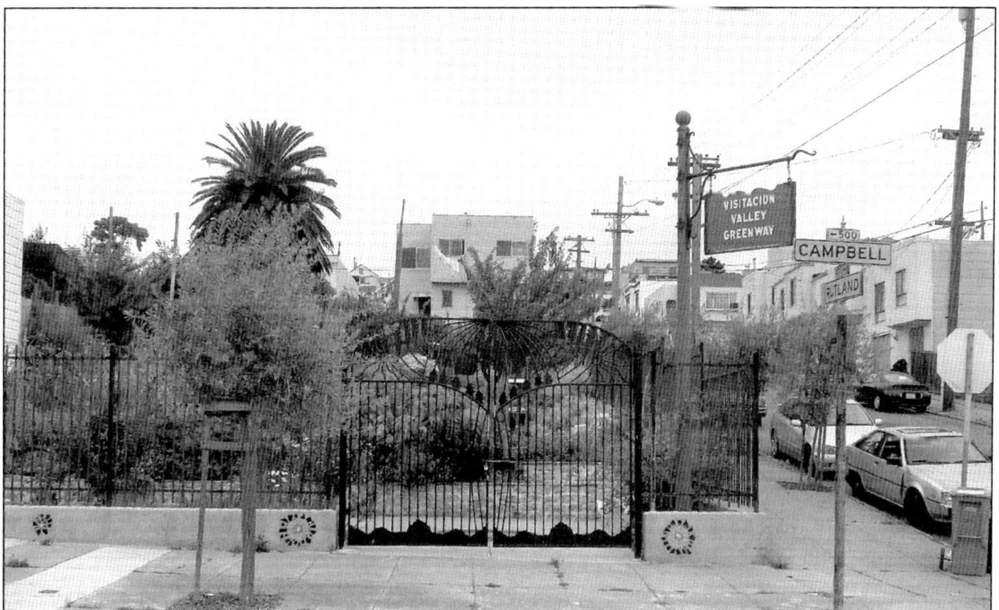

The Greenway Project's Agriculture Garden between Tucker and Campbell, graced by an entrance gate designed by Valley artist Jim Growden, was the second of the six lots to be completed. Local school groups, neighborhood volunteers, and city organizations worked to develop the garden and share in the enjoyment of the fruits of their labor. (Courtesy Russel Morine.)

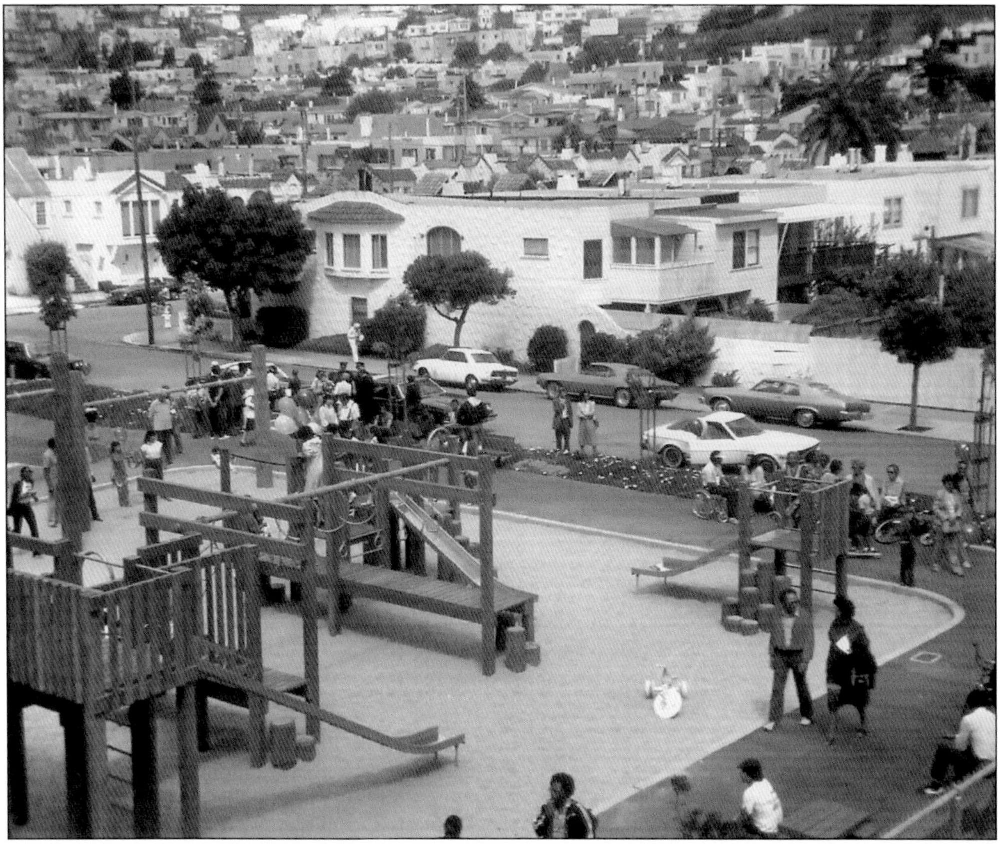

Neighborhood negotiations with the Sunset Scavenger Company led to the development of the Little Hollywood Community Park. In 1983, this open space on Lathrop was dedicated to longtime resident Clarence Fleming for his efforts on behalf of all Little Hollywood residents. (Courtesy Ron Gibson.)

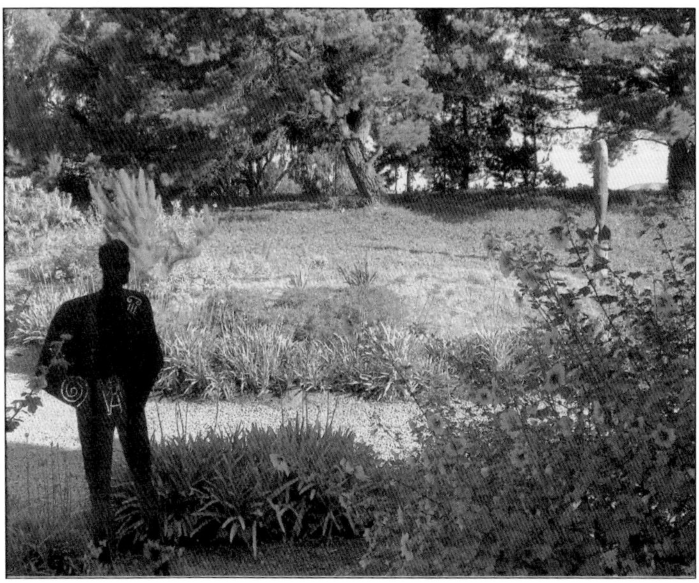

In addition to serving as the transfer point of refuse destined to become landfill, SF Recycling and Disposal also hosts a three-acre sculpture garden. Created in 1992 on top of a hill overlooking the bay, it features pieces created by a revolving series of resident artists from a collection of unlikely finds discarded at the center. The garden can be toured by appointment. (Courtesy Russel Morine.)

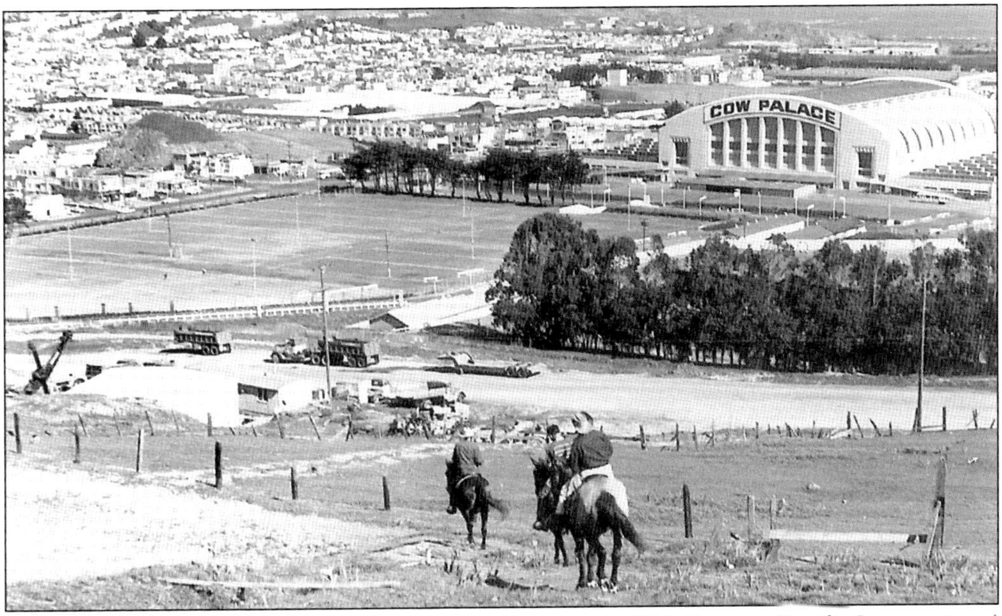

The popularity of a livestock pavilion at San Francisco's 1915 Panama-Pacific International Exposition led to the idea for a permanent exhibition hall, and construction began on the Cow Palace in 1935, during the Depression. In a newspaper editorial, a disgruntled citizen asked why, when people were starving, money should be spent on a palace for cows, and the name stuck. The building's construction as a WPA project did provide much-needed jobs, and the first Grand National was held there in 1941. Since then, the Cow Palace has hosted a wide variety of events, from presidential conventions, to a 1964 Beatles concert, to garden and sports shows, and more. (Courtesy Harriet Schindel Newhart.)

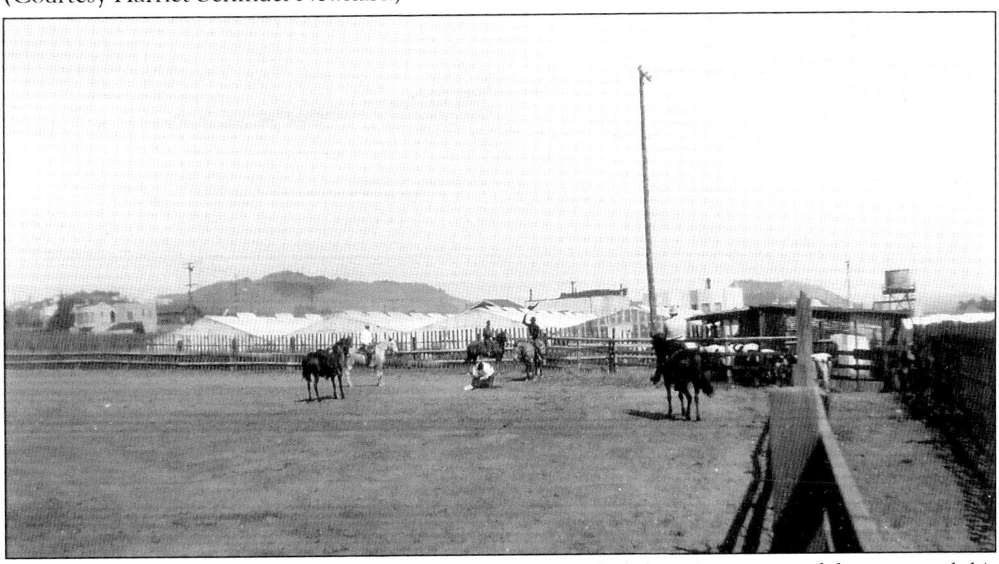

Lebano Orlando, who grew up in Visitacion Valley, provided this 1941 image of the roping club's large corral area at Hahn and Visitacion Avenue, near today's Coffman Pool. Rows of white greenhouses along Britton are in the background. Some of the ropers worked in Butchertown, some at non-riding jobs. All loved the sport, as did spectators who parked around the arena to watch the action. (Courtesy Lebano Orlando.)

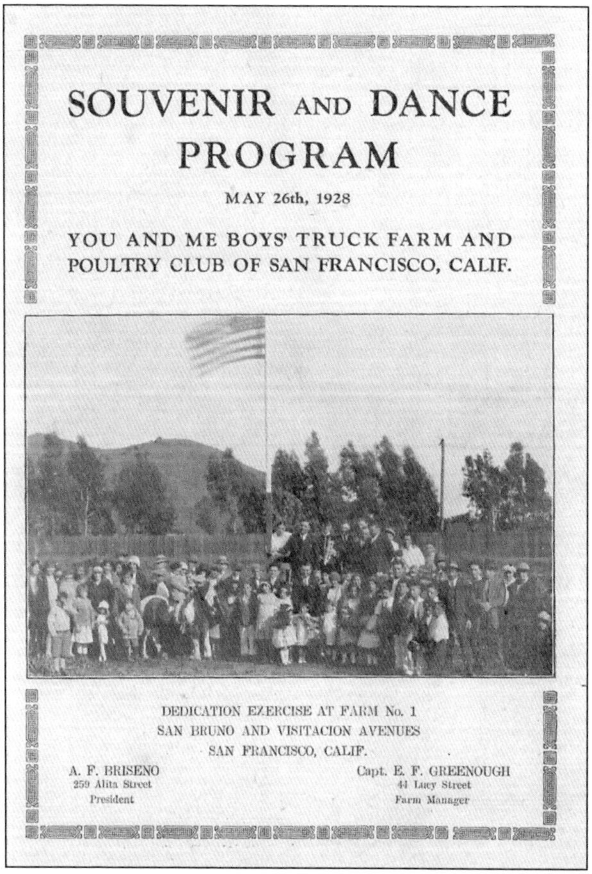

SOUVENIR AND DANCE PROGRAM

MAY 26th, 1928

YOU AND ME BOYS' TRUCK FARM AND POULTRY CLUB OF SAN FRANCISCO, CALIF.

DEDICATION EZERCISE AT FARM No. 1
SAN BRUNO AND VISITACION AVENUES
SAN FRANCISCO, CALIF.

A. F. BRISENO
259 Alita Street
President

Capt. E. F. GREENOUGH
44 Lucy Street
Farm Manager

Valley organizations often combined entertainment with good works, as this 1928 program cover indicates. The You and Me Boys' Truck Farm and Poultry Club was organized to take at-risk youngsters off the streets, teach them the farming and poultry trades, and in so doing help them become self-supporting, constructive members of the community. (Courtesy Visitacion Valley Community Center.)

The San Francisco Auto Camp on Sunnydale Avenue provided recreation for its customers and also for nearby residents. Besides catering to vacationing tourists, it also provided housing for people living in the Valley temporarily. Pictured here are Ruth Englefield and her son Johnny. In 1952, the family lived in a trailer at the camp while her husband was working for Southern Pacific. (Courtesy Ruth Englefield.)

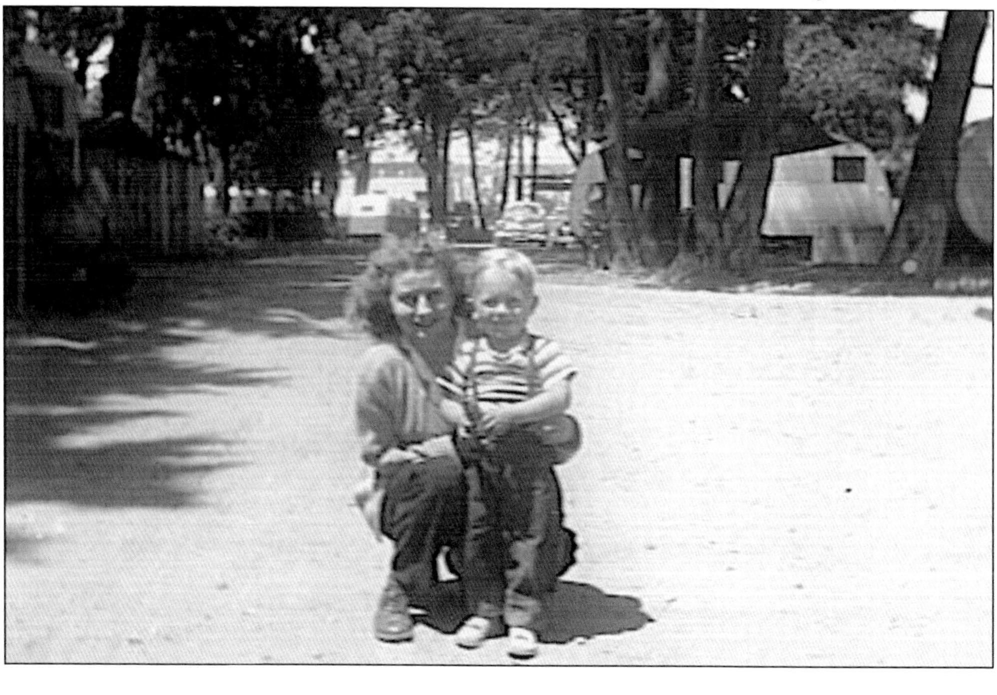

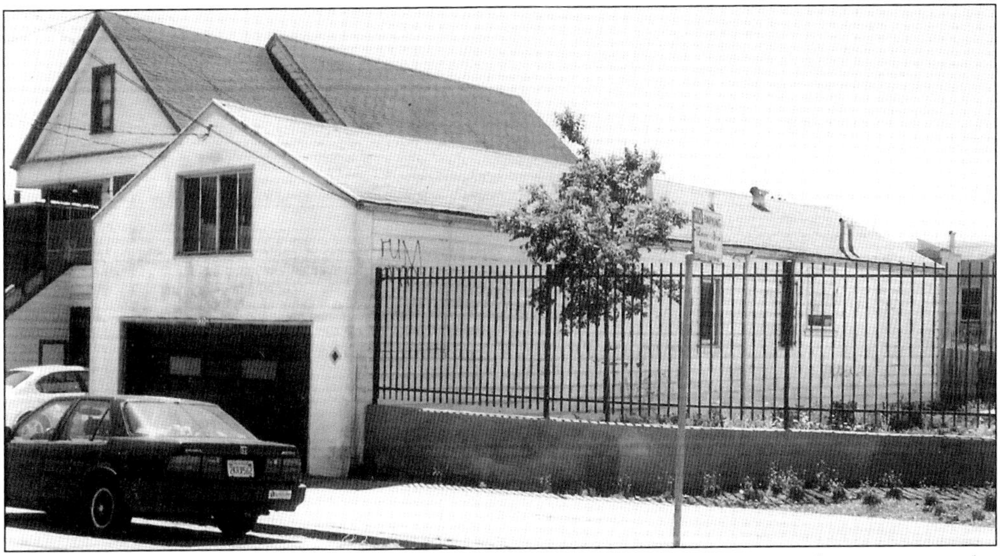

There were "flickers" at the nickelodeon on Raymond Avenue, now a private home next to the Greenway's Schiller Plaza. The old movie theater was constructed of sheet metal, with fireproof walls embossed with designs. Out front, a player piano and blue mercury lamp attracted attention. (Courtesy Edie Epps.)

The Bayshore Theatre at 2428 Bayshore Boulevard (above left), known affectionately as the Flea House, brought the movies to Visitacion Valley in 1926. There were 350 seats, where patrons could enjoy double bills and collect a dinner set just by attending the weekly "dish night." With the advent of television, the Bayshore, whose marquee can be seen in the photograph on the right, suffered the same fate as many other neighborhood theaters and closed in October 1957. It was then home to the Mt. Olivet Missionary Baptist Church for many years until the building was destroyed in a fire. (Courtesy J. E. Tillmany.)

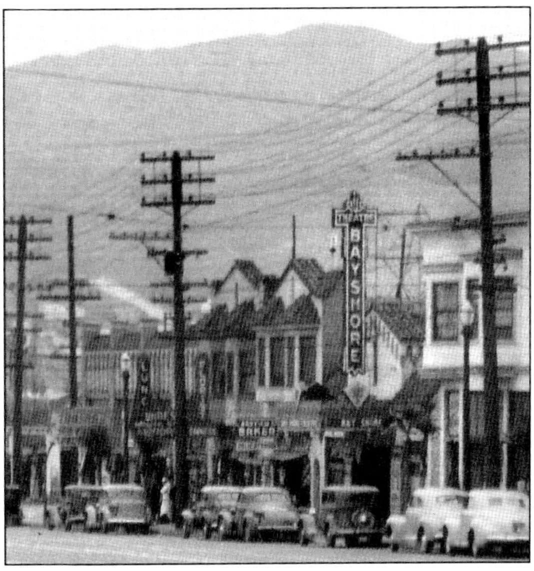

In 1947, a double feature of *Yes Sir, That's My Baby* and *Miss Grant Takes Richmond* was playing at the Bayshore. (Courtesy *San Francisco Chronicle*.)

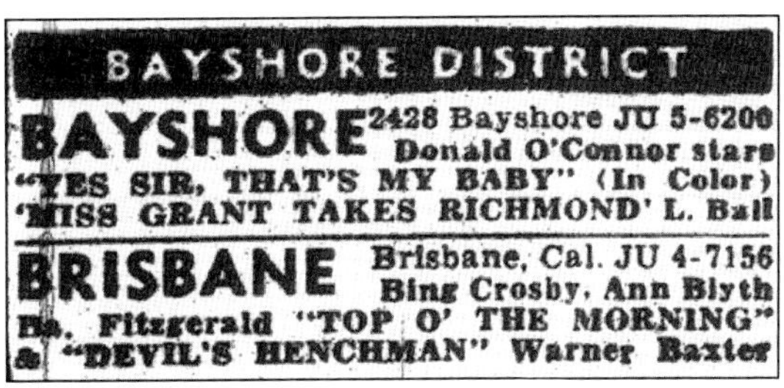

BAYSHORE DISTRICT

BAYSHORE 2428 Bayshore JU 5-6200 Donald O'Connor stars "YES SIR, THAT'S MY BABY" (In Color) 'MISS GRANT TAKES RICHMOND' L. Ball

BRISBANE Brisbane, Cal. JU 4-7156 Bing Crosby, Ann Blyth Ba. Fitzgerald "TOP O' THE MORNING" & "DEVIL'S HENCHMAN" Warner Baxter

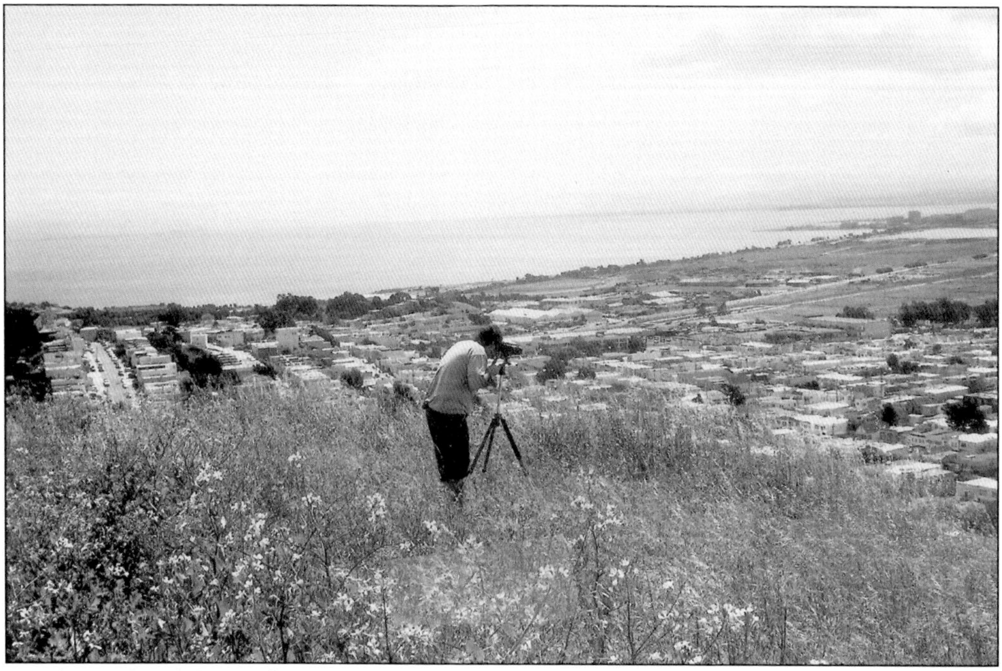

In a letter dated September 1932, a camera buff wrote to his girlfriend, "It was quite windy throughout McLaren Park today. The park is on a high hill right on the edge of the bay—the view is really marvelous—many chances for good pictures. I want you to see it if possible but if it is as windy as it was today, I [would] have to tie a rope around your waist and then around mine to keep a light weight like yourself from blowing away." In this 2005 photograph, Anthony Janigian adjusts the angle of his camera for a picture of Visitacion Valley. (Courtesy Edie Epps.)

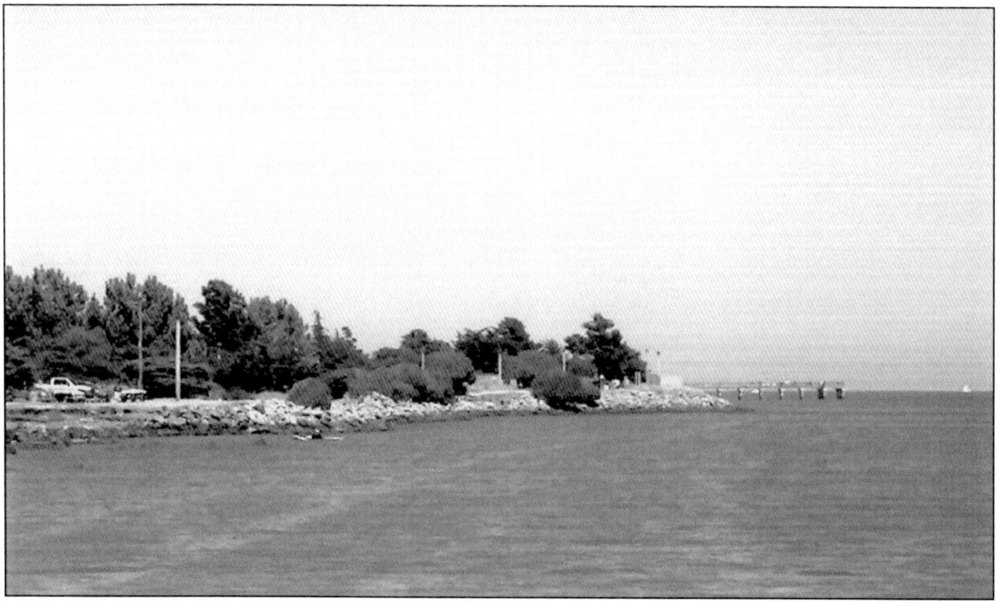

The wind that powered the windmills long ago still blows across the Valley and the Cove, where windsurfers put it to good use. People also picnic, jog, fish from the piers, and enjoy the great views off the shore of Candlestick Point State Park. (Courtesy Edie Epps.)

Five

Homes and Buildings

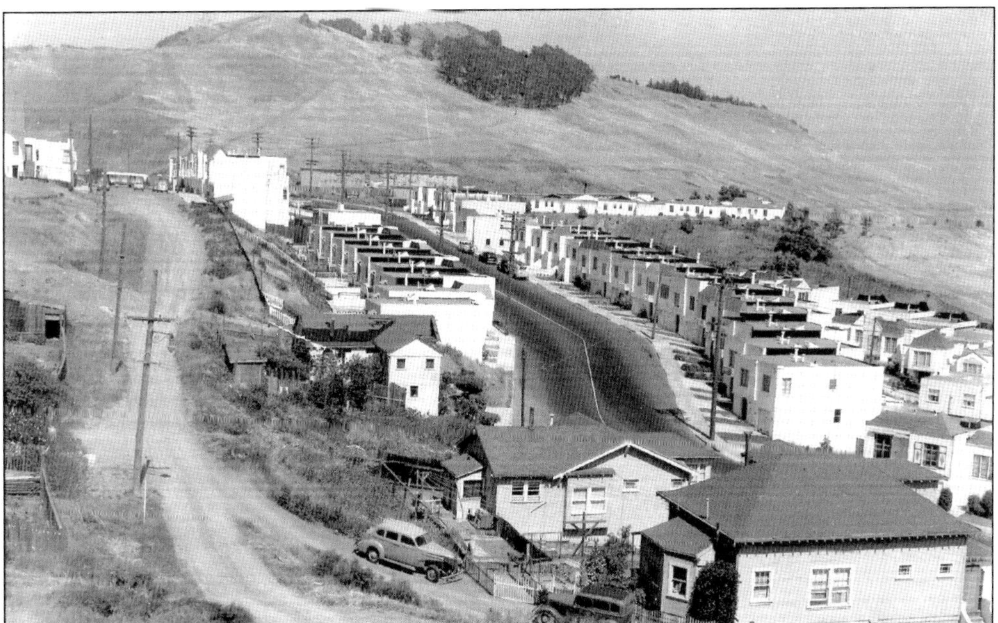

Part of the charm of Visitacion Valley, as in many parts of San Francisco, is the variety of housing. In this photograph, the old and the new stand side by side. The World War II–era homes on the right line the paved San Bruno Avenue, while the older homes in the forefront stand at the intersection of Campbell and Somerset, not yet paved at the time. (Courtesy a private collector.)

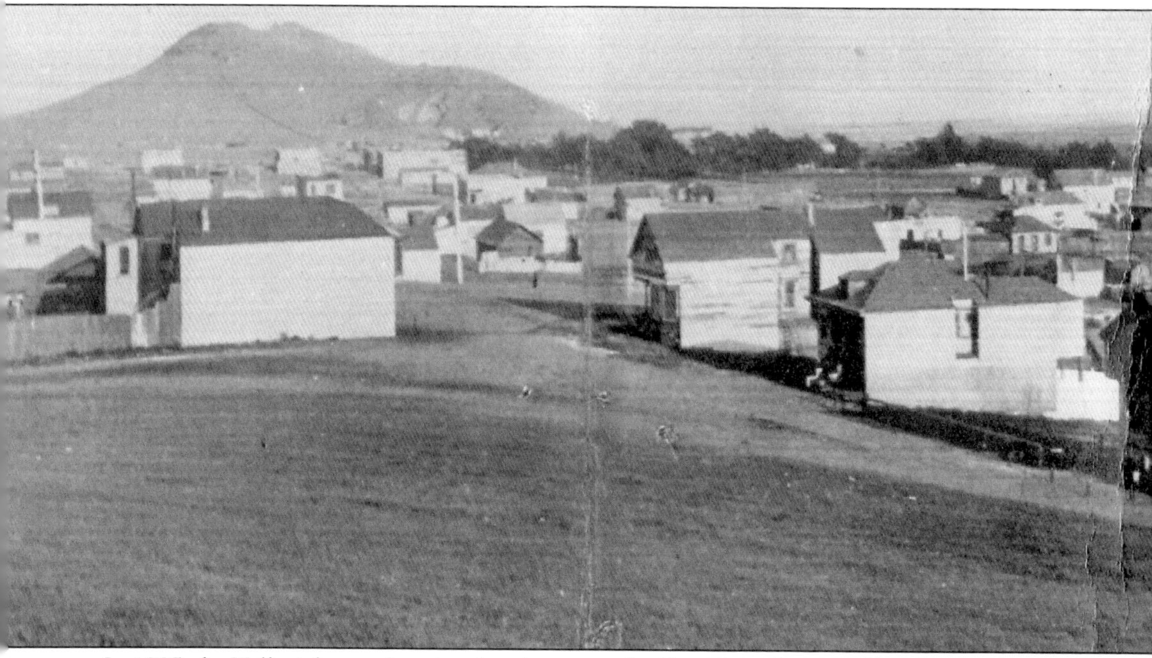

In 1905, the Valley's largest housing development, the Reis Tract, began selling lots for $125—$1 down and $1 a week. Selling points included the construction of a new power plant and Southern Pacific's Bay Shore Cut-off, expected to employ thousands of men, as well as the best water in the

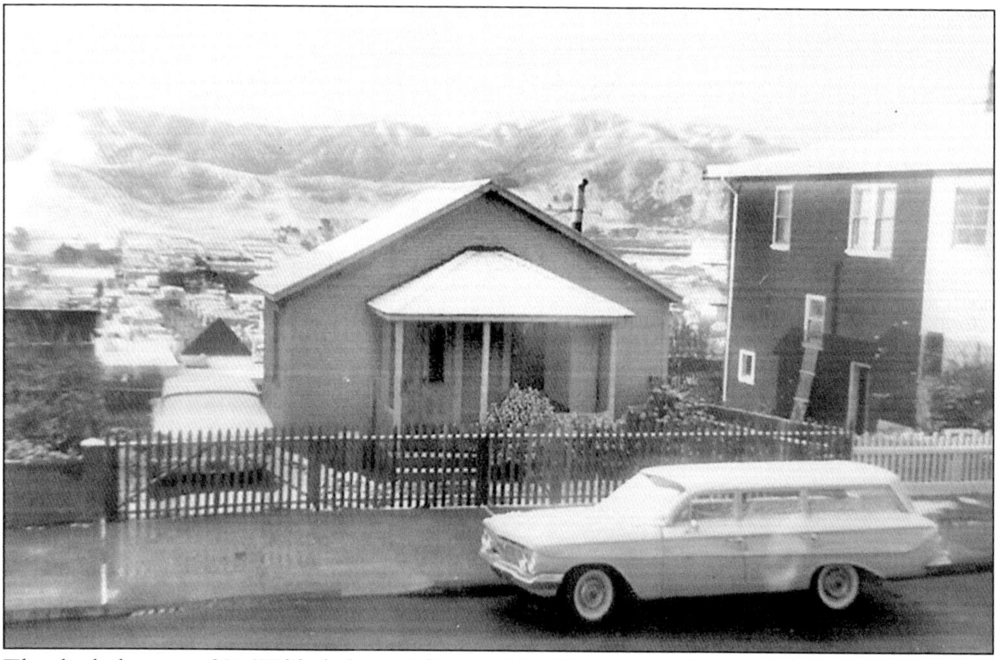

This little home at 391 Wilde belonged first to Mrs. Hearne and later to a popular bus driver. A couple of times a year, he brought home two sheep from his family's ranch to keep the grass down. There was a lot of fun the day the little flock got out and ran around the block twice before being caught. This 1962 photograph depicts one of San Francisco's rare snowfalls. (Courtesy Betty Parshall.)

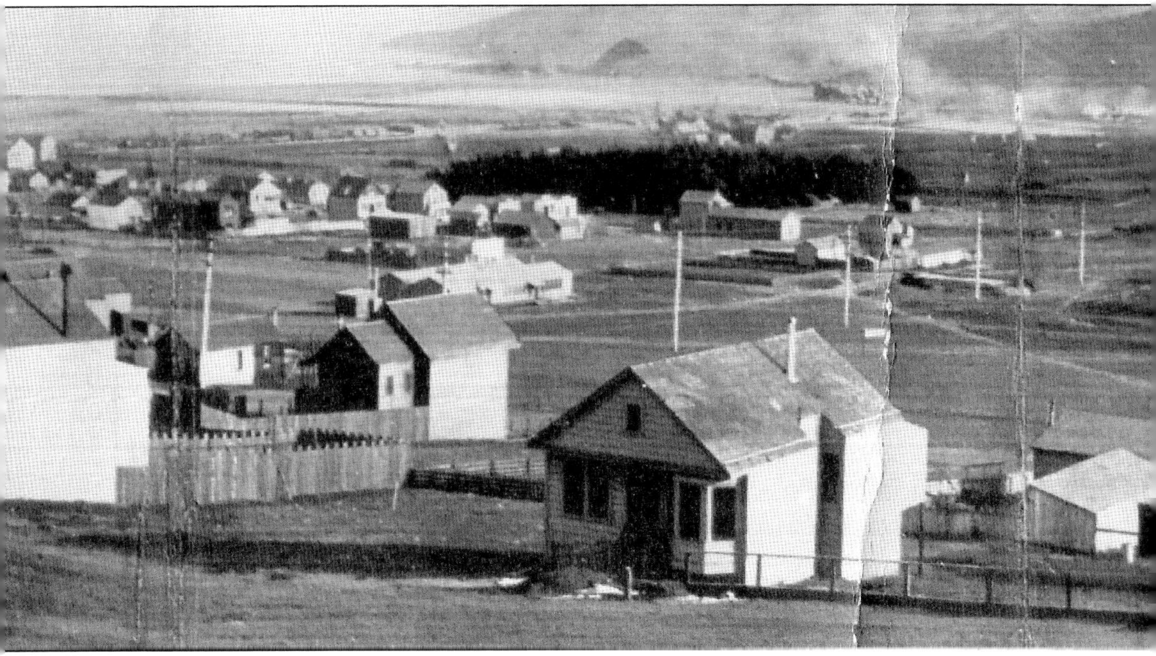

city, a "wide-awake Improvement Club," and the "most beautiful building sites in San Francisco." The developers boasted, "Lots sold on easy terms; homes built on easy terms; money loaned on easy terms." (Courtesy Taylor family.)

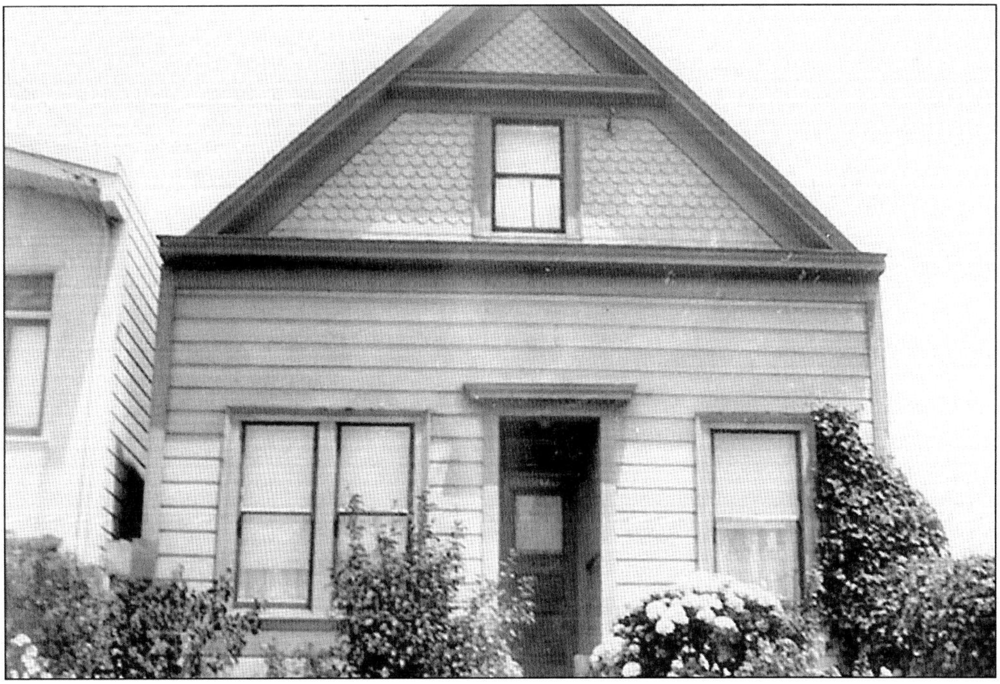

Bill Schwartz grew up in this home, built in 1903, on Leland Avenue. An avid athlete, he ran the Dipsea marathon and trained many of the neighborhood boys, making good use of the hills that surround the Valley. After Bill and Mary Leotta married, they built a home next door to this one. (Courtesy Mary Schwartz.)

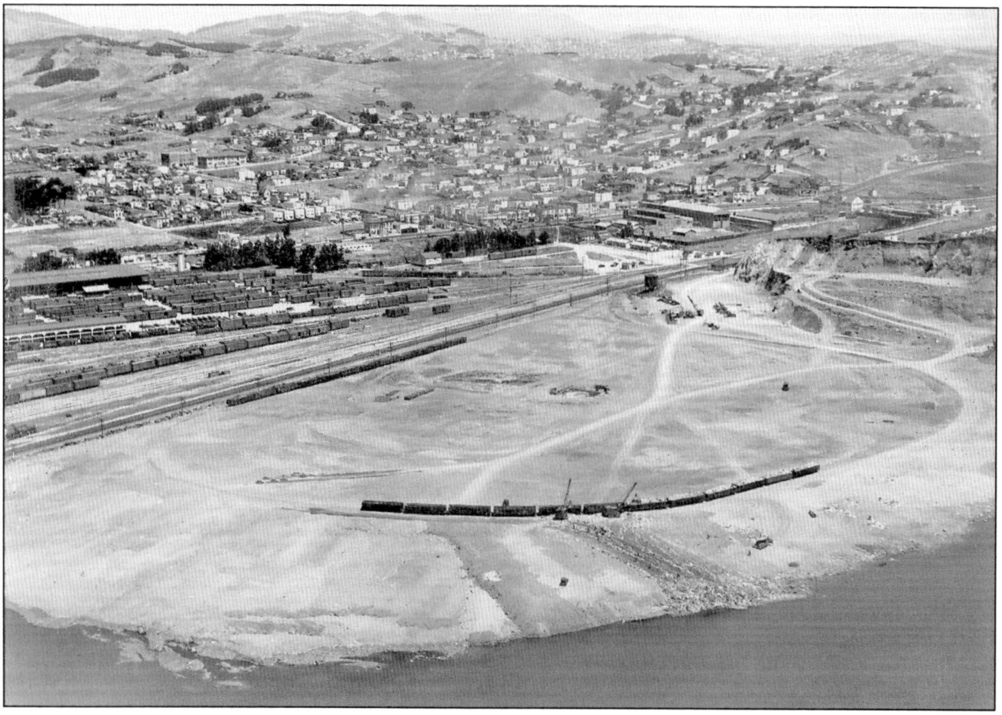

In this *c.* 1925 photograph, houses dot the landscape across the Valley, although much open space is still available. In the foreground, a train carries refuse as landfill for the bay. (Courtesy Arosio family.)

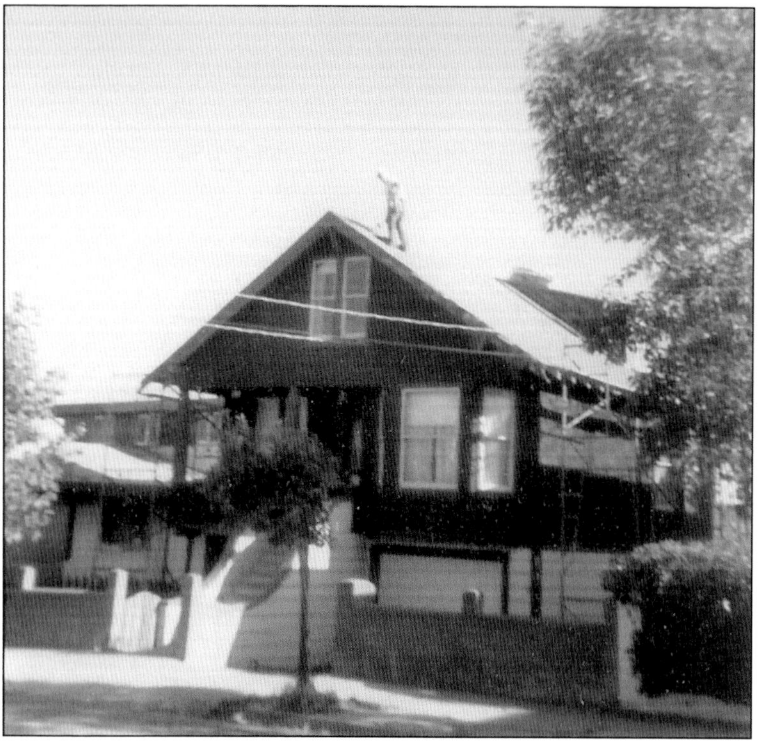

Mike Lister lived in this home on Wilde Avenue. He and his brothers, Walter and Frank, were all remembered as outstanding baseball players, Mike being a first baseman. Mike's front porch was a favorite hiding place when children played hide-and-seek and kick the can in the days before traffic made playing in the street too risky. (Courtesy Betty Parshall.)

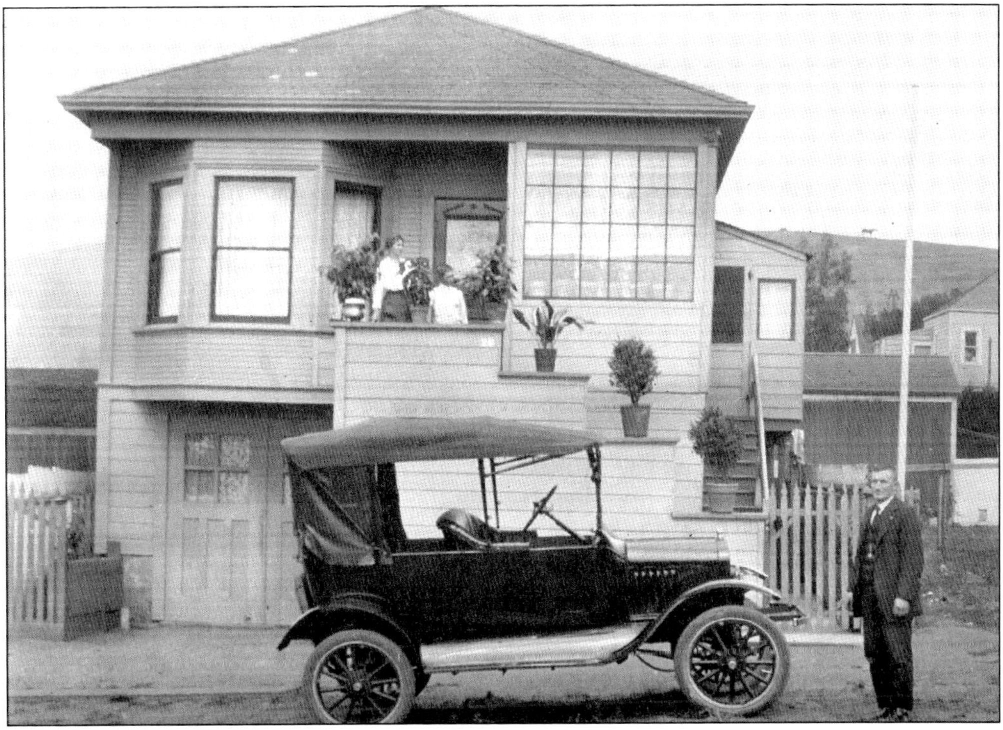

In this photograph, Mrs. Guttner and son Clarence stand on the steps of the family home at 26 Rutland. When he reached adulthood, Clarence took over his father's grocery store on Wilde and became an active neighborhood leader of the Reis-Paul Tract Improvement Club. (Courtesy Taylor family.)

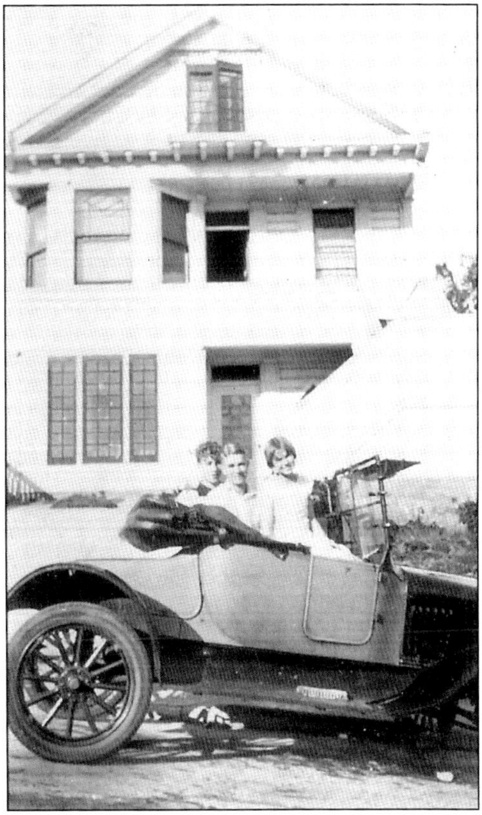

Harry Pierce lived on Tioga. "My brother and I decided to fix up our bedroom. We covered the walls with plywood, sunk dressers into the wall . . . The family had a phonograph and my sisters had stacks of records. We had these big French window–doors up there and we sailed those records out the window toward Tucker to see how far down we could sail them. There should be a lot of broken records down there." (Courtesy Harry Pierce.)

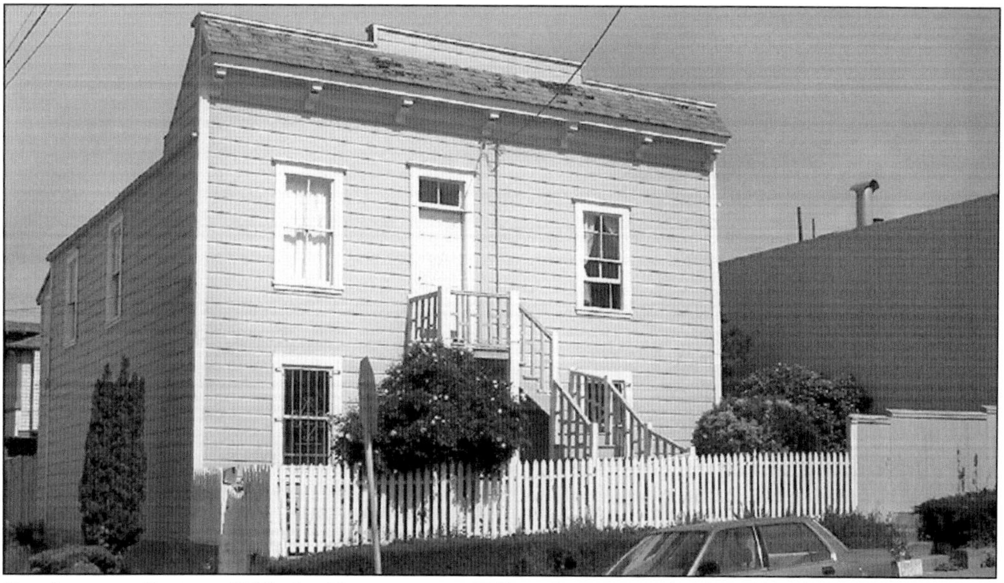

On the city rolls since 1885, this Victorian, on Talbert Street, may be the oldest house in Visitacion Valley, built in the false-front style popular in towns across the West. (Courtesy Edie Epps.)

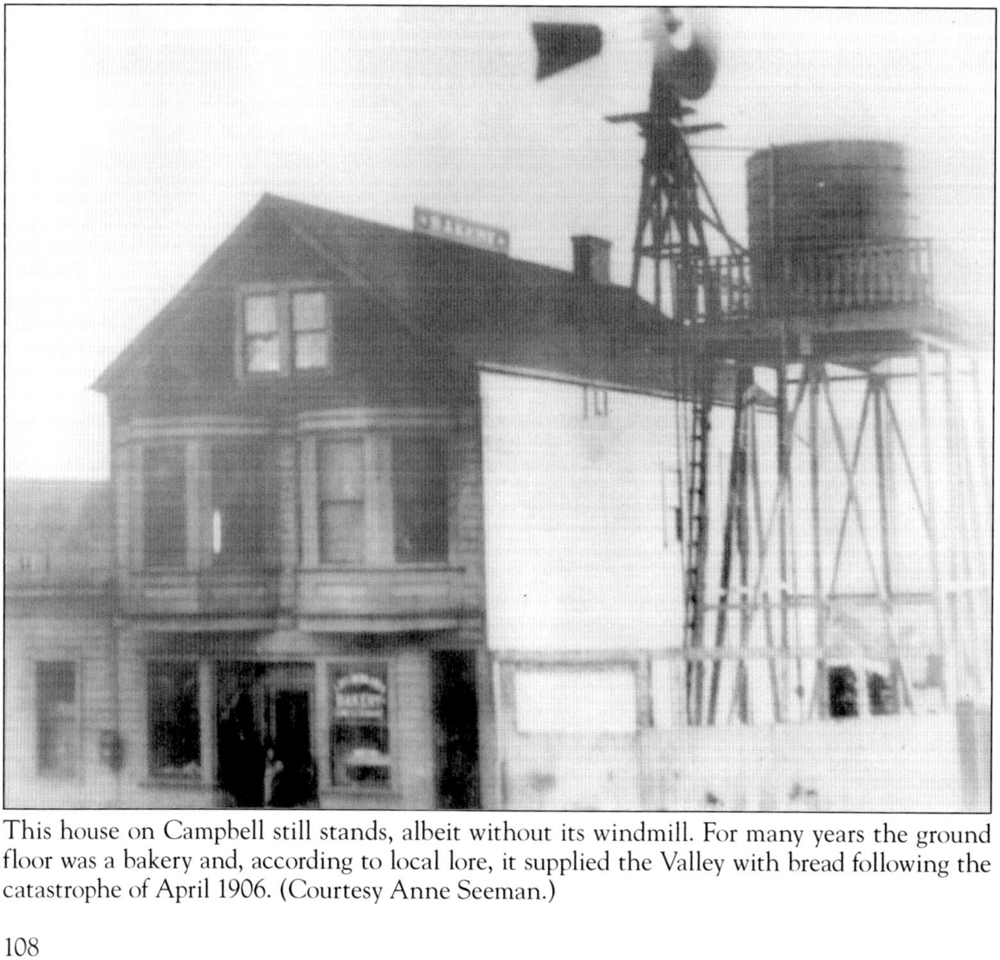

This house on Campbell still stands, albeit without its windmill. For many years the ground floor was a bakery and, according to local lore, it supplied the Valley with bread following the catastrophe of April 1906. (Courtesy Anne Seeman.)

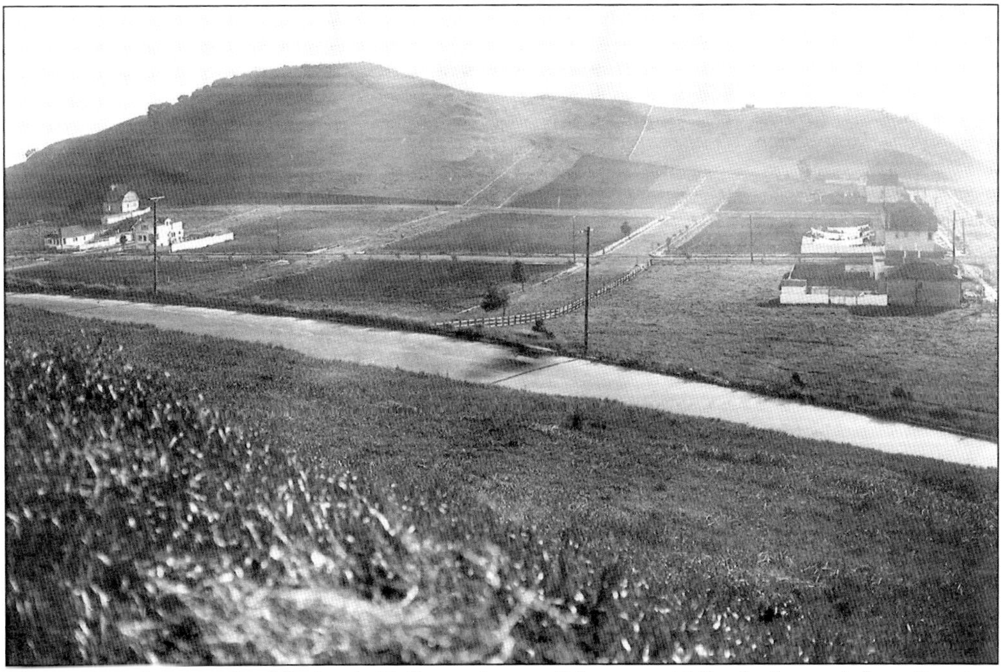

This c. 1918 photograph of the Little Hollywood area of Visitacion Valley looks south from Bayview Hill. The wide street in the foreground is Hester. In the distance on the left is a private home that still stands, known locally as the "Dutch farmhouse." (Courtesy a private collector.)

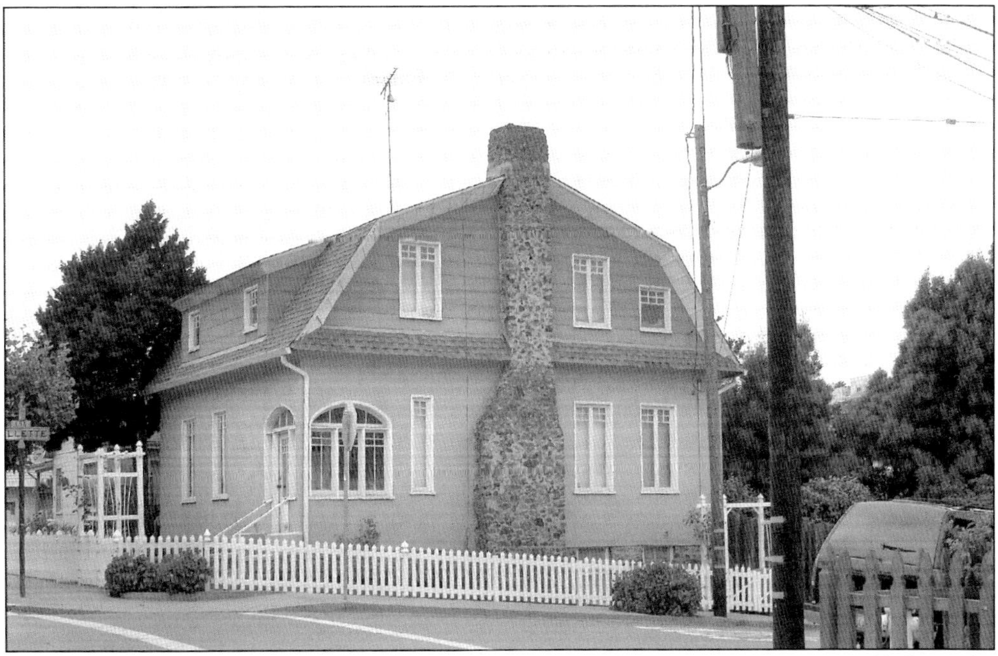

The Dutch farmhouse on Lathrop at Nueva was built by the current owner's grandfather. The foundation and chimney are made of rocks collected from the adjacent hillsides. (Courtesy Russel Morine.)

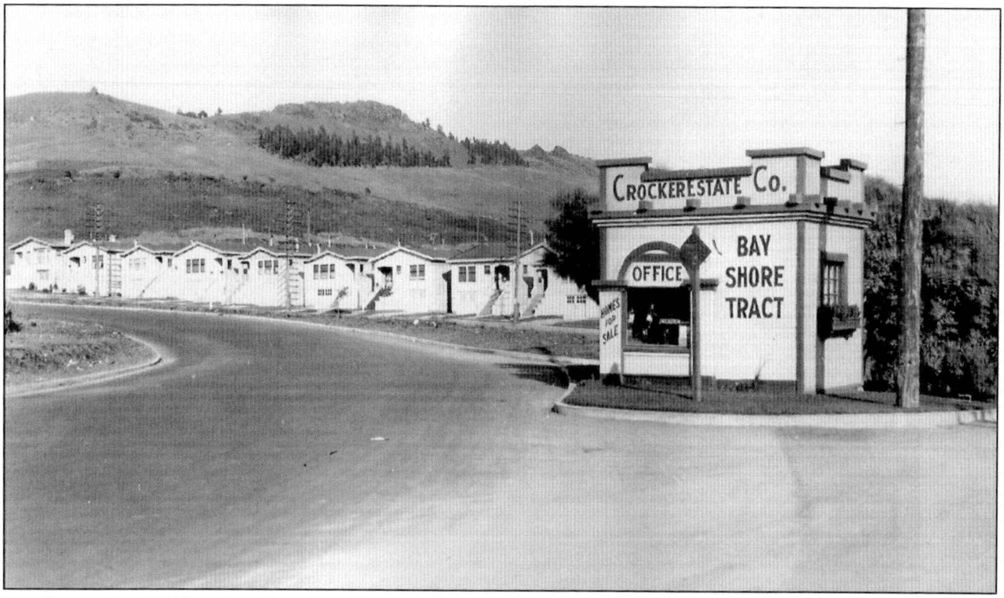

In the early 1920s, the Crocker Estate Company opened a sales office at what is today the intersection of Bayshore Boulevard and Blanken Avenue. The area now known as Little Hollywood was gradually developed, with many of its homes being built by local craftsmen. (Courtesy a private collector.)

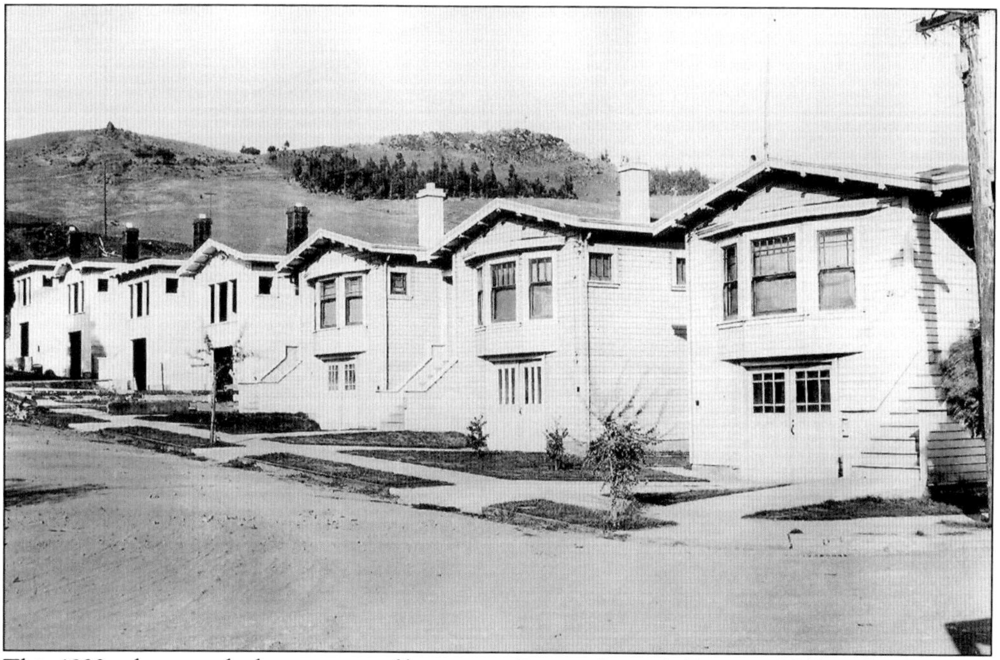
This 1920s photograph shows a row of houses on Peninsula, with Bayview Hill in the distance. The 1926 Reis Tract sales pamphlet noted that the "Crocker Bay Shore Tract consists of the extreme eastern part of Visitacion Valley where land and water meet. This tract has about seventy modernly built homes . . . if you wish to examine the tract, call upon Mr. John Wickstrom who is sales manager; he will give you prompt, courteous attention." Mr. Wickstrom built his own house at 125 Tunnel Avenue. (Courtesy a private collector.)

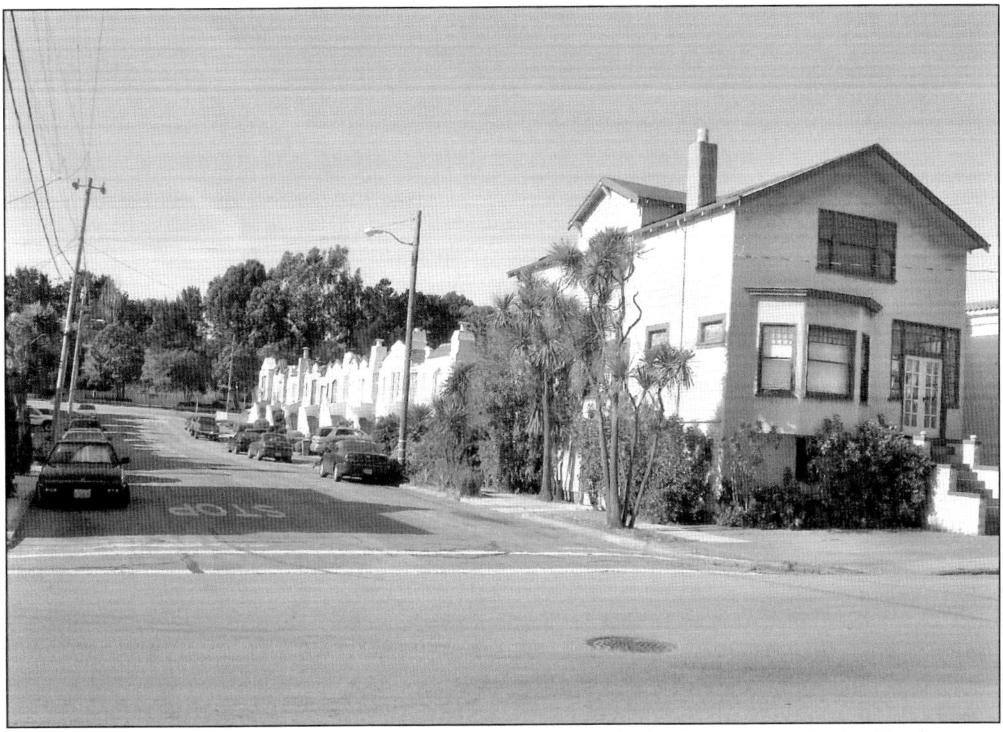

This c. 1910 Arts and Crafts home on Little Hollywood's Blanken Avenue is flanked by far more modern homes on the appropriately named Nueva Street. (Courtesy Russel Morine.)

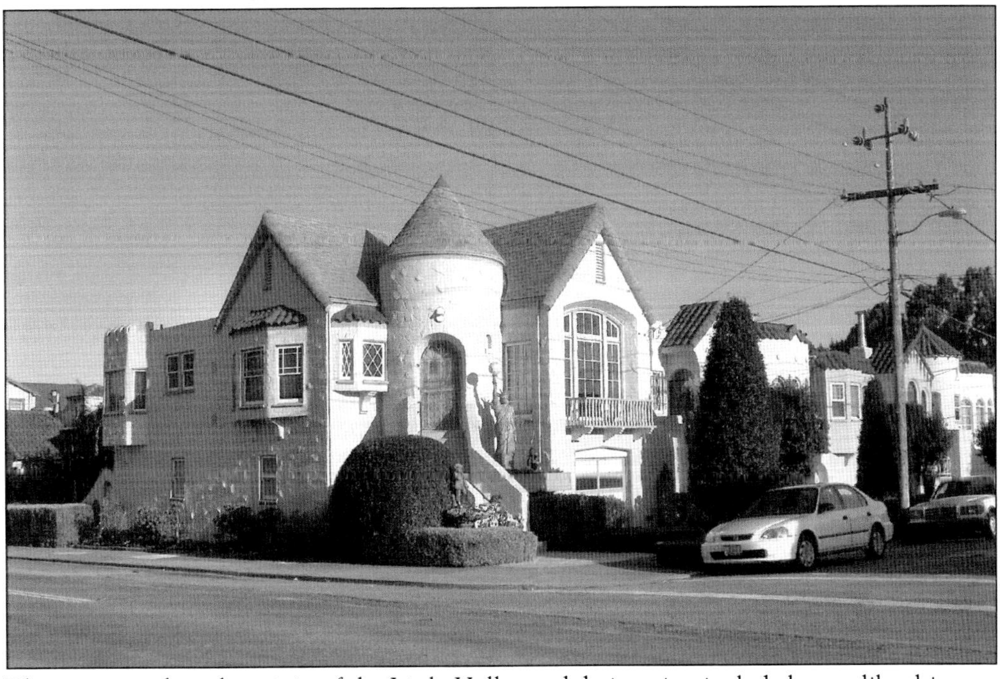

Theories regarding the origin of the Little Hollywood designation include homes like this one, possibly built with blueprints originally used in the southern part of the state. The replica of the Statue of Liberty beside the staircase adds an interesting accent. (Courtesy Edie Epps.)

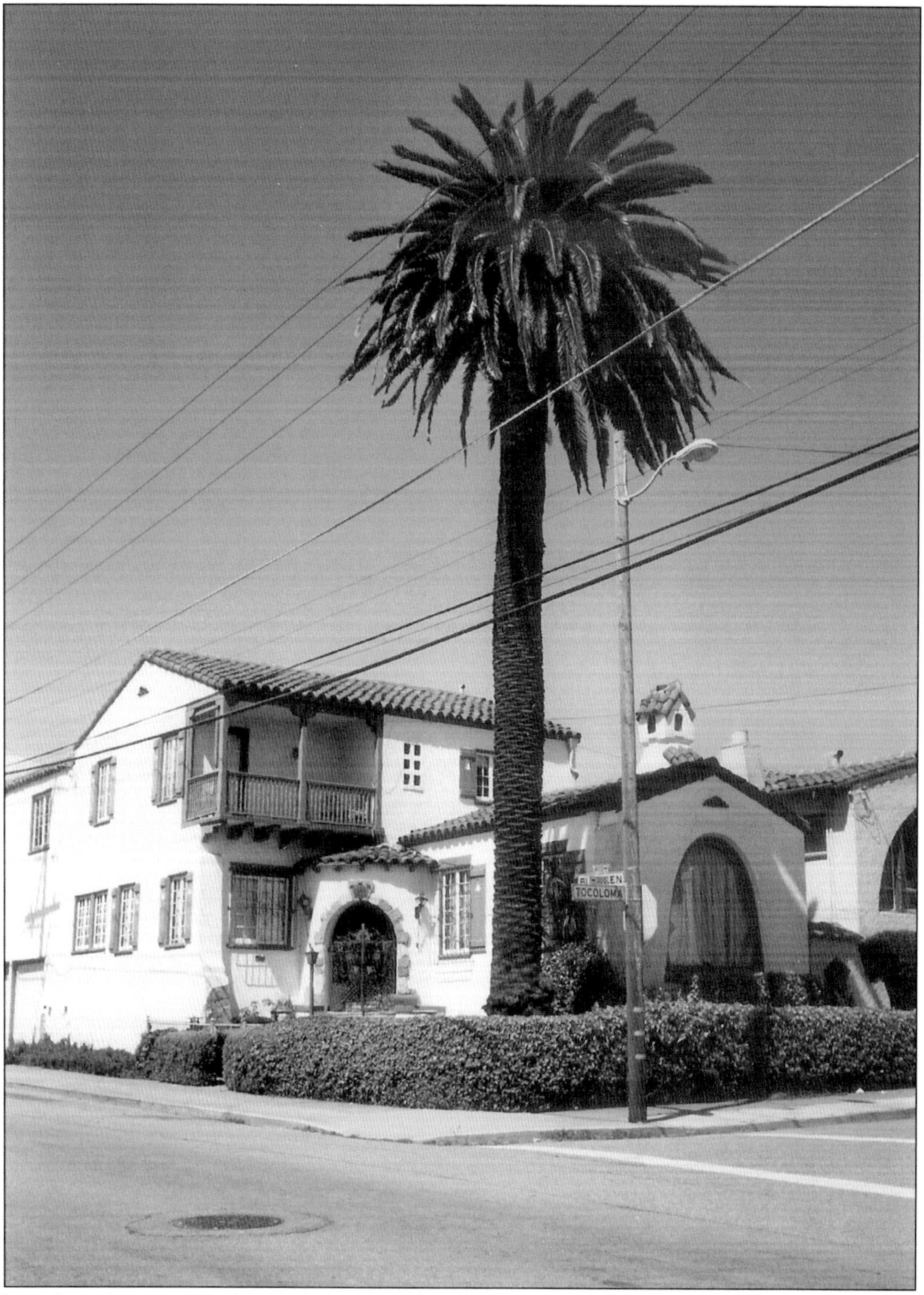

This large home at Blanken and Tocoloma is called Casa Bahia Loma. Although long rumored to have been a hidden retreat for movie legend Mae West, no proof of this has been discovered. The area's many palm trees and abundant sunshine add to the charm of this quaint neighborhood. (Courtesy Edie Epps.)

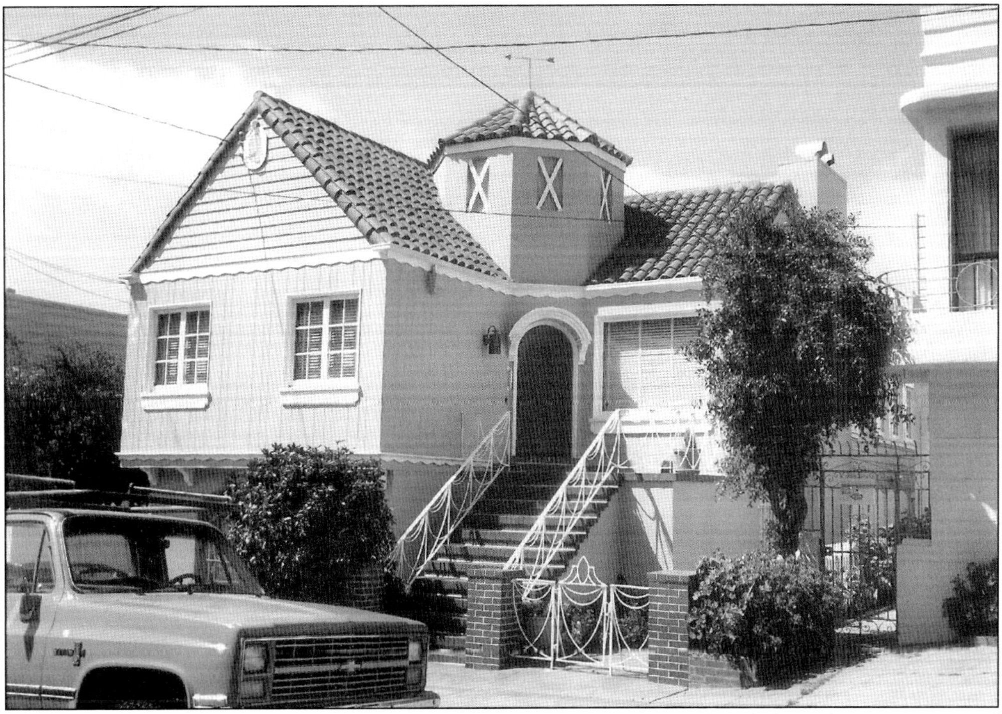

This home, built in 1937 on Schwerwin Street, is a good example of the eclectic variety of architecture found in the Valley. (Courtesy Edie Epps.)

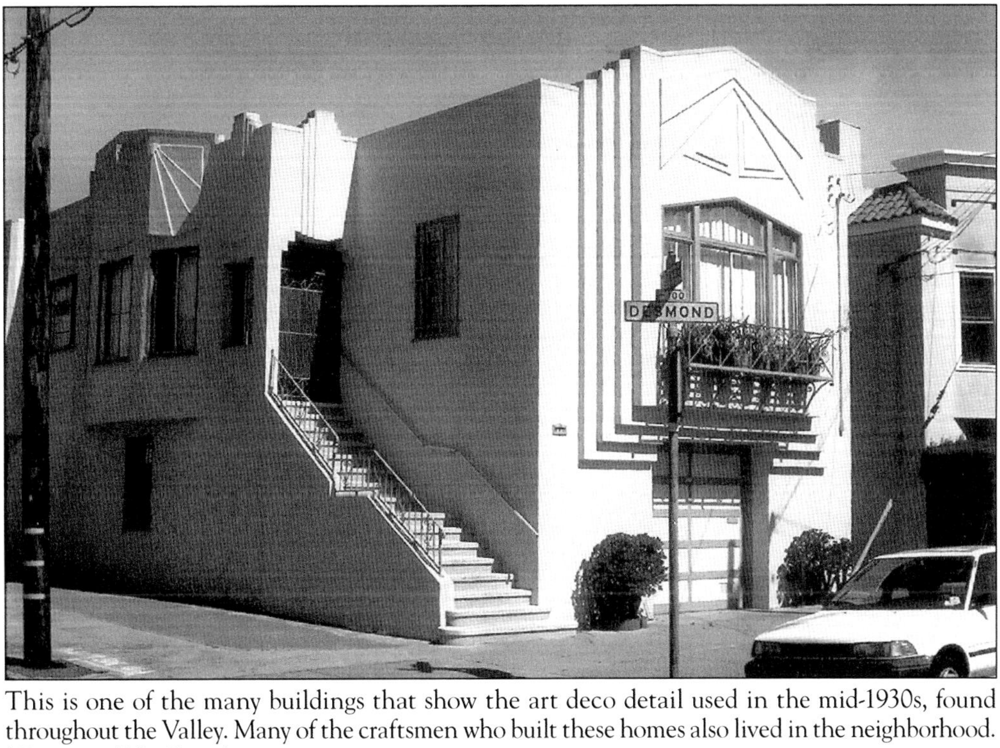

This is one of the many buildings that show the art deco detail used in the mid-1930s, found throughout the Valley. Many of the craftsmen who built these homes also lived in the neighborhood. (Courtesy Edie Epps.)

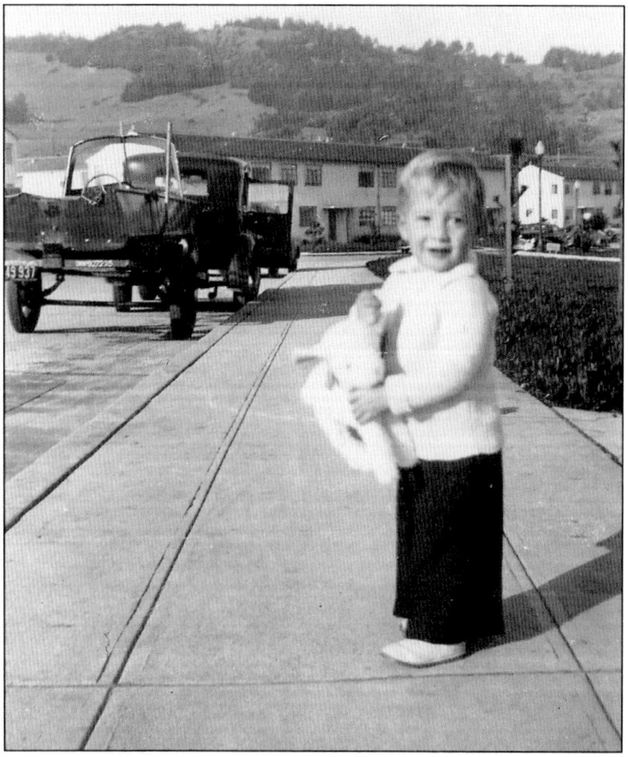

The Sunnydale housing project was built in 1942 and restricted to Caucasians. Of five projects completed in San Francisco during the World War II era, only one, Westside Courts, housed African Americans. When the issue was addressed after the war, the San Francisco Housing Authority first denied and then later admitted using so-called "neighborhood patterns" for tenant location. Because this equaled discrimination, the agency was forced to change its policy. (Courtesy a private collector.)

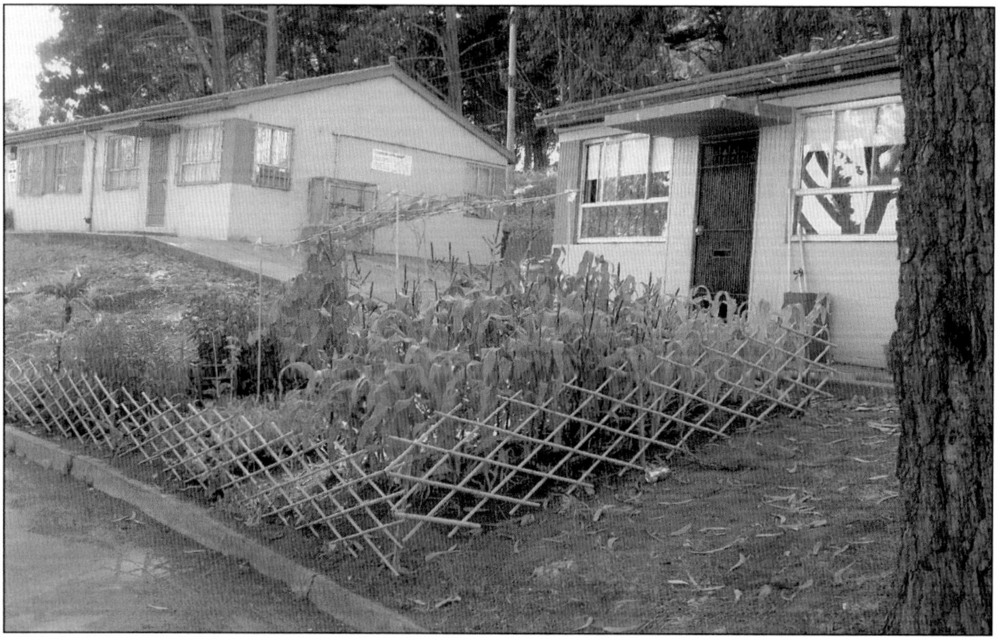

The Sunnydale housing project has 767 family units in its 91 buildings, and personnel at the community center work hard to address the needs and concerns of children and adults. One innovative program begun in 2004, the "Phoenix Project," was inspired by a resident who planted a garden. Proving successful in Sunnydale, it may become a model for other housing blocks in the city. (Courtesy Russel Morine.)

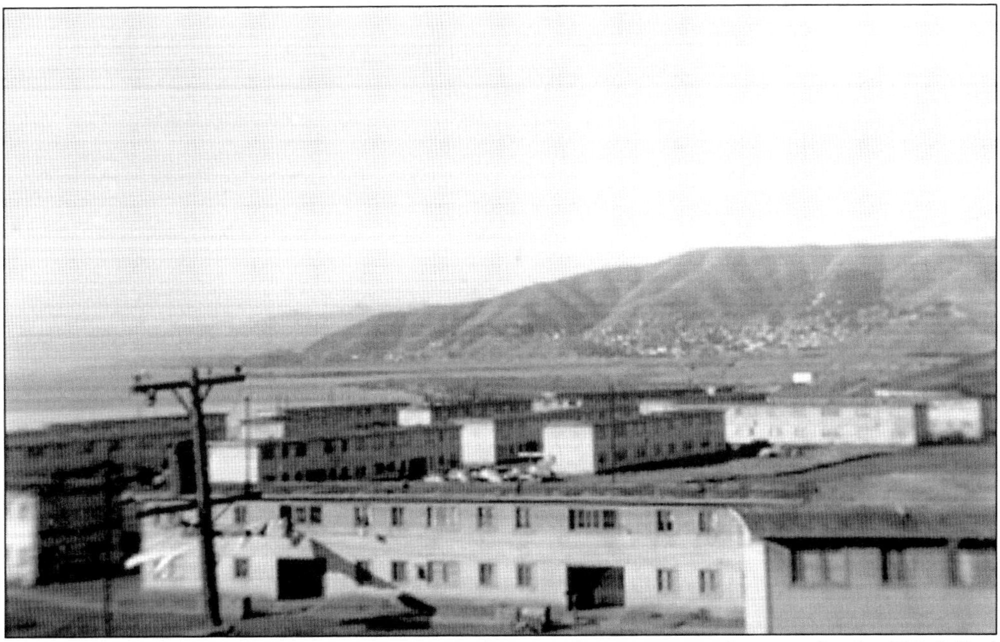

The Candlestick Cove housing project was built in 1943 as temporary housing for the 992 skilled craftsmen and their families who formed the Hunters Point Naval Shipyard core crew during and after World War II and was occupied until at least 1957. The buildings covered the flat land of the Cove and climbed the hillsides, where dairy cows once grazed. (Courtesy Richard Kerr.)

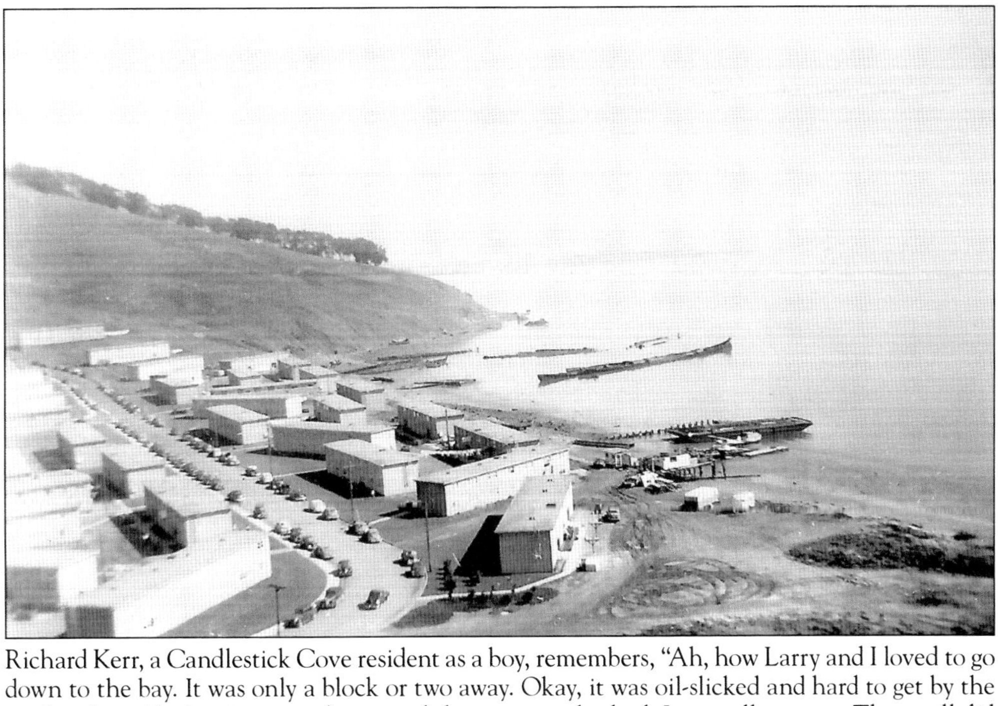

Richard Kerr, a Candlestick Cove resident as a boy, remembers, "Ah, how Larry and I loved to go down to the bay. It was only a block or two away. Okay, it was oil-slicked and hard to get by the stink at low tide, but it was a playground that no one else had. It was all ours . . . The smell did subside the longer you were there, but it was our new world to conquer. It was also strewn with wrecks of old ships." (Courtesy Ron Parshall.)

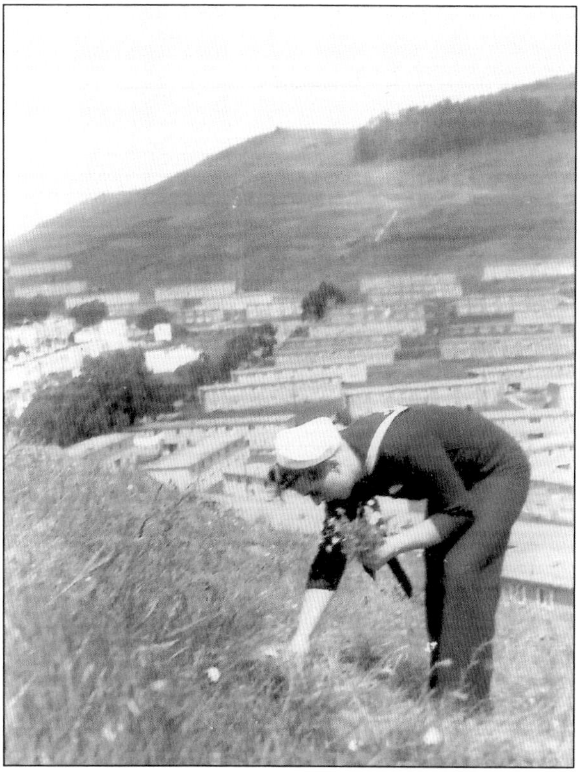

In this 1940s photograph, a sailor home on leave picks wildflowers for a loved one on the hillside above the Candlestick Cove housing project. Bayview Hill can be seen in the background. This same site now hosts Executive Park's office buildings and new condominium developments. (Courtesy Ron Parshall.)

Looking south from Bayview Hill, this now-vacant property was the former site of the Candlestick Cove housing project. Current development plans for the land specify nearly 500 units of housing, including town homes, mid-rise condos, and retail space. Overhead Highway 101 bisects this site and the Little Hollywood neighborhood. (Courtesy Russel Morine.)

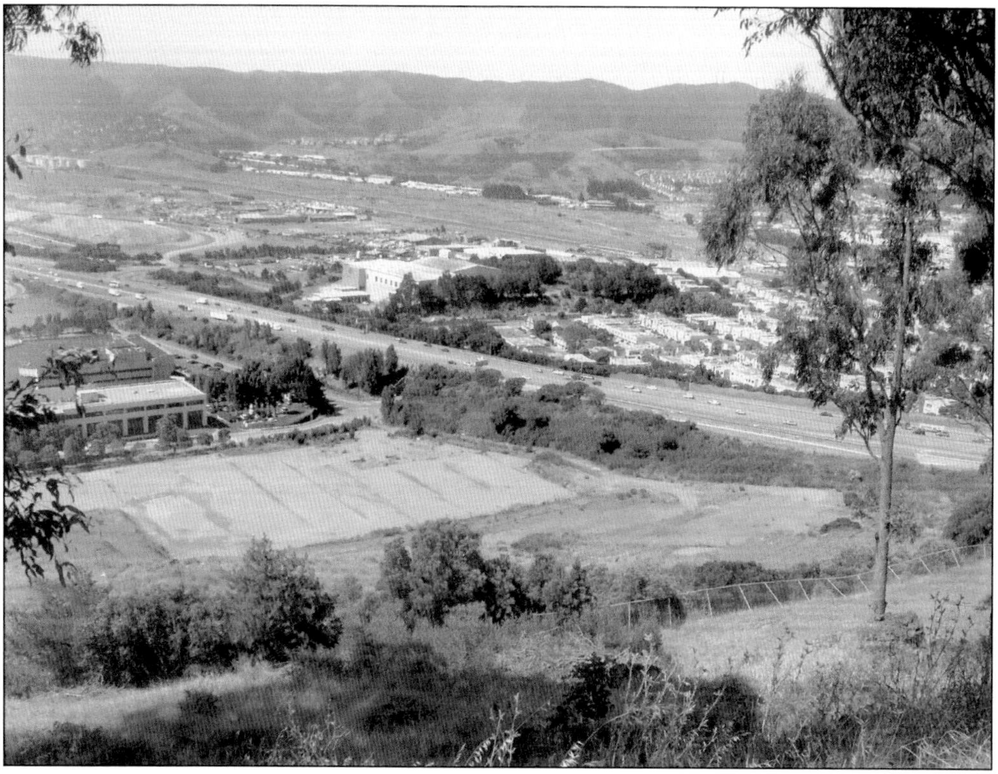

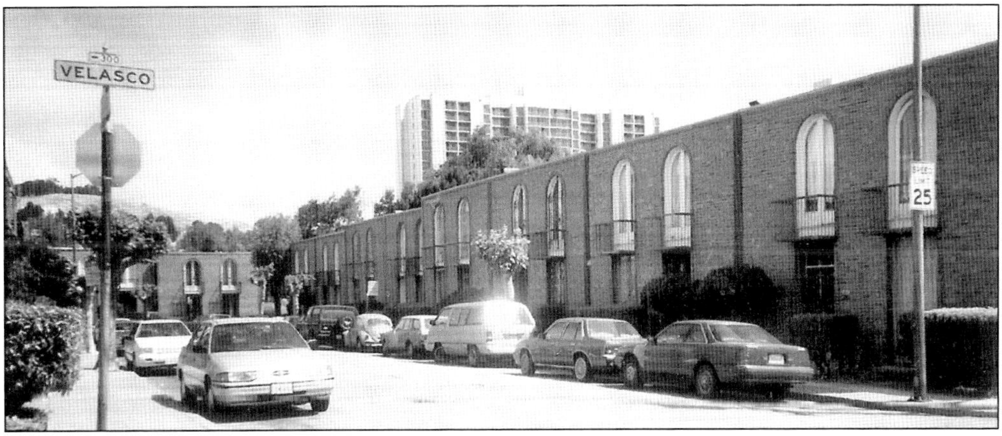

Geneva Towers literally towered over Eichler's brick townhouse development, built in the 1960s along Sunnydale Avenue. This was a new look for the area formerly associated with farming and nursery buildings of glass. (Courtesy Taylor family.)

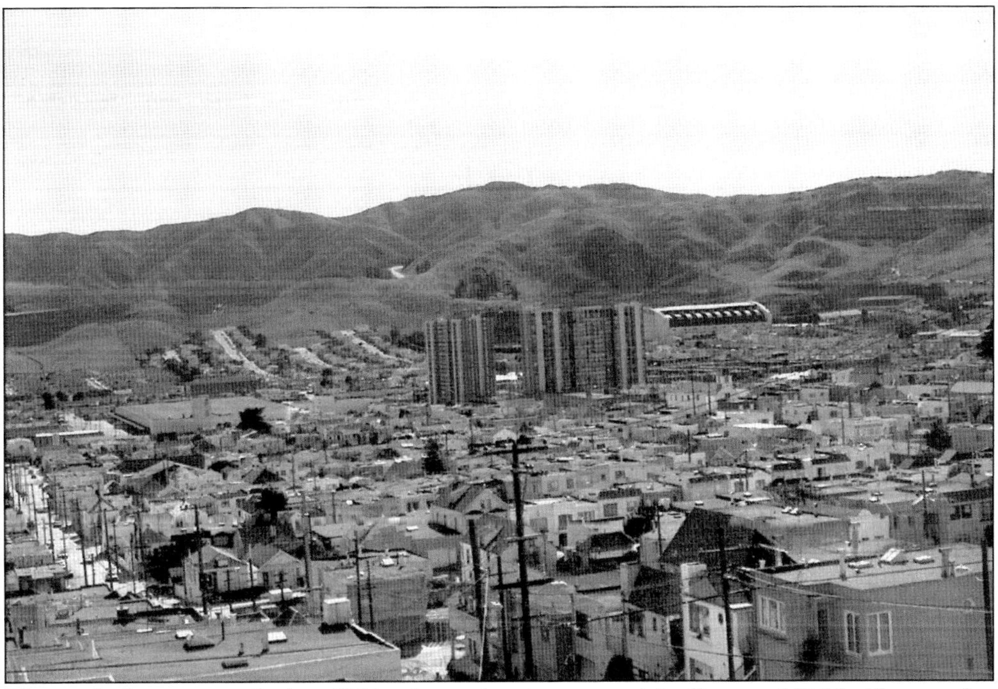

The two high-rise towers built in 1964 as luxury housing were originally named Eichler Towers, after their developer. Joseph Eichler's later claim of financial difficulties resulted in their conversion to subsidized housing under HUD jurisdiction. Renamed Geneva Towers, their condition deteriorated by the 1980s and the buildings were eventually slated for demolition. (Courtesy Ron Gibson.)

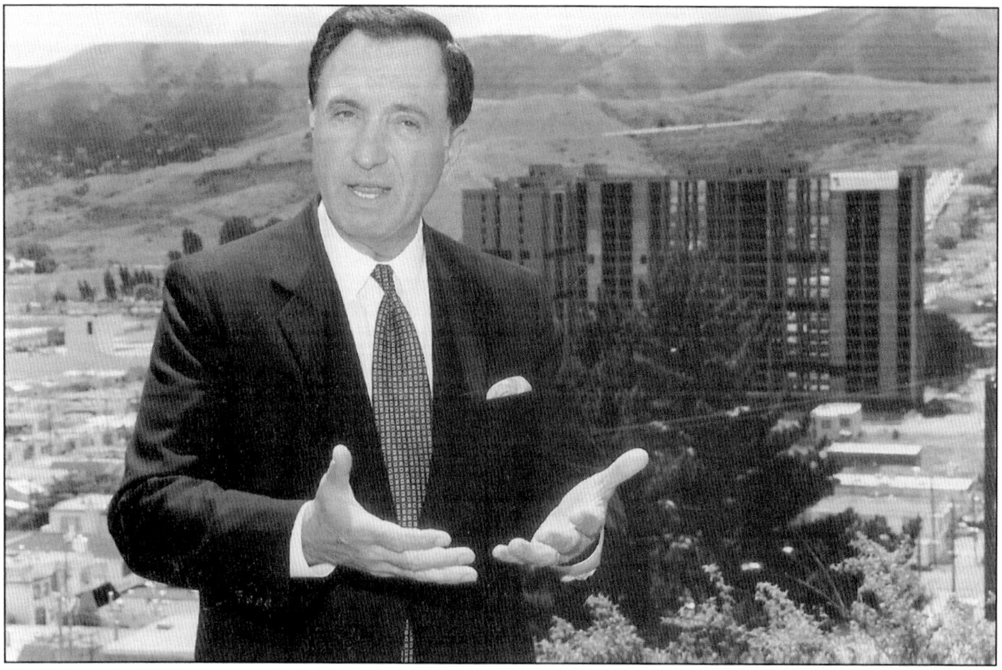

On May 17, 1998, former San Francisco mayor Art Agnos spoke to the crowd gathered to view the impending implosion of the towers, gutted in preparation for the dramatic event. (Courtesy Judith Williams Sandoval.)

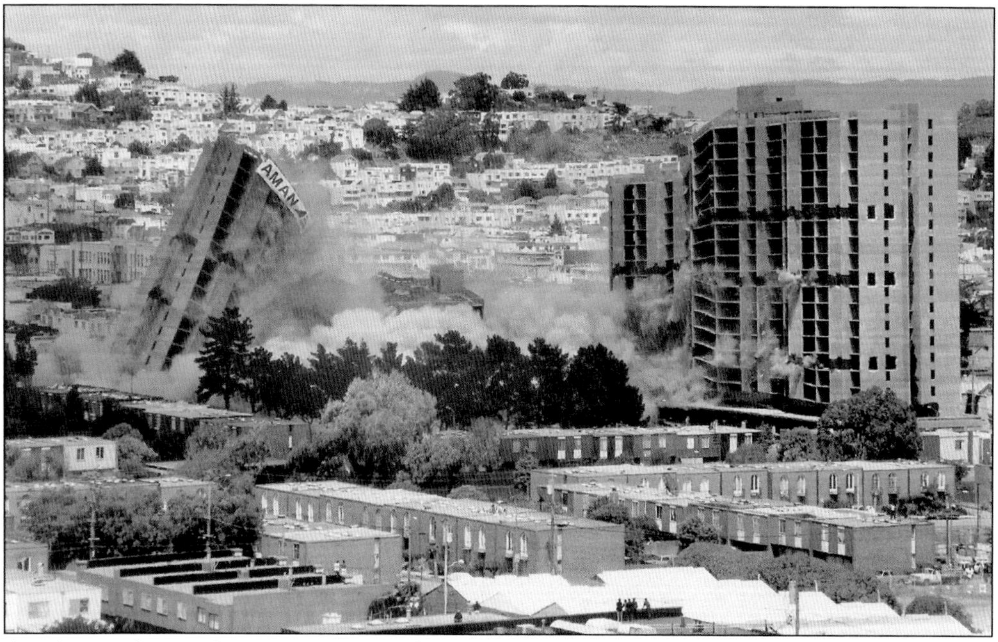

Art Agnos, former Geneva Towers resident Shanica Knowles, and Rep. Nancy Pelosi together pressed the ceremonial plunger and the two buildings were imploded in a spectacular 10-second show. Thousands watched from nearby hills. Some shed tears to see their former home destroyed, while others cheered with the excitement of the moment as well as with optimism of better housing to come. (Courtesy Judith Williams Sandoval.)

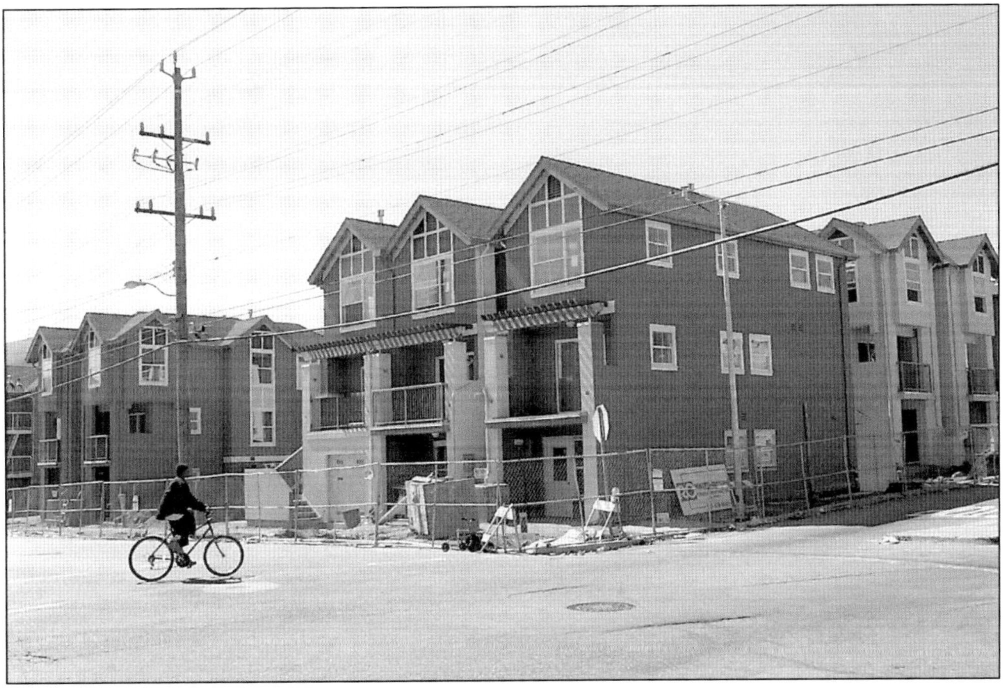

Heritage Homes, 146 units of affordable housing, were built on the site formerly occupied by Geneva Towers. Former residents were given the first opportunity to return to their old neighborhood and move into the attractive new townhouses. (Courtesy Russel Morine.)

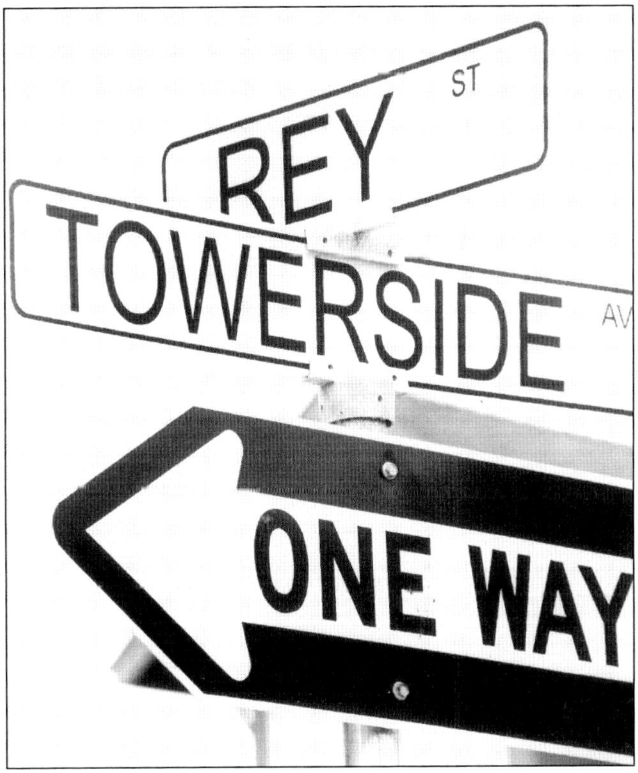

As this sign indicates, new streets and housing were constructed as part of the replacement of Geneva Towers with Heritage Homes. Although former residents originally selected "A" and "B" as names for the new streets, paralleling the names of the two towers, they were already assigned. Instead streets "Towerside" and "Heritage" now honor the past. (Courtesy Judith Williams Sandoval.)

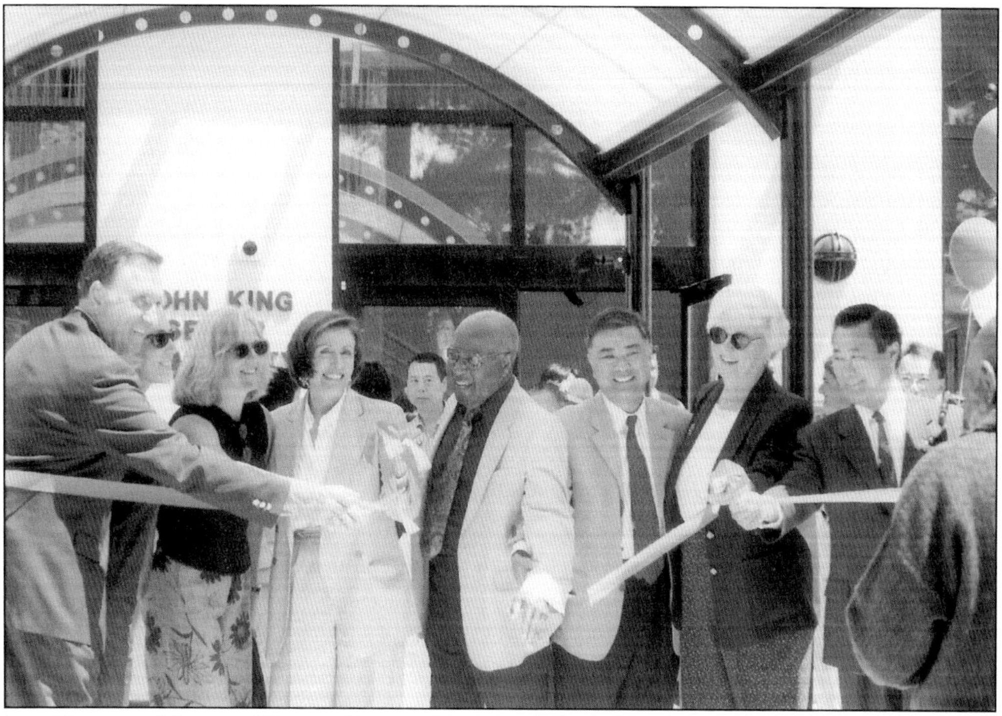

In addition to Heritage Homes, Britton Court and the John King Senior Community Center also offered replacement housing for former Geneva Towers residents. On May 11, 2002, John King (center) cut the ribbon with an assist from former mayor Art Agnos. Rep. Nancy Pelosi (left of Mr. King) and other dignitaries attended the grand opening. (Courtesy Judith Williams Sandoval.)

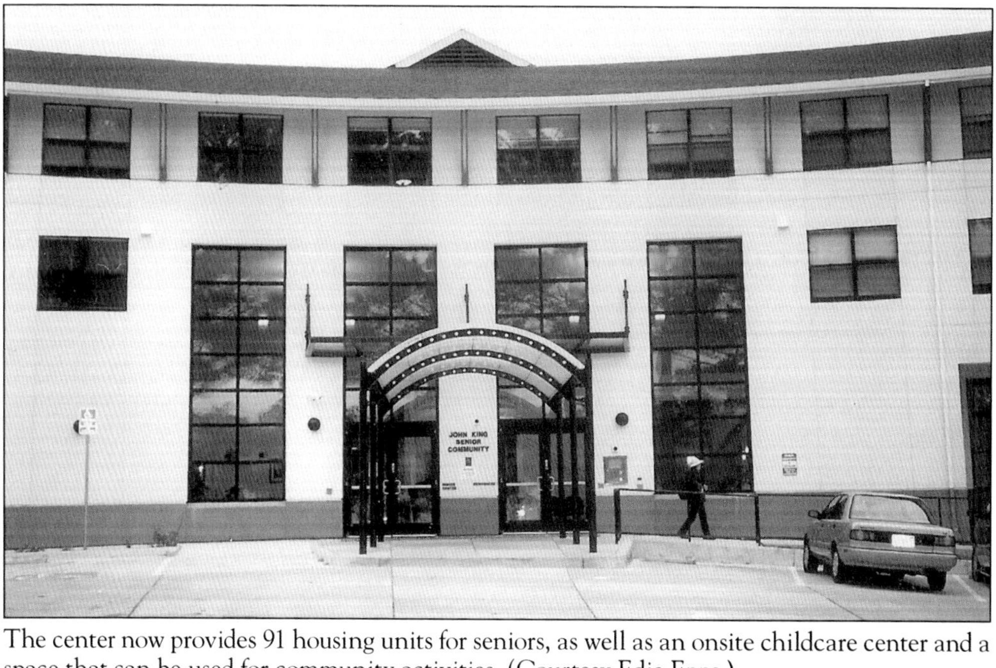

The center now provides 91 housing units for seniors, as well as an onsite childcare center and a space that can be used for community activities. (Courtesy Edie Epps.)

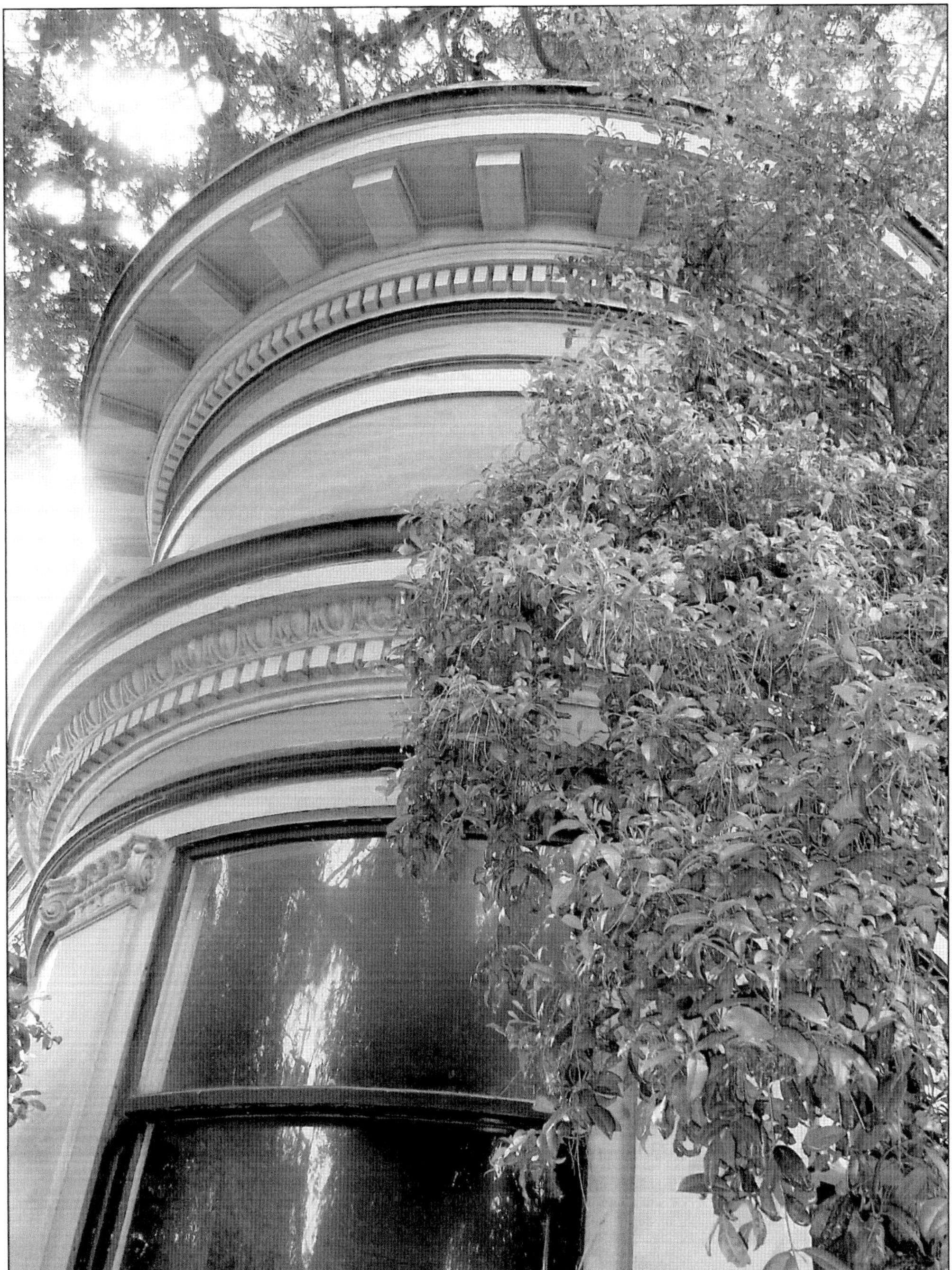

Sculptor Mikal Cartor lives in an Edwardian on Hahn Street. Legend holds that this is one piece of a house amicably divided among sisters who equally loved their family home and physically split it into two or three parts. Perhaps you can identify the current location of the missing part(s), or otherwise solve this mystery! (Courtesy Russel Morine.)

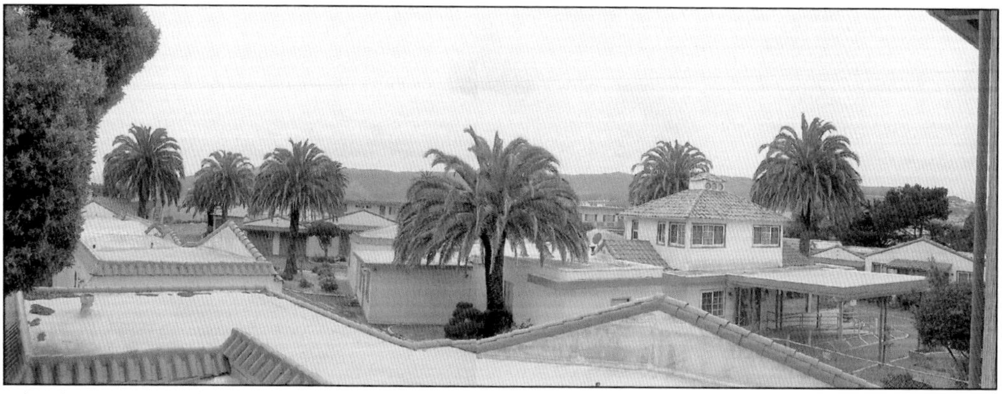

The former Bayside Motel, atop Bayshore Boulevard, sits vacant in 2005, with plans moving forward for demolition and construction of multiple housing units. Nearby residents hope that at least some of the palm trees will remain on the site. (Courtesy Russel Morine.)

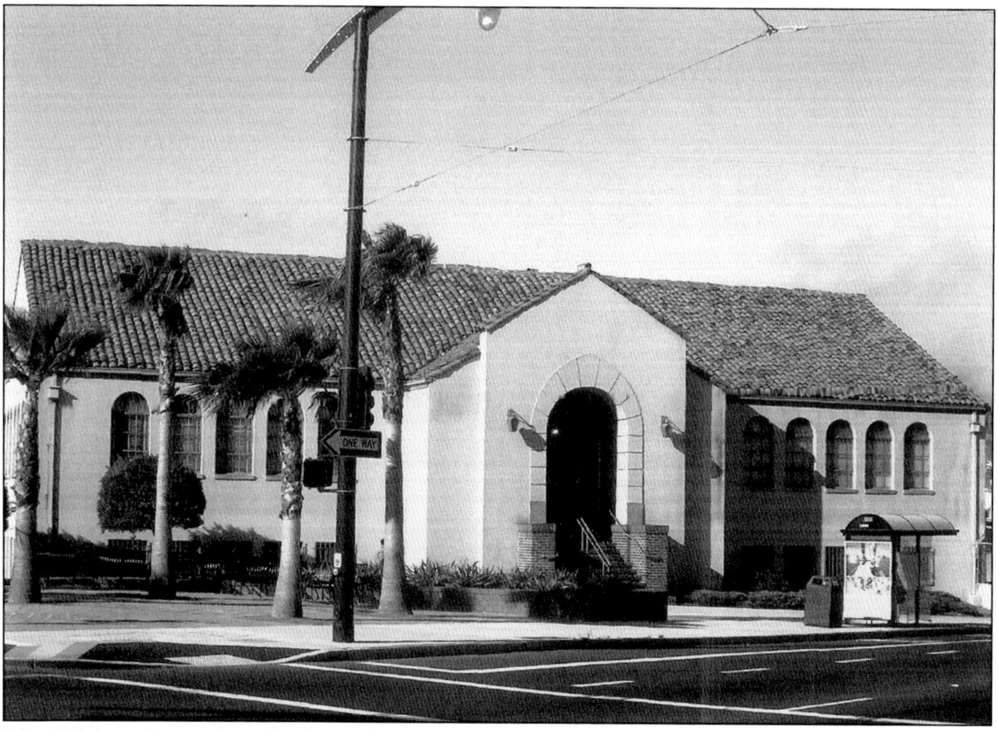

The Schlage shops where locks and keys were once manufactured closed in 1998 and are slated for demolition to make room for new housing. But the Mediterranean-style office building is supposed to be preserved for community use. (Courtesy Edie Epps.)

Six

A Few More Faces and Places

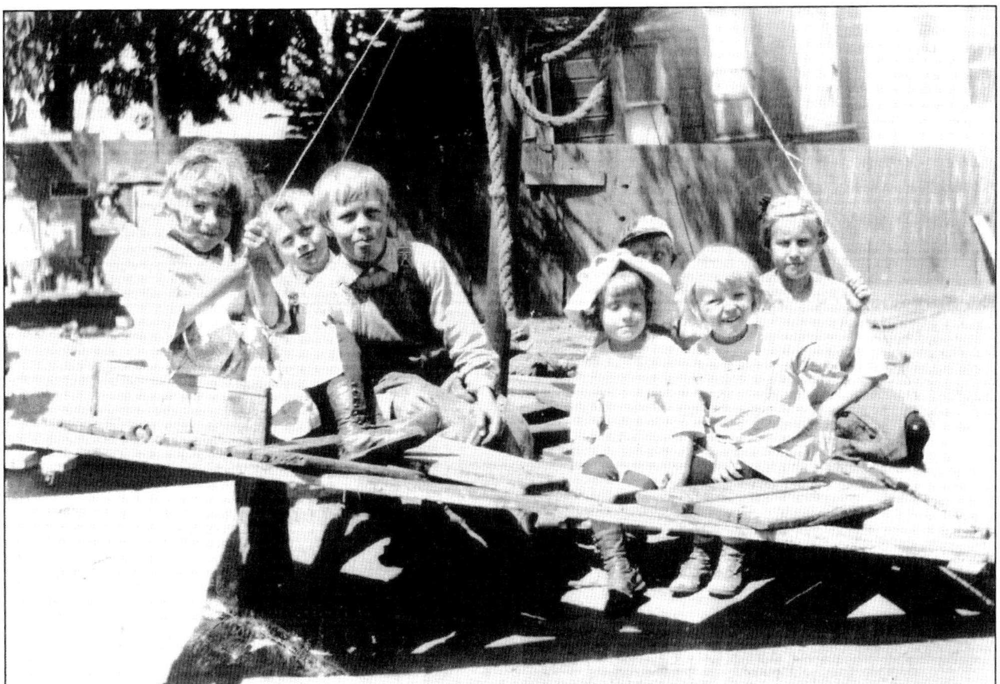

In this c. 1915 photograph, neighborhood children enjoy their homemade merry-go-round built by big brother Irving Stevenson. From left to right are Loretta Bauman, Walter Bauman, Irving Stevenson, Paula Bauman, Alma Stevenson, and Eleanor Stevenson. Albert Stevenson peeks out from the back. (Courtesy Taylor family.)

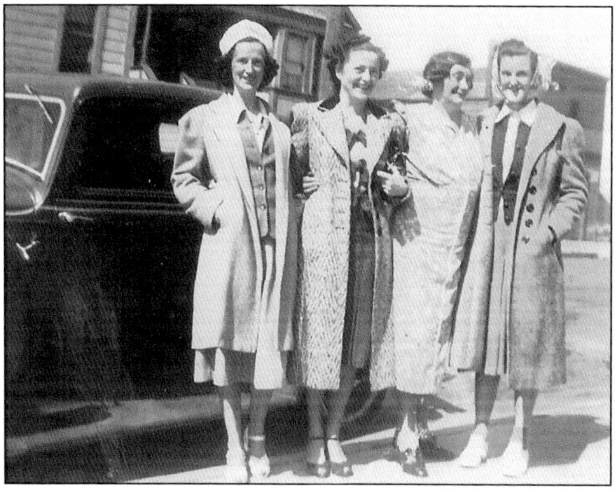

From left to right in this 1939 photograph are Mary, Agnes, Mary (mother of the three younger women), and Theresa Mullen. The Mullen family moved to Visitacion Valley about 1927 and lived on Raymond across from the Bonvitas (now Thutmose) Hall. A family with two sons and five daughters, at least two of the girls were avid San Francisco Giants fans, as so many people in the Valley are—not surprising, since the team played at the Candlestick Cove stadium for many years. (Courtesy Carol Conway.)

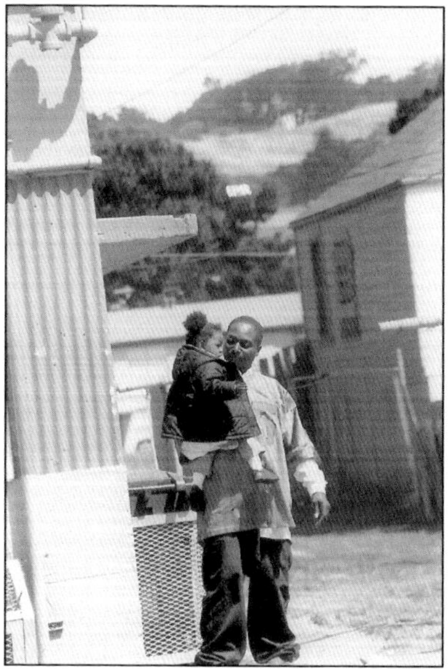

A proud father holds his child in front of a Sunnydale home. (Courtesy Visitacion Valley Community Center.)

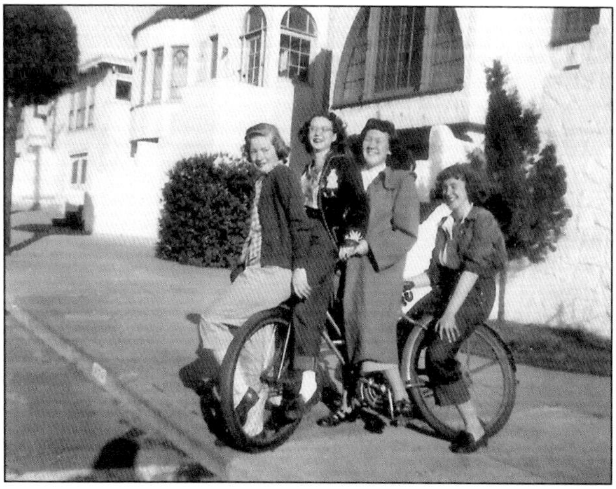

In this 1949 photograph, four future Lowell High students pose with a bicycle on Wheeler Street in Little Hollywood. The homes in the background show the Spanish-influenced style that may have played a role in the naming of this neighborhood. Pictured from left to right are Nancy Boblitt, Eleanor Baggetto, Pat Villegas, and Cristina Sutti. (Courtesy Cris Sutti-Janigian.)

In this c. 1955 photograph, Mrs. Susan Scott holds onto her hat on a typical windy afternoon while visiting her daughter Martha Arnott on Wilde Avenue. (Courtesy Betty Parshall.)

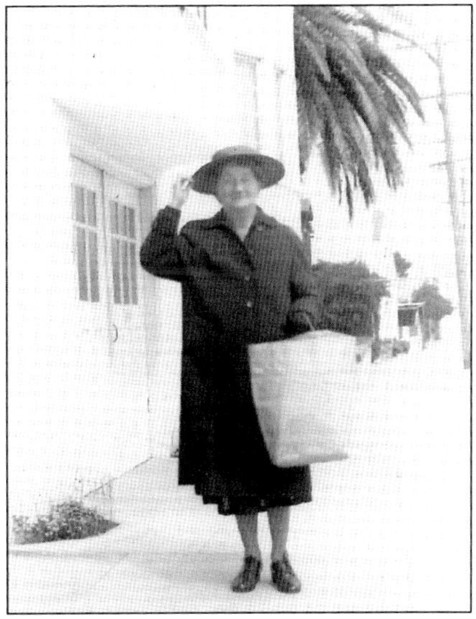

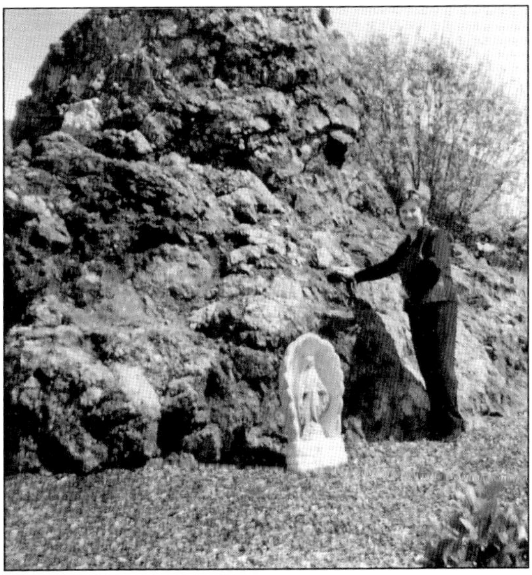

Realtor and longtime resident Cathy Kline-Saunders poses in front of "The Rock" in this 1980s photograph.

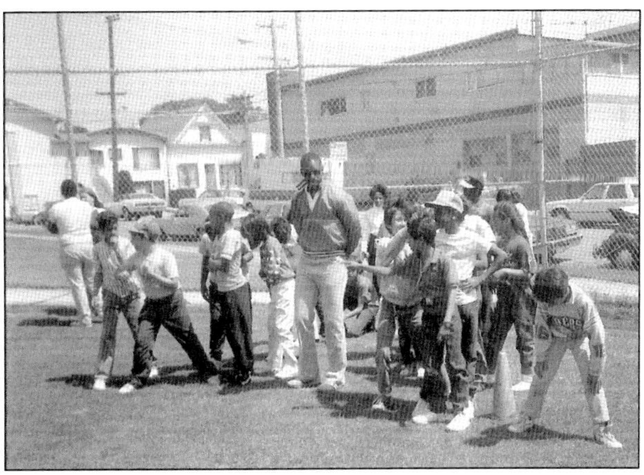

At Visitacion Valley Park, kids gather around a patient coach prior to some sort of race or sports practice. (Courtesy Visitacion Valley Community Center.)

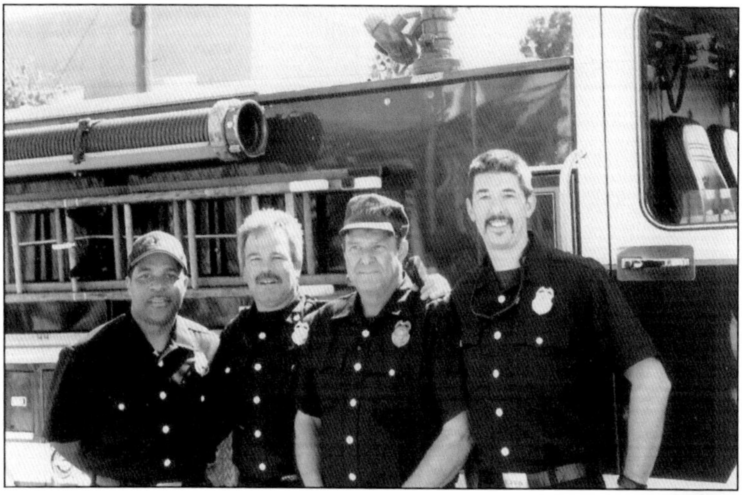

Besides protecting our lives and property, the firefighters of Engine Company No. 44 often join in many community events. They also visit the Valley's schools, providing fire safety education and spreading goodwill. (Courtesy Judith Williams Sandoval.)

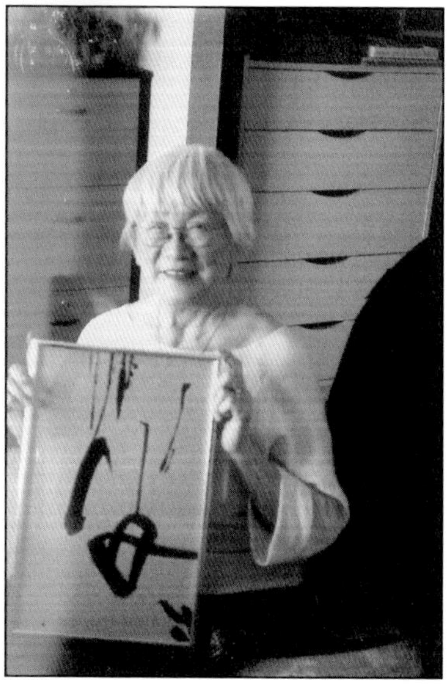

Sue Tom was the art instructor in the multicultural resource department at Visitacion Valley Elementary School in the 1970s. Here she holds a painting by her son, who was two years old at the time. (Courtesy Edie Epps.)

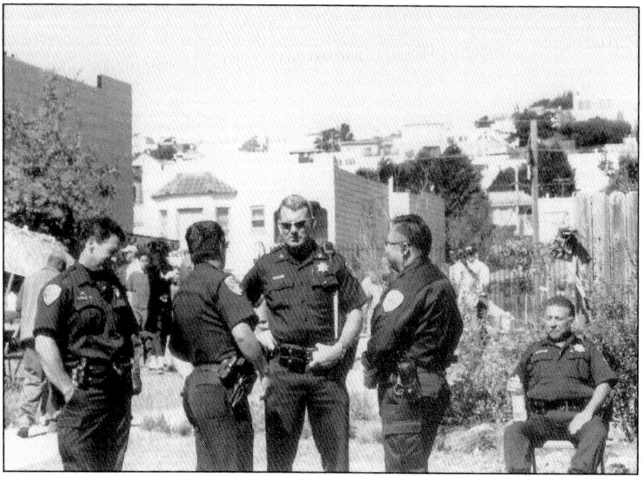

Visitacion Valley is served by the San Francisco Police Department's Ingleside Station. Although the station is located outside the neighborhood, the department maintains frequent contact with Valley residents. A monthly meeting is held at the new clubhouse at Visitacion Valley Park, and officers often attend other community gatherings to provide information and answer questions. (Courtesy Judith Williams Sandoval.)

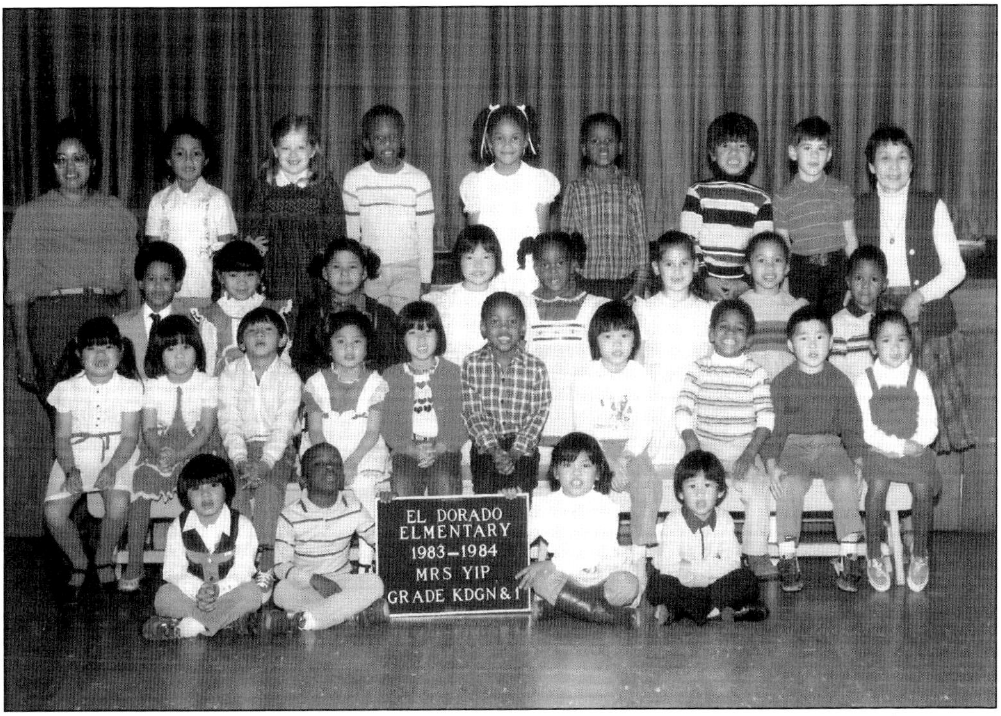

The sign says it all in this class photograph of one-time El Dorado students. (Courtesy Edie Epps.)

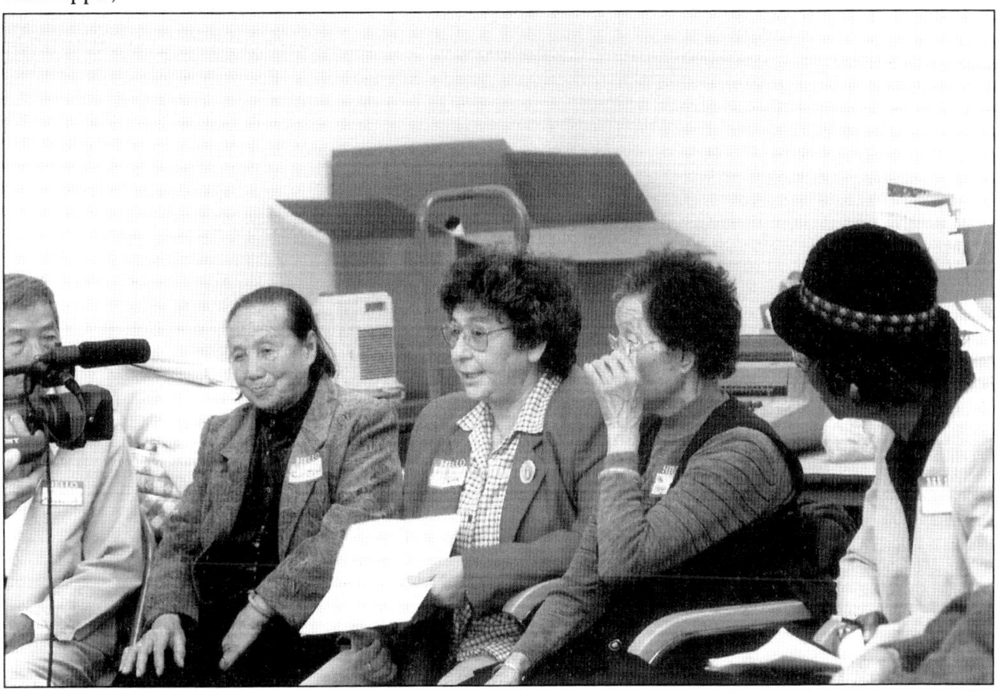
This 2003 photograph depicts some of the attendees at the initial Circle of Elders meeting at the John King Center. Plans for an oral history project were announced and discussed. (Courtesy Judith Williams Sandoval.)

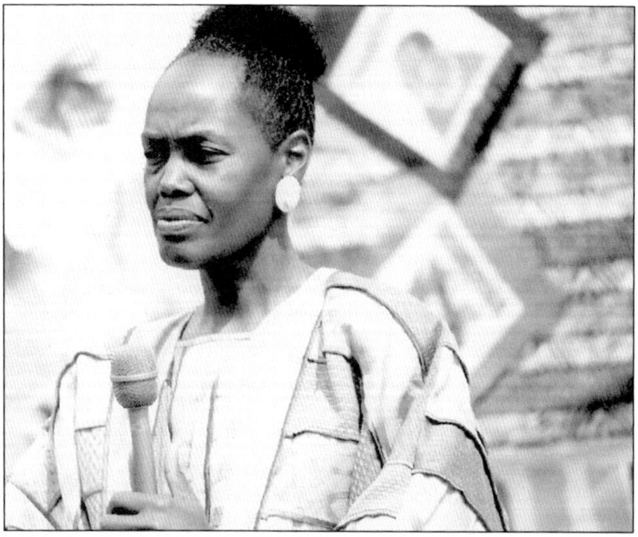

Supervisor Sophie Maxwell represents Visitacion Valley and the other San Francisco neighborhoods of District 10. She notes, "I believe Visitacion Valley's greatest asset, historically and today, is its diverse and active residents. I am proud when I come to visit or work in the Valley . . . [whose residents'] work is a model for other neighborhoods." (Courtesy Judith Williams Sandoval.)

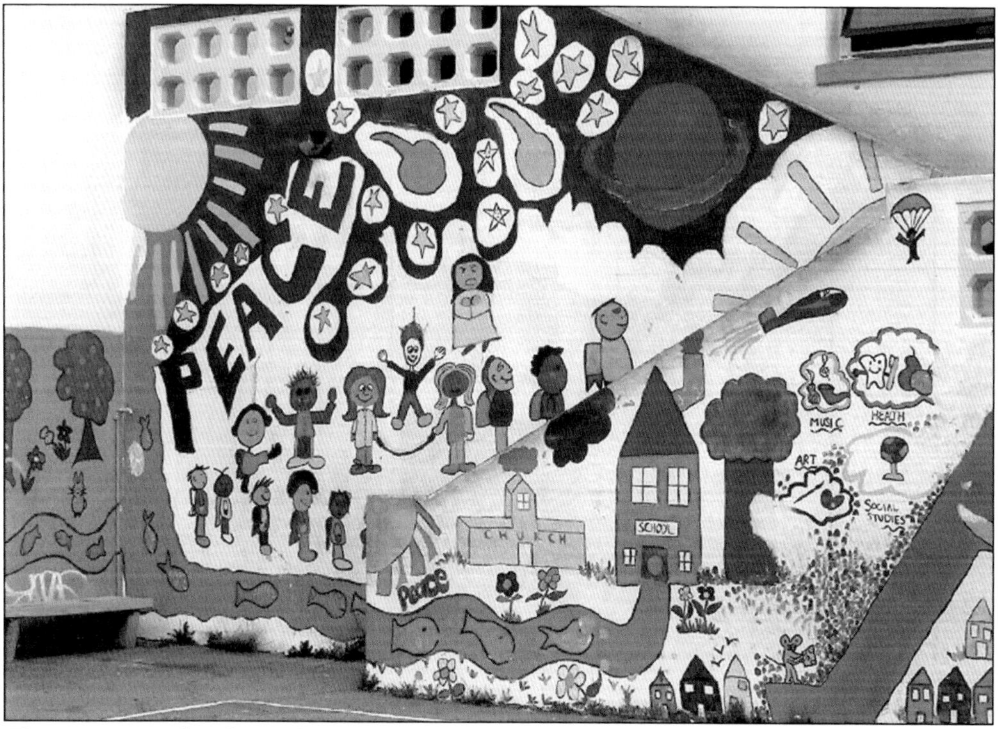

The "Peace Mural" is located at the Visitacion Valley Elementary School playground. (Courtesy Edie Epps.)

We could talk about the old times forever. But times change.
About every decade something changes in sports and in life too.
And that's how it's been all the way down the line.

—Visitacion Valley resident and famed Pacific Coast League pitcher Walter Lister